Lobbying

LOBBYING

Understanding and Influencing the Corridors of Power

SECOND EDITION

CHARLES MILLER

Basil Blackwell

Copyright © Charles Miller 1987, 1990

First published 1987
Second edition 1990

Basil Blackwell Ltd
108 Cowley Road, Oxford, OX4 1JF, UK

Basil Blackwell, Inc.
3 Cambridge Center
Cambridge, Massachusetts 02142, USA

All rights reserved. Except for the quotation of short passages for the purposes of criticism and review, no part of this publication may be reproduced, stored in a retrieval system, or transmitted, in any form or by any means, electronic, mechanical, photocopying, recording or otherwise, without the prior permission of the publisher.

Except in the United States of America, this book is sold subject to the condition that it shall not, by way of trade or otherwise, be lent, re-sold, hired out, or otherwise circulated without the publisher's prior consent in any form of binding or cover other than that in which it is published and without a similar condition including this condition being imposed on the subsequent purchaser.

British Library Cataloguing in Publication Data

A CIP catalogue record for this book is available from the British Library.

Library of Congress Cataloging in Publication Data
Miller, Charles.
  [Lobbying government]
  Lobbying: understanding and influencing the corridors of power/
Charles Miller. – 2nd ed.
     p. cm.
  Originally published as: Lobbying government. 1987.
  Bibliography: p.
  Includes index.
  ISBN 0-631-17212-2
  1. Lobbying – Great Britain. I. Miller, Charles. Lobbying
government. II. Title.
JN329.P7M55   1989
324′.4′0941–dc20   89-35528
                            CIP

Typeset in 10 on 12 pt Plantin
by Joshua Associates Ltd, Oxford
Printed in Great Britain by
T.J. Press (Padstow) Ltd, Padstow, Cornwall.

Contents

Preface to the Second Edition — vii
Acknowledgements — x
Introduction – the need to understand and work the system — xi

1 Government – the components of power — 1
   1.1 Political leadership and policy formulation — 2
   1.2 Implementation of policy — 24
   1.3 Policy scrutiny and endorsement — 36
   1.4 Parties — 46
   1.5 The power structure: influence, strengths, weaknesses — 51

2 Decision-makers – how do they work? — 57
   2.1 Legislation — 57
   2.2 Policy management and administration – the work of Ministers and officials — 77
   2.3 Can Ministers exercise power? — 91
   2.4 Whitehall: its mentality and its dealings with outsiders — 92
   2.5 Policy scrutiny and endorsement – the work of MPs and Peers: their mentality; pressures on them; their links with outsiders — 97

3 Dealing with Government — 122
   3.1 Fundamentals — 123
   3.2 Getting information — 136
   3.3 Techniques of advocacy — 156
   3.4 Promoting and amending legislation — 193
   3.5 Using help — 206

Appendices

1 The courts and the Ombudsman: action against executive and administrative decisions	213
2 Components and mechanics – finding out more	216
3 Movement of officials to the private sector – rules and concerns	217
4 Departments – responsibilities and ministerial duties 1989	224
5 All-Party subject and county groups	241
Index	245

Preface to the Second Edition

How do we gain Government contracts, aid or assistance?
How can we change policies that may harm us?
How can we promote or amend legislation?
Who in Government should we liaise with, and why?
Do we negotiate with Government, or apply pressure to it?
How do we acquire information about Government's plans?
How do we react if a Select Committee investigates us?
How do we influence Party policies?
Can Government promote our products or organization?
How can we get a Minister to visit us?
How do we react if a campaign is launched against us?
What are the ethics and techniques of Government liaison?

As a professional consultant on public policy and legislative dealings with Government, I am constantly being asked those questions. Many people either fear officials, Ministers and legislators, or do not understand them, or treat them like journalists.

There are many fine books on Government. In writing this one, I have drawn from them liberally. Yet few have described the infrastructure of decision-making on policy, commercial or legislative matters and none have explained in detail to those outside Government both how to ensure that they are not caught out by policy planning that could affect them and how to influence decision-making in Government as a whole.

The UK Government is large and complex. Dealing with it is a science – understanding its power balances and the way its policy-making processes work – coupled with the art of advocacy and negotiation.

This book aims to take the science and art of dealing with the UK Government out of the often lightweight province of an exercise in public relations and put it into its proper perspective. As in the United States, it is really an extension of the law: a serious, technical business which nonetheless can and should be mastered by all who could be affected by Government activity.

It may, however, be more constructive first to say what this book is not meant to do.

It is not an academic analysis of our system of Government.

It is not an exhaustive description of the way Government works and of all the techniques of working with Government. We have deliberately excluded detail on certain areas, such as monopolies and mergers, the Establishment side of Departments, and commercial negotiations involving the Government as contractor or dispenser of aid. Each really justifies a separate volume and it is hoped that outsiders will soon be able to learn about these subjects.

Another omission is guidance on dealing with the EEC. The work of the European Commission, Council of Ministers, European Parliament, and European Court of Justice, and their influence on UK legislation should be learnt and understood by any serious lobbyist, but the decision-making methods and techniques of working with community institutions are significantly different to those applicable to the UK also to warrant consideration in a subsequent book. Nonetheless, we should note that the increased role of EEC legislation and regulation in our own policy system is the most marked change between 1986, when the first edition was completed, and today. In many areas an organization's attention should now be turned at least as often to Brussels as to Whitehall and Parliament.

It is not intended to be a rulebook. Compared to the practice of law, accountancy and other professional and technical fields, there is a lack of established precedent and procedure in the business of dealing with Government. Any assessment, even by insiders, of the nature of power, the work of power centres, and particularly their concerns and susceptibilities is innately subjective. The practice of government liaison involves sound judgement as much as factual knowledge and leaves much room for innovative thinking and techniques, but we have been helped by many MPs and officials in producing what we feel is an accurate guide to Government rather than a complete exposition of its inner workings: an idea of where power really lies, how decisions are really taken and policy formed and implemented. What happens when a letter is sent to an MP or Minister? What considerations influence the thinking of MPs, officials and Ministers? What are the techniques of professional lobbyists? In seeking to address these issues, we have geared our observations only to the User of Government – the companies, trade associations and interest groups concerned with monitoring the policy process and influencing it – and have not included detail that would be irrelevant to an explanation of the way the structure of Government works and, in turn, how to work it to mutual advantage. We have set out fundamental principles of working with Government and, where the book appears to list imperatives, they are based on experience and on the accepted practices of leading government affairs consultants.

Preface to the Second Edition ix

Another reason why this book cannot be studied in the same way as a legal textbook is that the techniques of advanced negotiation with, and lobbying of, Government are not accessible by reading: it is more a matter of applying experience to the basic techniques described here. There can be no substitute for that experience, even in professions with more defined practising principles: a barrister of ten years' call is likely to be better than one of two years' standing.

In concentrating on technique, we are not decrying the value of friendships with Ministers made at school, on relationships forged with MPs and officials at parties or on holiday; but users of Government cannot count on that – decision-makers will never grant favours. Not only does it pay, therefore, to understand the principles of monitoring, legislative analysis, negotiation and lobbying, but strong contacts are unlikely to be repeated across the full range of a user's interests. Membership of a Party hierarchy may allow him to develop a close relationship with MPs and Ministers, but what about officials? What if the Government changes?

We therefore have aimed to advise on acquiring information, analysing it, accessing decision-makers and advocating a case to them. In short, answering the questions posed at the start of this preface.

One problem in writing this manual has been the level which its advice should be pitched. Too basic and it would appear laborious, and possibly patronizing, to those with some experience of working with Government. Too detailed and only professional consultants could understand its concepts without explanation. We have therefore produced it as a series both of questions to guide users' thoughts and statements of fact. Those with already established dealings with Government may therefore be able to add some new considerations to their existing knowledge.

I would like to thank the former officials, MPs and Ministers in Public Policy Consultants, who know far more than I, for their assistance. I hope, as a result of their advice, and that of many others within and outside the power structure who have lent their experience to us, that the techniques of Government liaison will now be understood and accepted as essential corporate tools.

One final point. One critic of the first edition commented on my exclusive use of the masculine pronoun throughout the book. I should have made it clear that this usage is not gender specific.

Acknowledgements

My grateful thanks go to the following: Peter Hennessy for his enthusiastic assistance; Patrick Nealon, Joanna Hurst, Michael Duncan, Berkeley Greenwood and Anna Hall for their help in revising the first edition; all those officials and legislators who have been so helpful in providing and checking opinions and information; the members of Public Policy Consultants whose collective experience and skill is far superior to the modest ability shown in this book.

The author and publisher wish to thank the following for permission to use copyright material:

The Controller of Her Majesty's Stationery Office for Crown copyright material;

Financial Times for 'Commons committee attacks handling of BT privatisation' by Lucy Kellaway, *Financial Times* 18.12.85;

Macmillan Publishers Ltd. for material from *Mastering British Politics* by F. N. Forman, 1985.

Introduction – the need to understand and work the system

This book brings up to date the reality of power in the British system of government. It is a guide to corporate dealings with today's Whitehall and Parliament. It is not an academic analysis or discussion of power or the historical role of government. It is a user's manual, setting out factually the structure of political and administrative decision-making and telling you how to deal with it.

Although the principles of democratic government in Britain can be traced back to Simon de Montfort's first Parliament in 1265, the structure of the system of political and administrative decision-making, as we know it today, is of surprisingly recent origin.

Forty or fifty years ago, people were as interested in politics as they are today, but were less politicized in a national sense. The media did not bring the work of Government into every sitting room; MPs represented local communities, not national Party issues; and pressure groups and business contacts with Government were less sophisticated.

Nor did they need to be any better: the size and role of central Government was far smaller before the Second World War than it is now.

In 1939 there were 615 MPs; now there are 650 and a range of backbench, All-Party and Select committees that would have been unknown to the pre-war parliamentarian. There are now over 350 Life Peers and far less of an Establishment imbalance in the Upper House. Parliament has nonetheless become more of a scrutinizing and endorsing body than one that exerts real influence on policies. MPs have also changed. From being largely financially independent, many now rely on their parliamentary salary and seek outside consultancy work to make ends meet.

In 1939 there were 19 Departments; in 1930 there were 84 Ministers, Whips and Parliamentary Private Secretaries. Now there are 25 Departments and 144 MPs and Peers are involved in Government.

Moving further back, Peel as Home Secretary in 1822 had a staff of fourteen clerks, a precis writer, a librarian, and various porters and domestic officials. The Foreign Office employed 20 in 1821.

As the world moves faster, reliance of Ministers on departmental and – a recent feature – specialist political advisers has become greater. Government has moved into a more dominant regulatory role, influencing corporate policies and individual lives to a far greater degree and becoming a major commercial entity as State procurement and trading concerns have grown.

Technological change has also accelerated the obsolescence of legislation. Copyright law, for example, which used to have an average life of 40 years or more, is now being constantly outdated by new uses of copyright material that had not been envisaged at the time of enactment of each Statute. Today's Copyright Act may require revision in ten years, not 40.

So times have changed and Government has become more complex, more pervasive, and harder to ignore. As its influence has increased, so has the need to understand both how it can affect our interests and the way it now works. Failure to do so inevitably means that the right to know and be heard – whether that right is exercised by a ratepayers' association or the CBI – cannot be used effectively.

One problem that any individual or company faces in understanding the framework of Government and its decision-making processes is, ironically, our tradition of parliamentary democracy. We are all educated to regard Parliament as the most important part of our constitutional structure. The media concentrates on Parliament as the most public, visible and accessible element of Government. We are justifiably proud of our parliamentary heritage, but power is a dynamic and should be considered without the romantic focus that led Bagehot, the great nineteenth-century political commentator, to observe that one does not let light in upon magic or the natural propensity to be impressed by the magnificence of the Palace of Westminster.

Yet that very dynamic that must make us reconsider the structure of power at regular intervals also means that no two issues or decisions in Government can be regarded in the same way. Power in the British constitution may rest within a number of institutions, and even individuals, depending on the issue. Britain is not like the United States, where individuals or business interests can rely on Congress as the central pivot of the system of government. Checks and balances are real concepts there but academic notions here. Power, and the influences on it, are the only factors that should concern those who want to know how the British system actually works and how they should work it.

Another factor deterring the desire to understand and work with Government is the over-emphasized role of lobbying. Contact with Government, we have been led to believe, is essentially a matter of pressure; of large-scale, expensive and time-consuming campaigns that are often high profile. For any business, these can be seen as set-piece battles; as something

Box 1 Government as a commercial entity

In 1988 the UK Government dispensed £86 million in aid and trade provision and £1387 million in multilateral and bilateral aid. Since 1964, it has given over £20 billion in regional industrial assistance.

It wholly owned the following nationalized industries in 1988:

British Coal
Electricity Supply Industry (England and Wales)[a]
North of Scotland Hydro-Electric Board[a]
South of Scotland Electricity Board[a]
Post Office
National Girobank[a]
British Rail
British Waterways Board
Scottish Transport Group
British Shipbuilders
Civil Aviation Authority
Regional Water Authorities[a]

And was involved with the following public corporations:

Bank of England
British Broadcasting Corporation
British Technology Group
Commonwealth Development Corporation
Covent Garden Market Authority
Crown Agents
Development Board for Rural Wales
Highlands and Islands Development Board
Housing Corporation
Independent Broadcasting Association
Land Authority for Wales
National Dock Labour Board
National Water Council
New Town Development Corporations and Commission
Northern Ireland Development Agency
Northern Ireland Electricity Service
Northern Ireland Housing Executive
Northern Ireland Transport Housing Company
Passenger Transport Executives
Pilotage Commission
Property Services Agency
Royal Mint
Scottish Development Agency
Scottish Special Housing Group
Her Majesty's Stationery Office
Trust Ports

Cont.

Box 1 (*Cont.*)

> Urban Development Corporations
> Welsh Development Agency
>
> It had substantial shareholdings in a further three large organizations:
>
> British Nuclear Fuels
> Harland and Wolff[a]
> Short Bros[a]
>
> [a] The Government announced its intention to privatize these industries.
>
> *Note*: Compare this box with that in the first edition to see the extent of the Conservative privatization programme.

rather special. However, as with any other form of crisis management, prevention is always preferable to cure and the first and most important requirement in dealing with Government is the *Need to Know*. That need, connected with Government's duty to communicate with the governed and the right to be informed, can be satisfied at two levels: by passive monitoring – making sure you know of everything that *has* happened; or through early warning – making sure you know in advance of likely policy planning or actions that may affect your interests.

At the next stage of work with Government comes the *Need to Inform* – to know and be known by those officials, MPs, Peers and Ministers who could formulate, consider, scrutinize, amend or endorse policies or commercial matters that concern organizations; and to establish a relationship of trust that makes Government willing to use individuals, firms or trade associations as a source of the information it needs in order to produce representative policies, whether public or commercial.

Higher still is the *Need to Negotiate* – to make representations to the components of the power structure where there is a need to change policy or where Government is a trading partner. It may, however, be necessary to ally outside influences – the media and public or associated groups' opinion – for one's point to get across. This final need, the *Need to Lobby*, is what many believe to be the most common form of requirement in dealings with Government. That belief is generally only justified in the case of pressure groups.

In any guide to dealings with Government, it is important to clarify ethics at the outset. There are many who feel that, while the four needs are undeniable, their satisfaction involves a buckling of the perfect wheel of democracy; an inevitable exercising of undue influence and interference with the efficiency of the policy process. Since it is also undeniable that abuses of the system have been, and still are legion, this argument cannot lightly be dismissed.

The counter-case is best made by first appealing to history. Magna Carta in 1215 gave our nobles the right to petition the King – the source of power. The First Amendment to the United States Constitution also provides for the right to plead for redress of grievances. Our Government, no less than that in the United States, is one by the people and for the people. It is not meant to be a self-satisfying system. The modern notion of making Government accountable for its actions, or of professional advocacy to persuade decision-makers of the validity of a point of view, is no different from the long-established principles of administrative law, which provides for court orders to make Government perform its duties or prevent abuses of power.

Government is a court. It cannot make up its mind in a vacuum and today, more than ever before, it encourages all shades of opinion to state their case rather than risk the charge of making unrepresentative decisions. If the governed – either individuals or corporate bodies – do not state their demands to those they elect or whose salaries they pay, they have only themselves to blame when democratic institutions make undemocratic decisions. If those decisions favour a few at the expense of many, it is because the majority has forgotten to make its point or has made it badly. After all, skilful advocacy has secured the acquittal of many a criminal, yet the right to take a case to a legal, rather than a governmental tribunal is accepted unchallenged.

As with the law, the balance of interest lies in encouraging unrestricted access to Government. The best guarantee against abuse, and the objective of this book, is that this right is professionally exercised.

This book is divided into three sections. In section 1 we describe the way Government works. We identify the components of the power structure and assess their importance. In section 2 we look inside Whitehall and Westminster to examine the working lives of their members and consider legislative and non-legislative decision-making. In section 3 we explain how to work with Government. How to become better informed. How to deal with officials, Ministers and parliamentarians. How to construct a strategy of dealing with Government. The techniques of advocacy to Government. And when and how to use outside advice. At each stage we use graphic examples and checklists for easy reference in future.

The information in *Lobbying* was up-to-date on 1 October 1989.

1
Government – the components of power

The UK Government is rather like a larger European group of companies, with the Prime Minister as Chief Executive, Departments as line companies with Ministers as directors, the Cabinet as the group management board serviced by a secretariat and a second tier board, Parliament, which exists to supervise corporate policy and put forward the consumers' point of view. Each Department will have separate staff responsible for administration and production. Although the management's men often dominate the lower board, the Chief Executive and his directors have to make sure it is kept reasonably happy because a voice against upper board policy means that both boards may have to offer themselves for re-election by the shareholders – the UK electorate.

In attempting to understand the modern power balance in our system of government, a working knowledge of its parts must first be established. Power rests in three main groups of bodies covering

- political leadership and overall policy formulation;
- implementation of policy; and
- scrutiny and endorsement of policy.

Distinctions between these three areas can often be blurred, however. Government can be set out graphically as a route map, with each part of the power structure being linked to a number of others by paths of command, influence, and the checks and balances that have evolved in our unwritten Constitution of accepted principles. Box 2 illustrates that power structure in simplified form. As we can see, a number of components straddle the boundaries between two sectors. They combine political and administrative functions or act as a link between formulators and endorsers to ensure that the latter do just that.

2   Government – the components of power

Box 2   The route map of Government

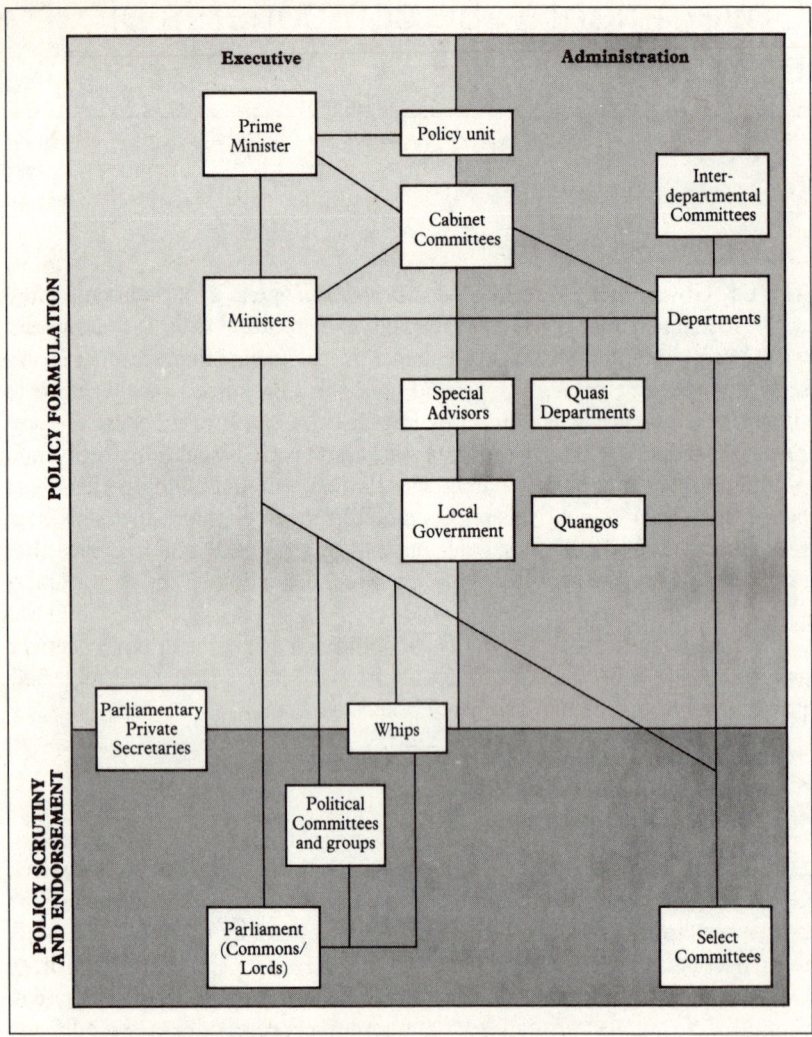

1.1 Political leadership and policy formulation

These functions are otherwise known as the Executive arm of government. The Prime Minister and his Ministers, within the broad mandate given to them by their Party, decide on the subject matter and tone of important policy changes. As the main board of our company, they formulate its corporate plan.

The Prime Minister

The Prime Minister is political leader of the country, leader of the majority Party and Chairman of the group of Ministers represented in our model as directors. He appoints and dismisses Ministers, is the only regular link between the power structure and its constitutional head, the monarch, and is the ultimate determinant of policy. Ministers have a specific remit and power framework: the Prime Minister has the ability to be almost presidential or appear to be no more than part of a team. To the contemporary reader, the former might best be exemplified by Margaret Thatcher; the latter by Stanley Baldwin. In both cases, however, the potential power of the Prime Minister's office remains the same. The ability to secure the confidence of his Party, both in Parliament and nationally, is the key to his position. Parties need leaders, and strong leadership provides a focus of expectations both by the electorate and legislators. Strong Prime Ministers can dominate and influence their Ministers and gain allegiance from those MPs whose position on the Government benches, or even their seat, may depend on the public's perception of that strength.

In addition to providing his Ministers' job descriptions, where they have not already been set by ongoing departmental commitments, the Prime Minister is also the ultimate reconciler of policy differences between Departments. He chairs many interdepartmental Cabinet Committees (see page 14) and may either call on conflicting Ministers to establish liaison between officials on specific issues or ask his Policy Unit of personal advisers to produce recommendations, as happened in 1984 when British Airways and British Caledonian had both lobbied the Department of Transport, Treasury and Department of Trade and Industry over allocation of air routes against a background of BA privatization and Ministers were initially unable to reach a satisfactory solution.

The Prime Minister can combine any of the responsibilities of State in his office. Margaret Thatcher took a personal interest in departmental organization and efficiency and became Minister for the Civil Service. Yet the Prime Minister has no Department of his own, with a mass of specialists to advise on the logistics and implications of policy proposals. Instead, he has at his disposal a large personal staff at 10 Downing Street, his official residence and office; the resources of the Cabinet Office, which services and guides, under the Prime Minister's ultimate instruction, the board he chairs; and, in the place of a Permanent Secretary, the most senior official adviser to Ministers in each Department, he enjoys the close counsel of the

Secretary of the Cabinet, currently regarded as the head of the Civil Service. Together they formulate and control the agenda of Cabinet meetings, setting the parameters within which ministerial discussions on policy can take place, and of Cabinet Committees, to influence policy decisions involving more than one Department. Within Departments, the Prime Minister's word on the shape of policy formulation, either agreed by the Cabinet or dictated to a Department by normal administrative necessities, is invariably conclusive when passed to Ministers.

In 1989, the Prime Minister had 27 main staff at 10 Downing Street, divided between her Private, Political and Press offices. In total, there were 63 people supporting Mrs Thatcher.

The *Private Office*, manned by civil servants, provides the Prime Minister with administrative support. It is led by a Principal Private Secretary, an official of senior (Under Secretary) grade who will have had at least 20 years' policy advisory experience. Even the most senior Ministers in the Cabinet are given Principal Private Secretaries who in the main have served for only half that length of time and who are usually two grades below the level of the Prime Minister's Private Office manager. The Principal Private Secretary has constant access to the Prime Minister and has strong control over the flow of information to him, including listening to all but the most private telephone calls in case immediate action must be taken on his own initiative. Two Assistant Private Secretaries process the Prime Minister's correspondence, excepting that involving his Party's affairs, and help the Principal Private Secretary to manage the vast amount of letters, memoranda and documents that flow to and from the Cabinet Office, Ministers, officials and outsiders. Four Private Secretaries, who are officials at Assistant Secretary and Principal grades seconded from other Departments, provide specialist advice on foreign, home and Treasury matters, draft answers to Parliamentary Questions to the Prime Minister, monitor Parliament generally and keep his diary.

Finally, the Appointments or Patronage Secretary handles recommendations on the public positions wholly or largely filled by Prime Ministerial decision or advice – bishoprics, Permanent Secretaries, the Governor of the Bank of England, chairmen of nationalized industries, and so on.

The Private Office functions very much as a team in linking the Prime Minister to Whitehall Departments, the offices of the Chief Whip – who is charged with the maintenance of loyalty among the Government's MPs and Peers – and the Leaders of the House of Commons and Lords, who are responsible for ensuring that the Government's schedule of legislation and debate is completed within the time available for parliamentary discussion. While each Private Secretary specializes, as described above, business is dealt with by any of them if necessary. The organization of meetings and visits, either in this country or abroad, may involve all the Office's members in conjunction with relevant Departments.

Mrs Thatcher also exercises her position's freedom to create whichever posts are deemed necessary by the Prime Minister in appointing a senior diplomat as Adviser on Foreign Affairs. The appointment was made to assist the Private Secretaries' continuous contact with the Foreign Office and provide the Prime Minister with more senior advice on international relations.

The *Press Office* is the main point of contact between the general public and media and Number 10. The Prime Minister's Press Secretary is responsible for the management of his relations with the media, for his public relations more generally, and the presentation of the Government's policies as a whole. For this purpose the Press Secretary coordinates the work of his counterparts in all other Whitehall Departments through a weekly meeting and daily contact. He deals directly with the media, but especially with the Parliamentary Lobby correspondents, a group of journalists accredited by the two Houses of Parliament who receive off the record briefings from MPs and Peers, Ministers and, every day, from him. He and his staff are civil servants, on secondment to the Prime Minister's office from other Departments. In addition to the Press Secretary, there is a Deputy Press Secretary and three Press Officers. A further Press Secretary in the Political Office deals with Party publicity.

The *Political Office* services the leader of the Government Party in the same way that the Private Office services the leader of the Government. It handles the great volume of communications between the Prime Minister, his Party's head office and regional or local organizations and prepares for Party Conferences, rallies, election campaigns and other meetings involving the Prime Minister as a political figure as distinct from Chairman of the Board in our model of Government. It also provides advice on issues independent of the Civil Service. Rarely are the Political Office's members officials. They are usually Party supporters recruited from Head Office or the Prime Minister's former Opposition office in Parliament or from business, industry or academe.

The Political Office has four components. At its head, the Political Secretary and his assistant are the Prime Minister's in-house advisers on Party affairs, speeches and Election campaign planning. They help the Prime Minister to maintain a presence in his constituency, a difficult task when the pressures of office invariably prevent the weekly meetings with constituents or the local constituency association that are part of the working life of most backbench MPs. There is a Policy Unit, which exists to maintain and develop the Government's strategic policies, offer independent advice to the Prime Minister and provide solutions to some

6   Government – the components of power

Box 3   The Policy Unit – members and backgrounds 1989

Head	
Prof. Brian Griffiths	Education, housing
Members	
Greg Bourne (Seconded from BP)	Energy, transport
Andrew Dunlop (Ex Special Adviser, M.o.D.)	Scotland, tax, employment, social security, defence
George Guise (Seconded from Consolidated Goldfields)	Industry, R&D
Howell Harris Hughes (Seconded from Touche Ross)	City matters, industry
John Mills (Seconded from DTI)	Local government, water
Carolyn Sinclair (Seconded from the Treasury)	Home affairs, agriculture
Ian Whitehead (Seconded from the Bank of Montreal)	Health, inner cities

interdepartmental problems. In 1989 the Policy Unit had nine members, drawn from a variety of backgrounds (box 3).

Lastly, the counterpart of the Private Secretary specializing in parliamentary matters is the Prime Minister's Parliamentary Private Secretary, who is appointed by him from among his backbenchers to act as the day-to-day liaison with them. The post of PPS, as it is normally abbreviated, is unpaid but the number of PPS appointments has grown in recent years, particularly in Mrs Thatcher's second Government, with a very large number of MPs in the majority Party being offered the job, which is traditionally seen as the first step towards a ministerial appointment. The Prime Minister's PPS, however, is often an experienced MP who may have held a ministerial position and is more than likely to be rewarded for loyal and useful service to the Prime Minister with another office of state.

In 1988, in addition to the Prime Minister, all Secretaries of State, most Ministers of State and even some Parliamentary Under Secretaries of State had PPSs – as Box 4 shows, there were 40 in total. The PPS performs the same role for all of them:

Box 4 Parliamentary Private Secretaries – a growing band

	1900	1920	1940	1960	1979	1988
PPSs	9	13	25	36	28	40

- advising on parliamentary reaction to ministerial policies or future measures;
- acting as a forum for complaint or enquiry by MPs where the Minister may not be immediately accessible. This is particularly important in the case of the Prime Minister;
- acting as one of the conduits for parliamentary representations to Ministers and as a means by which outsiders can raise confidential or personal matters with the Minister without officials being involved, either as intermediaries or eavesdroppers.

Ian Gow, a past PPS at Number 10, was dubbed 'Supergrass' by backbenchers, a graphic but concise description of the PPS's role. Since a Minister is to some extent distanced from the House of Commons by departmental responsibilities, he needs to be kept up to date. PPS's are the link between Ministers and Parliament.

Parliamentary Private Secretaries, in return for gaining an insight into and experience of departmental life and the pressures of ministerial office, are by convention constrained from exercising some of the freedoms of their fellow MPs. They do not normally sign Early Day Motions (page 117), must give up their place on Select Committees, and cannot ask questions or speak on subjects covered by their own Minister. For them to vote against the Government would normally be regarded as incompatible with their status. Occasionally, that restriction may weigh heavily on a PPS. Dissent by them may be taken to show that their master, particularly if he is a Cabinet Minister, has disagreed with Government policy and has either been overruled or is bound by the principle of Collective Responsibility from openly expressing opposition. The PPS may sacrifice his position under such circumstances as a subtle signal to the Leadership.

They will also have to devote a great deal of time to the job. In addition to assessing pitfalls in debates, votes or question times for his Minister, he will be required to sit on Standing Committees considering his Department's Bills. So, apart from rewarding promising backbenchers and providing much-needed help to Ministers, the creation of more and more PPS posts can be seen as a means of finding work for restless MPs, particularly when Government majorities are great, and of effectively limiting major backbench votes against the Executive. A PPS who has been in the same post for more than two years or three years without promotion may feel that he has been shackled without any real privilege and return to the backbenches.

The role and work of Parliamentary Private Secretaries should be compared with that of the Whips, who are discussed on page 8.

Ministers

In 1989 there were 83 Ministers, with responsibility for the ultimate setting, management and approval of policy in 25 Departments (not all Departments have controlling Ministers).

Ministers are appointed by the Prime Minister, usually on the advice of the Secretary of State concerned and the Chief Whip, and may be selected from either the Commons or the Lords. While it is usual nowadays for Secretaries of State, who have ultimate departmental responsibility, to be members of the Commons, there were three Peers in the 1989 Cabinet and Prime Ministers are conscious of the need to have strong Ministers in the Lords, where Party discipline is less marked than in the Lower House.

While Ministers may be drawn from any Party, in practice they are only selected from the majority faction unless there is a coalition (the last one being during the Second World War) or the largest Party has no overall majority and may offer ministerial posts to members of the Party holding the balance of power as a means of buying voting allegiance in the Commons. Edward Heath, Conservative Prime Minister between 1970 and 1974, offered Liberal leader Jeremy Thorpe the office of Home Secretary in 1970 for that reason. One official of ministerial status, the Comptroller and Auditor General, whose Department controls the issue of money to Whitehall Departments, checks that the Treasury's demands are in accordance with the sums authorized by Parliament, and audits departmental accounts to ensure that money has been properly spent, is appointed by Parliament as an officer of the House of Commons. Those exceptions aside, Ministers are selected for several reasons:

- as a recognition of ability;
- as a reward for loyal support for the Prime Minister and Party;
- to emasculate backbench dissidents; and
- as a personal concession to a Secretary of State who may wish particular MPs to join his ministerial team.

So policy management abilities, while desirable, are not necessarily paramount in the Prime Minister's thinking when new Ministers are chosen. Many hold one or two junior ministerial posts and are then returned to the backbenches. Some, however, remain as Ministers because the Prime Minister may feel their position as a member of the Government, with its Collective Responsibility bar to dissent, is safer than having them attack the Executive and possibly undermine its credibility in the Party and country.

That doctrine of Collective Responsibility is important. It means that Government policies must be adhered to and supported by all Ministers. Failure to reconcile personal conscience with this principle leaves a Minister only with the option of resignation. Similarly, within a Minister's own Department, Ministerial Responsibility declares that, whether it is truth or fiction, he has sanctioned all the actions or omissions of his officials and is responsible for them. Thus in 1982 Lord Carrington and his Foreign Office Ministers resigned following suggestions that officials had ignored forewarnings about the Argentine invasion of the Falklands. Even though the oversight may have been committed without Ministers' knowledge, they were bound to take responsibility for it. (One Minister, Richard Luce, was eventually reappointed.)

One final personal circumscription is the convention that a Minister should divest himself of all sources of income apart from his ministerial salary as a safeguard against influence by outside interests. In practice, that means either appointing nominees for shareholdings and other assets, or transferring them into their spouse's name. In 1988 Ministers were paid between £18,219 (Parliamentary Under-Secretaries) and £34,479 (Secretaries of State) as well as a reduced parliamentary salary of £18,148. More than one MP has found himself unable to accept ministerial office, since to have done so would have meant giving up directorships, consultancies and other business income well in excess of the Crown's remuneration.

There are a number of other limitations, which mainly apply to the Prime Minister's right freely to appoint anyone as a Minister:

- If he appoints from outside Parliament, convention demands that the new Minister should become a member of either House virtually immediately. Since it is most unusual for an MP to resign his seat in mid-term, particularly to make way for another, this principle in practice means that a peerage would be created to enable the Minister to be directly accountable to Parliament.
- The number of Ministers and Parliamentary Under-Secretaries who are members of the Commons is limited by the House of Commons (Disqualification) Act 1975 and the Ministers of the Crown Act, 1975–95.

This means that, with today's requirements, the Prime Minister has to create a nucleus of Ministers in the Lords.
- Where the head of a Department is in the Lords, his deputy must be drawn from the Commons.

The ministerial hierarchy in almost all Departments is:

- *Secretary of State* – with overall responsibility for all departmental policy;
- *Minister(s) of State* – with line responsibility for broad sectors of policy;
- *Parliamentary Under Secretary(ies) of State* – who understudies Ministers of State and may take responsibilty for individual projects.

Regardless of level, all Ministers have the following roles:

- ensuring that agreed manifesto and Cabinet policy is implemented by officials;
- protecting their Department and the sectors it sponsors in interdepartmental negotiations;
- acting as the ultimate departmental forum for representations by individuals or organizations;
- being accountable to Parliament.

The last of these, accountability to Parliament, illustrates the ambivalence of the Minister's position. It has often been commented that a change is wrought in an MP when he becomes a Minister. From being an outsider who seeks information on and influence over departmental activities, he often finds himself heavily reliant on his officials to defend himself and his Department against parliamentary and public probing. The one-time Select Committee member, who may have taken particular pains over interrogating civil servants and Ministers, usually finds himself delivering anodyne responses to Parliamentary Questions and resisting wherever possible legislative amendments even where they have been tabled by his own backbenchers.

The main opposition Party in the House of Commons also appoints a team of MPs and Peers as spokesmen to 'shadow' Ministers of the main Departments. As with the Government, the Opposition has three or four MPs responsible for each departmental area. At least one Shadow Minister will sit on appropriate Standing Committees (page 38) and will respond for the Opposition to ministerial speeches during the various parliamentary stages of legislation or in policy debates. The Shadow Cabinet meets in the House of Commons every Wednesday evening.

Many Departments now have *Special Advisers* appointed by Ministers to provide political advice to Ministers and act as a buffer between them and their officials. They perform an equivalent function to the Prime Minister's

Box 5 Departmental Special Advisers (as of September 1989)

Ministry of Agriculture	
Richard Gueterbock	European Democratic Group & Milk Marketing Board
Office of Arts and Libraries	
Dr Elizabeth Cottrell	Centre for Policy Studies
Ministry of Defence	
Keith Simpson	Conservative Research Department
Department of Education	
Eleanor Laing	Shopping Hours Reform Council
Department of Employment	VACANT
Department of Energy	
Guy Black	Conservative Research Department
Department of the Environment	
Patrick Rock	Conservative Research Department and No 10 Political Office
Tim Collins	Conservative Research Department
Foreign Office	
David Lidington	Special Adviser, Home Office; BP; RTZ
Maurice Fraser	Conservative Research Department
Department of Health	
Tessa Keswick	Cluff Resources
Home Office	
John Godfrey	Daiwa
Scottish Office	
Graeme Carter	PA to the late Sir Alex Fletcher MP
Department of Social Security	
Charles Hendry	Special Adviser, DHSS and DTI; PR consultant
Department of Trade & Industry	
Katherine Ramsay	Special Adviser, DTp and DoE
Michael Simmonds	Adam Smith Institute
Department of Transport	
Elizabeth Buchanan	Conservative Research Department

Cont.

Box 5 (*Cont.*)

Treasury	
Judith Chaplin	Conservative Research Department and IOD
Andrew Tyrie	Special Adviser, DOE and OAL
Warwick Lightfoot	Special Adviser, Employment; Hill Samuel
Downing Street	
John Whittingdale	Special Adviser, DTI
Lord Privy Seal's Office	
Anthony Teasdale	Special Adviser, FCO; European Democratic Group

Policy Unit and, like the Policy Unit, will be supporters of the Government and its policies. In essence they are political civil servants but, like Parliamentary Private Secretaries, they provide a valuable direct conduit to Ministers without recourse to officials. That does not necessarily mean that Ministers will take their advice in preference to that of their civil servants, but they do provide a second opinion from a known sympathizer. However, as with PPSs, the status of Special Advisers is dependent on the way Ministers decide to treat them: some are trusted senior counsel, others may be no more than political speech writers for their master. One rule is common – if a Minister is moved or dismissed, his Special Adviser must resign immediately, although he may be reappointed by another Minister.

While Ministers have for many years introduced personal political advisers into Departments on a piecemeal basis, the Labour Government of 1974 established them as a long-term and widespread phenomenon. Their place under future administrations looks assured.

Cabinet

The Cabinet has been compared in our analysis to the board of directors in our system of government and in constitution, work and role it is very similar. In 1989 it consisted of the Prime Minister and 22 Ministers including, uniquely, both the Chancellor of the Exchequer and the Chief Secretary to represent the Treasury and reinforce its senior position. (Mrs Thatcher also exceptionally included two Department of Employment Ministers in 1985–7 and two Department of Trade and Industry Ministers in 1989.) It meets every Thursday morning, rather more often than

Box 6 Members of the Cabinet 1989

> The Prime Minister
> Lord Chancellor (who presides over the House of Lords and is the most senior law officer in the country)
> Lord Privy Seal and Leader of the House of Commons
> Lord President of the Council and Leader of the House of Lords
> Chancellor of the Duchy of Lancaster (and Chairman of majority Party)
> Minister for Agriculture
> Secretary of State for Defence
> Secretary of State for Education and Science
> Secretary of State for Employment
> Secretary of State for Energy
> Secretary of State for the Environment
> Secretary of State for Foreign and Commonwealth Affairs
> Secretary of State for Health
> Secretary of State for Home Affairs
> Secretary of State for Northern Ireland
> Secretary of State for Scotland
> Secretary of State for Social Security
> Secretary of State for Transport
> Chancellor of the Exchequer
> Chief Secretary to the Treasury
> Secretary of State for Wales

company boards, and exists to decide on the Government's major domestic and foreign policies, amend or fill in manifesto and other political commitments, coordinate interdepartmental policies and decisions and take emergency decisions on major problems.

The Cabinet's agenda is under the control of the Prime Minister, who decides with the Secretary to the Cabinet, who is also currently the Head of the Home Civil Service, what to include and in which order. Its meetings are secret and its agenda and discussions are only reported through hearsay. However, every regular Cabinet agenda includes a consideration of the coming week's parliamentary business; a summary by the Foreign Secretary of international developments affecting the UK; and a statement on economic affairs from the Chancellor of the Exchequer.

Cabinet meetings are brief, usually lasting around two hours. The Cabinet can work this quickly because only matters that need to be discussed collectively rather than individually are selected, with others being cleared by interdepartmental meetings and informal discussions between Ministers or with the Prime Minister in advance; because Cabinet papers summarizing arguments and recommendations are circulated at least a day or two before each meeting; because Prime Ministers have been in the practice for many years of consulting on major issues with an 'Inner Cabinet' of senior Ministers or personal favourites; and, lastly, because subjects that are to be discussed in some detail are usually examined in advance by one of the series of Cabinet committees. Any Cabinet member may apply to the Cabinet Secretary for an item to be included on the agenda for a meeting, but such requests are often turned down and the subject referred instead to one of those committees. *Questions of Procedure for Ministers*, the guidebook on Cabinet procedure that all ministers receive when they take office, makes it clear that, where there is a conflict of interest between Departments, it should not be referred to Cabinet until all other means of resolving it have been exhausted.

Although the Cabinet is made up of Ministerial heads of Departments, with the exception of the Chief Secretary to the Treasury, the Chief Whip, and one or two Ministers of State if their departmental head is a member of the Lords, the Attorney-General would also attend if a legal issue were involved and more junior colleagues may deputize if their masters are absent for any reason. Civil Servants and outsiders are occasionally invited to make presentations after the Cabinet's main business has been concluded.

Cabinet committees

Cabinet committees are, in a sense, the real Cabinet decision-makers. Each day between 10 and 15 such committees meet in the Cabinet Office or, if schedules only permit afternoon meetings during parliamentary sittings, in the offices reserved for Ministers in the House of Commons. They are constituted either as permanent or *ad hoc* groups. Currently, it is believed that some 25 Standing Committees and around 110 *ad hoc* groups exist. If this total seems high, it should be remembered that Attlee accumulated 466 such committees and Callaghan 190.

There are two levels of Cabinet Committee, the first in which only Ministers and Chief Whips sit, with a lower level, known as 'shadow' committees, comprising civil servants who iron out interdepartmental policy issues prior to ministerial discussion.

The Prime Minister has the power to appoint, amalgamate or abolish Cabinet committees. In the 1985 list in box 7, which is not exhaustive, social policy has been largely incorporated by Mrs Thatcher into H whereas her two predecessors had several *ad hoc* groups handling social issues. Mrs Thatcher in particular was known for bypassing the Cabinet Committee structure completely by assembling informal committees of Ministers, aides and Policy Unit members to handle difficult or delicate issues.

Box 7 Cabinet Office – committees 1985 (selection)

Committee initials	Chairperson	Functions
Economic and Industrial		
EA	Margaret Thatcher (*Prime Minister*)	Economic strategy, energy policy, changes in labour law, the most important EEC matters
E(EX)	Margaret Thatcher	Exports policy
E(NI)	Margaret Thatcher	Public sector strategy and oversight of the nationalised industries
E(NF)	Nigel Lawson (*Chancellor of the Exchequer*)	Nationalised industry finance
NIP	Nick Monck (*Treasury official*)	Official committee on nationalised industry policy
E(PSP)	Nigel Lawson	Public sector and public service pay policy
E(DL)	Nigel Lawson	Disposal and privatisation of State assets
E(PU)	Leon Brittan (*Trade and Industry Secretary*)	'Buy British' policy for public purchasing
E(CS)	John MacGregor (*Chief Secretary*)	Civil Service pay and contingency plans for Civil Service strikes
E(OCS)	Anne Mueller (*Cabinet Office official*)	Official committee for preparing contingency plans for E(CS)
PESC	John Anson (*Treasury official*)	Committee of finance officers handling the annual public expenditure survey
Oversea and Defence		
OD	Margaret Thatcher	Foreign affairs, defence and Northern Ireland
OD(O)	Sir Robert Armstrong (*Cabinet Secretary*)	Permanent secretaries' group working to OD
OD(E)	Sir Geoffrey Howe (*Foreign Secretary*)	EEC policy
EQ(S)	David Williamson (*Cabinet Office official*)	Committee of Deputy Secretaries steering OD(E)
EQ(O)	M R H Jenkins (*Foreign Office official*)	Official committee on routine EEC business
OD(SA)	Margaret Thatcher	Committee on the South Atlantic, the so-called 'War Cabinet' of 1982

Cont.

16 Government – the components of power

Box 7 (*Cont*)

Committee initials	Chairperson	Functions
OD(FOF)	Margaret Thatcher	Committee on the future of the Falklands
Northern Ireland	Lord Whitelaw (*Lord President*)	Preparation of future initiatives
Home, Legislation and Information		
L	John Biffen (*Leader of the House*)	Progress and planning of legislation
QL	John Biffen	Preparation of the Queen's Speech
H	Lord Whitelaw	Home affairs and social policy, including education
CCU	Douglas Hurd (*Home Secretary*)	The Civil Contingencies Unit of the Cabinet Office which plans for the maintenance of essential supplies and services during industrial disputes
H(HL)	Lord Whitelaw	Reform of the House of Lords
HD	Douglas Hurd	Home (i.e. Civil) defence
HD(O)	David Goodall (*Cabinet Office official*)	Official committee shadowing HD
HD(P)	David Heaton (*Home Office official*)	Updating of central and local government civil defence plans
TWC	Sir Robert Armstrong	Transition to War Committee which updates the 'War Book' for the mobilisation of Whitehall and the Armed Forces in a period of international tension
EOM	Anne Mueller	Monthly meeting of Whitehall Establishment officers on industrial and personnel policy
MIO	Bernard Ingham (*No 10 Press Secretary*)	Weekly meeting of chief information officers
MIO(E)	Bernard Ingham	Special group for handling economic information. Now meets infrequently due to persistent leaking

Cont.

Box 7 (*Cont*)

Committee initials	Chairperson	Functions
Intelligence and Security		
MIS	Margaret Thatcher	Ministerial steering committee on intelligence which supervises MI5, MI6 and GCHQ and fixes budget and priorities
PSIS	Sir Robert Armstrong	Permanent secretaries' steering group on intelligence: prepares briefs for ministerial group
JIC	Sir Anthony Duff (Cabinet Office official)	Joint Intelligence Committee which prepares assessments for ministers collating intelligence from all sources and circulating them weekly in the 'Red Book'
JIC(EA)	Sir Antony Duff	Economic intelligence assessments
SPM	Sir Robert Armstrong	Security and policy methods in the Civil Service
Official Committee on Security	Sir Robert Armstrong	Permanent secretaries' group on internal security
Personnel Security Committee	Sir Robert Armstrong	Official group supervising the working of positive vetting, polygraphs, etc.
Ad hoc		
MISC 3	John Dempster (*Lord Chancellor's Dept. official*)	Public records policy
MISC 7	Margaret Thatcher	Replacement of the Polaris force with Trident
MISC 14	Nigel Lawson	Policy innovations
MISC 15	Formerly head of Think Tank; post now defunct	Official group for briefing MISC 14
MISC 21	Lord Whitelaw	Ministerial committee which meets each autumn to fix the level of rate and transport support grant for local authorities
MISC 32	Robert Wade-Gery (*Cabinet Office official*)	Deployment of the Armed Forces outside the NATO area

Cont.

Box 7 (*Cont*)

Committee initials	Chairperson	Functions
MISC 42	Robert Wade-Gery	Military assistance (e.g. training of personnel) for the armed services of friendly powers
MISC 51	Robert Wade-Gery	Commodities needed for strategic purposes, e.g. oil
MISC 57	Robert Wade-Gery	Contingency planning for a miners' strike
MISC 58	John Dempster	Liberalising the declassification of official documents
MISC 62	Lord Whitelaw	The 'Star Chamber' for forcing spending cuts on departmental Ministers
MISC 79	Lord Whitelaw	Alternatives to domestic rates: rate capping
MISC 83	David Goodall	Internal constitutional arrangements for the Falkland Islands
MISC 87	Nigel Lawson	De-indexing of benefits
MISC 91	Margaret Thatcher	Choice of ALARM anti-radar missile
MISC 95	Margaret Thatcher	Abolition of the GLC and the metropolitan counties
MISC 97	Nicholas Barrington (*Foreign Office official*)	Preparation of 1984 London Economic Summit
MISC 101	Margaret Thatcher	Day-to-day handling of the 1984–85 miners' strike
MISC 107	Lord Young (*Employment Secretary*)	Training of 14–18 year olds
MISC 108	Lord Young	Freeing small businesses from red tape
MISC 111	Margaret Thatcher	Future of the Welfare State

Notes: The existence of Cabinet Committees is not officially acknowledged. This list represents the most recent attempt to cover them. Many will have changed by now and the list should be used as illustration only.

Source: *Social Studies Review*.

Cabinet Office

Cabinet committees are serviced by the Cabinet Office, the two components counting as one power centre in our structure of the system of government in Britain. For that reason we will deal with the Cabinet Office at this point rather than in our consideration of Whitehall Departments (pages 24–33). In addition to its work for Cabinet committees, it coordinates the management and organization of the Civil Service; secondment from and recruitment into it; and training, efficiency, personnel management and senior appointments.

Cabinet Office staff are both permanent and seconded from other Departments. The main Secretariat staff supporting Cabinet committees, includes the Chief Scientific Adviser (a Deputy Secretary), and is under the day-to-day leadership of a Permanent Secretary who has come to be recognized not only as the most powerful of the Permanent Secretaries and head of the Home Civil Service, but also as the Prime Minister's chief official adviser, briefing him both on Cabinet matters and on the general running of the Government. He attends all Cabinet meetings as its secretary (although one of his Private Secretaries actually takes the minutes). An indication of the prestige of the Cabinet Office is that he is one of four Permanent Secretaries there; other Departments, with many times more staff, mostly have only one. There are six groups of officials under the Cabinet Secretary who advise the Prime Minister and Cabinet in liaison with line Departments.

- The Economic Secretariat – covering economic, industrial and energy policy;
- The Oversea and Defence Secretariat – covering foreign and defence policy and also liaising with:
- The Security and Intelligence Secretariat – which considers monitored intelligence and pools it with some of our allies;
- The European Secretariat – covering EEC affairs;
- The Home Secretariat – covering social policy, law and order, environment, education, housing, local government and the planning of the government's legislative programme; and
- The Science and Technology Secretariat.

In advance of meetings, the Cabinet Office circulates Cabinet papers, which consist of statements by Departments, memoranda, supporting documents and recommendations for action; prepares agendas for each committee; and records and circulates discussions and decisions through Ministers' Private Offices to those Ministers and departmental Divisions that have to act on them.

Within the Cabinet Office, the Management and Personnel Office (MPO) is also led by a Permanent Secretary, the current office-holder being only the third woman to be appointed to a post of such seniority in the Civil Service. As the title suggests, it controls personnel management policy for the Civil Service, including appraisal, pay, and efficiency. It also advises on transfer of ministerial responsibilities; is the official link with the Treasury and Civil Service Select Committee (page 39); and maintains the central list of people who wish to be considered for appointments to public bodies. Security vetting and advice on acceptance of outside appointments by civil servants or others employed by the State is another part of the MPO's work.

In recent years, bilateral exchanges between business and industry executives and officials have increased dramatically. It is now common for officials at Principal and Assistant Secretary grades (mainly the former) to be allowed postings lasting from three months to two years to private sector areas relevant to their work. Merchant banks, major accountants and large industrial organizations have not been slow in forging contacts with MPO and individual Departments, both of which have been keen to allow officials contact with issues in context while mindful of the dangers of better conditions and salaries luring high-fliers from the Civil Service for good. Secondments to Government have in the main taken a different form, with gifted individuals of senior experience being invited by Ministers to become Special Advisers (many of whom under Mrs Thatcher, were seconded from Conservative Central Office – see box 5), members of the Policy Unit and Cabinet Office for limited terms or more permanent leaders of areas of Government requiring commercial management skills.

Currently, some 280 officials are on secondment, with 200 outsiders working for limited periods in the Civil Service. Around 8 per cent of officials do not return. The Civil Service has become concerned over the number of high-quality officials being recruited into the private sector, the result of comparatively poor pay and conditions relative to responsibility, a grading structure that makes rapid promotion unlikely even for the most able, and the increased role and influence of Government in corporate planning (see appendix 3). The officials moving to the private sector are of two main types: high-flying Principal or Assistant Secretary grade civil servants who feel blocked or under-paid; and more senior grades, often transferring on retirement, who are recruited for their inside knowledge and ability to obtain results, often from the same officials of whom they were in charge. At the top of the tree, Permanent Secretaries are also respected public figures who receive an automatic knighthood in return for being Managing Director of a Department employing several thousand and for the responsibility of controlling the formulation and administration of policy.

Whips

The composition of the Executive is completed by the Whips who, like Parliamentary Private Secretaries, provide a regular link between Ministers and Parliament. Unlike PPSs, however, who advise individual Ministers on Party feeling and convey responses to backbenchers, the Whips, comprising the Chief Whip and, currently thirteen Deputy and Junior Whips, maintain day-to-day discipline within the Government Party and ensure that the Executive's decisions are endorsed by a majority on their side.

A Whip's task can be very difficult and requires the ability to be firm and to know about the concerns, problems and habits of a large number of MPs since each Whip is given responsibility for his Party's MPs within a geographical area. They are also assigned a subject responsibility and are involved in any parliamentary business relating to that subject. This responsibility, which changes each year, involves them in meeting Ministers of the appropriate Department once a week to keep them informed of Party opinion. Box 8 lists the distribution of both sets of duties among the Government Whips in 1989.

Box 8 Government Whips

Officers	Responsibilities (as at October 1989)	Areas
Tristan Garel-Jones Treasurer of HM Household	DEPUTY CHIEF WHIP	
Alistair Goodlad Comptroller of HM Household	Accommodation Constitutional	*South London*
Tony Durant Vice-Chamberlain of HM Household	Messages Arts and Heritage	*Wessex* Berkshire Buckinghamshire Hampshire W. Sussex
David Lightbown Lord commissioner of the Treasury	Defence Energy	*East Midlands* Hertfordshire Leicestershire (Part) Lincolnshire Northamptonshire Nottinghamshire
		Cont.

22 Government – the components of power

Box 8 (*Cont.*)

Officers	Responsibilities (as at October 1989)	Areas
Kenneth Carlisle Lord Commissioner of the Treasury	PAIRING WHIP Foreign and Commonwealth Affairs	*Eastern* Bedfordshire Cambridgeshire Essex Norfolk Suffolk
Stephen Dorrell Lord Commissioner of the Treasury	Finance Private Members' Bills and Motions	*South-East* East Sussex Kent Surrey
David Heathcoat-Amory Lord Commissioner of the Treasury	Environment	*Western* Gloucestershire Avon (Part) Shropshire Cornwall Hereford and Worcester
John Taylor Lord Commissioner of the Treasury	Home Affairs Media Euro Affairs Legal, Wales	*Wales and the Marches* Avon Gloucestershire Shropshire Hereford and Worcester
Greg Knight Government Whip	Health Social Security	*West Midlands*
Irvine Patnick OBE Government Whip	Trade and Industry Shipping Aviation Transport	*Yorkshire and North Midlands*
Tom Sackville Government Whip	Agriculture Northern Ireland	*North-West* Cheshire Greater Manchester Lancashire Merseyside
Michael Fallon Government Whip	Scotland COI Liaison	*Scotland & Borders*
Sydney Chapman Government Whip	Education Employment	*North London*

Where votes are sufficiently important and the Government's guaranteed majority small, Whips may bargain concessions in exchange for voting support. For example, Whips make an input to the Prime Minister on recommendations for honours, the composition of some overseas parliamentary delegations, and worthy candidates for ministerial office. They can also help MPs gain votes or Executive approval for a Private Member's Bill (page 58). All PPSs are appointed on their recommendation. If an MP wishes to vote against his Party on matters of conscience or because there are extenuating constituency circumstances, it is normal for him to clear his dissent with his Whip. And, since Whips decide on 'pairing' – cancelling out votes on both sides of the Commons – they are in a similar position to a school housemaster in that MPs must be present at votes unless the Whips have granted them an exeat.

Every Thursday, all MPs receive a list of the forthcoming week's debates. This sheet of paper, also and rather confusingly known as The Whip, shows each debate underlined once, twice or three times. This means:

- once – attendance is requested but not obligatory;
- twice – MPs may be absent if paired or if the Whips permit;
- three times – attendance is essential.

The Whip also contains announcements of many parliamentary group meetings. Putting a meeting 'on the Whip' guarantees that it is noticed by all MPs.

Opposition parties also have Whips who perform the same functions as their Government counterparts and liaise with them to ensure that the business of the two Houses strikes a balance between the Government's timetable and the Opposition's desire for time to criticize and debate. This procedure is known as 'the usual channels', with the Whips from all Parties submitting to the Speaker lists of leading speakers for debates as well as proposals for subjects and timetables. The 'usual channels' is in fact the Chief Whip's Private Secretary, an official of Principal grade who is selected for his impartiality and his ability to balance the demands of Government and Opposition. He works both long term, with a broad future strategy for legislation and debate over several months, and day-to-day, in conjunction with the Chief Whip, Opposition Chief Whip and the Leaders of both Houses.

The Whips also perform the same 'antenna' function as that of a PPS, but for the executive as a whole. There is always one Whip on duty on the Government front bench to ensure that business is proceeding according to plan. Every back bench committee (page 40) and many All-Party meetings will have a Whip present; and they sit on every Standing Committee (page 38). They are not, however, allowed to speak in Committee or on the floor of the House.

Government Whips meet together four times a week to discuss tactics, duty rosters, speaking lists and other strategy. Each Wednesday they meet at the Chief Whip's house, 12 Downing Street – an indication of the importance of his position. During these meetings, they also deal with the maintenance of Party discipline in the Lords, which on occasion has been a more difficult task owing to the smaller influence of patronage, cross-Party dynastic ties and a strong tradition of 'conscience' voting. Regular offenders against their Party line may have the Whip withdrawn from them, meaning that they can no longer seek Party support for their amendments or proposed legislation.

Although they are not Ministers, Government Whips receive a salary in addition to their MP's pay. The more senior Whips also have titles, such as Comptroller of the Household, which date back to a time of royal influence but today are purely formal.

1.2 Implementation of policy

Traditionally, implementation of policy is called the administrative arm of government. The Civil Service advises the Executive on policy, carries out its commands, and administers ongoing policy commitments. It is the workforce in our corporate model; a workforce, however, in a very progressive company, since its influence is considerable yet underrated and misunderstood by outsiders.

Departments – areas of responsibility

While the 16 main Government Departments have titles more or less indicating their briefs, it is still not always certain that outsiders can find the correct pigeon-hole for their concerns since many subject headings are the responsibility of more than one Ministry. Thus aviation is handled (or, as it is termed 'sponsored') by the Department of Transport, but the aerospace manufacturers primarily deal with the Department of Trade and Industry.

VAT on books – a case study

In 1984 it was rumoured that books were among the candidates for the application of a positive rate of Value Added Tax in the 1985 Budget. The departmental relationships over this one subject were typically complex:

- the Budget is formulated primarily by the Treasury;
- but VAT is the responsibility of Customs and Excise;
- and the implications for education fell under the sponsoring responsibilities of the Department of Education or, in Northern Ireland and Scotland, the Northern Ireland and Scottish Offices;
- and Public Libraries and authors are sponsored by the Office of Arts and Libraries;
- lastly, the Department of Trade and Industry sponsors the publishing, bookselling and printing industries.

If interdepartmental decision-making seems complex to outsiders, it can also be cumbersome to officials. As an example, we may take the EEC Directive on Misleading Advertising. The sponsoring Department in the UK is the Department of Trade and Industry. However, its Consumer Affairs Division had a long circulation list to other Departments that were involved and possibly keen to comment on proposals. These included:

- Foreign Office;
- Lord Chancellor's Department;
- Scottish Office;
- Department of Economic Development, Northern Ireland;
- Office of Fair Trading;
- Cabinet Office;
- Treasury Solicitors;
- Home Office.

One key to developing a better understanding of decision-making in Government is an appreciation of the interdepartmental (and interministerial) networks and pressures that exist even on simple issues. We have explained that Cabinet committees are meant to provide a forum for interdepartmental debate, but they can create as well as disperse conflict between officials whose views will often be persuasive to their Ministers. Cabinet clashes can be solved by the Cabinet Office machinery, but may also reflect deep incompatibilities between the views of civil servants shadowing their masters. Conflicting interests also exist within Departments. The Channel Tunnel lobby, for example, would have had to target, among others, the Departments of Environment, which sponsors construction, and Transport, since this is a question of transportation by road or rail. Yet the former is also responsible for assessment of the implications to the Kentish environment of major engineering work and increased traffic flow and the latter had to consider the interests of its other sponsored industries – ferries, hovercraft, aviation – all opposing a fixed link across the Channel.

All Departments have a common link in that they have to bargain with the Treasury over the funds they need to implement the policies they propose and administer. Since taxpayers' money is not unlimited, the Department of Environment's gain may be the Department of Health's loss.

Departments – structure and staffing

Departments are similar to companies in that they have external and internal functions. Externally, they are policy managers and implementers. Their output is decisions ordered by the Executive and scrutinized and endorsed by Parliament. But they also require a sophisticated administrative infrastructure to manage their staff, premises and operational budgets. Like large companies, their management is structured, with two main types of closely graded staff within what is known as the AEC (Administrative Executive and Clerical) system:

Administrative officials who comprise only 0.5 per cent of the Civil Service but dominate all the grades hold policy management power:
- Permanent Secretary (Grade 1)
- Deputy Secretary (Grade 2)
- Under Secretary (Grade 3)
- Assistant Secretary (Grade 5)
- Principal (Grade 7)
- Higher Executive Officer (HEO).

Executive officials who supervise clerical officers and assist members of the Administrative Class. They may also act as secretaries to Government committees or as Assistant Private Secretaries to junior Ministers and senior officials. Since they are generally not graduates, and Civil Service requirements favour those with degrees, they cannot rise above HEO level unless promoted, under limited circumstances, to the Administrative Class. They may be likened to NCOs.

A typical Department may have one or two Permanent Secretaries, five Deputy Secretaries, each in charge of broad areas of policy such as public finance or higher education, and twenty Under Secretaries covering generic subjects within those areas, such as fiscal policy or universities. These three grades are known as the Higher Civil Service. Each Under Secretary might have four or five Assistant Secretaries reporting to him, each controlling perhaps two Principals and four Higher Executive Officers working on ever more specific areas. The Assistant Secretary in the Treasury who covers direct taxation has one Principal handling personal taxation and another sponsoring business taxes, as an example of the ever more specific delegation of responsibility within Departments.

Within the Administrative Class, high fliers are separated from their colleagues by a 'fast stream' which is designed to offer the most promising officials rapid advancement. At an early stage, they can be recognized by the title HEO (D) (for development). They are more likely to be selected at HEO or Principal Grade to run Ministers' or Permanent Secretaries' Private Offices; and may be eligible for promotion to Principal at 27 or 28 and to Assistant Secretary in their mid-thirties. While not infallible, age is a good indicator of whether an official is considered to have promise or to be passed over. Someone who is still a Principal after the age of 40 or an Assistant Secretary after 45 is unlikely to move much higher. Once they pass Assistant Secretary, however, promotion becomes far more difficult and many very able senior officials may remain Under Secretaries without proceeding further.

The responsibilities of each of the main Departments, together with staff numbers and ministerial duties, are detailed in appendix 4.

Departments – role

In a nutshell, the role of each Department, individually or interdepartmentally, is to sponsor, advise, formulate, and implement policy.

Sponsorship means that an official or group of officials within a departmental Division has the responsibility of supervising the relations with Government of an issue, industry (even individual firms) or group of people. It is the task of sponsoring officials to collect facts about their area of responsibility; represent it in interdepartmental discussion and act as the primary contact between organizations or individuals and senior officials or Ministers. Direct representations to Ministers are normally sent straight to the appropriate sponsoring Division for response; even if the representations are more relevant to another Department or a different Division in the sponsoring Department, the sponsoring Division would nonetheless receive copies.

Advise both to Ministers and to the public. Ministers come and go. They may only hold office in a Department for a few months before being transferred or dismissed. Since they are given responsibility for a wide range of issues they have to rely heavily on their officials for advice and support. In advance of any ministerial meeting with outside organizations or individuals, for example, officials prepare a brief for him. They draft answers to all correspondence and Parliamentary Questions, have a major input to ministerial speeches in Parliament, and are present for consultations throughout their Ministers' debates in the Chamber of either House or in committees. Indeed, the Fulton Committee examining the Civil Service in the 1960s found that up to a quarter of officials' time is spent on parliamentary matters. Since they administer ongoing departmental policy

28 Government – the components of power

Box 9 Structure of a Government Department – 1 April 1989

The Department of Energy is one of the smallest Government Departments. The Ministry of Defence is 160 times larger. Like all departments, it is organized into Directorates, run by Deputy Secretaries; Divisions (Under Secretaries); and Branches (Assistant Secretaries).

Role	Directorate / Area	Divisions	Branch	Count
Secretary of State / Minister of State / Parliamentary Under Secretary (×2) / Permanent Secretary	Deputy Secretary Directorate — Oil, gas, offshore-supplies, petroleum engineering, economics & statistics, energy policy (international issues)	6 Under Secretaries Divisions	Energy technology	3
			Offshore supplies	4
			Petroleum engineering	8
			Economics & statistics	4
			Gas	4
			Oil	5
			28 Branches (Assistant Secretaries)	
	Deputy Secretary Directorate — Coal, electricity, atomic energy, energy efficiency, energy policy (coordination of nationalized industries)	5 Under Secretaries Divisions	Energy efficiency	5
			Energy policy	4
			Atomic energy	4
			Electricity	4
			Coal	2
			19 Branches (Assistant Secretaries)	
	Under Secretary (Establishment)			4
			4 Branches (Assistant Secretaries)	

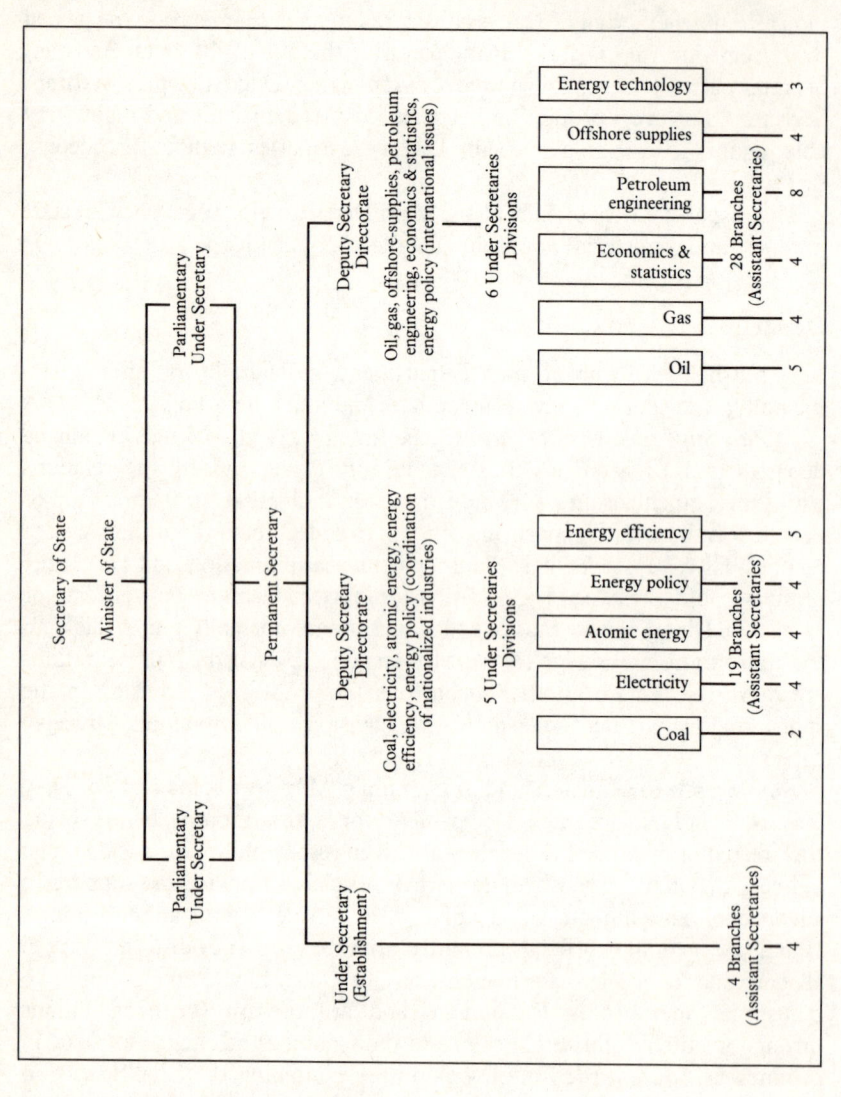

Box 10 Department of Energy sponsorship – examples

BRANCH 2
Emergency planning, home defence, security (including energy installations). Manpower and manpower related costs, staff inspection and complementing, management services and reviews. Accommodation and office services. Honours.
Grade 5
R Beasley

BRANCH 3
Estimates, Public Expenditure Survey forecasts, fees, charges and internal audit. Public Accounts Committee, financial propriety. Energy nationalised industries investment and financing.
Grade 5
C C Wilcock

BRANCH 4
Budget management and contracts for research, development and demonstration in the fields of offshore oil and gas technology, new and renewable sources of energy and coal technology.
Grade 5
G W Thynne

Coal, Electricity, Atomic Energy, Energy Efficiency Office, Energy Policy (co-ordination of energy and nationalised industries policy).
Grade 2
I T Manley CB

COAL DIVISION
Grade 3
R J Priddle
Enquiries: 01-211 3197
GTN 211 3197

BRANCH 1
Financial matters relating to the coal industry. Supply, distribution and demand for solid fuels. Corporate plan.
Grade 5
C P Carter

BRANCH 2
European Coal and Steel Community and other international organisations. Imports and exports of solid fuels. Environmental matters, opencast coal working. Mining subsidence. Redundancy benefits and other social costs. Manpower and industrial relations. Defence planning and civil emergencies. NCB appointments.
Grade 5
Ms A Beaton

ELECTRICITY DIVISION
Grade 3
A W Brown
Enquiries: 01-211 5861
GTN 211 5861

BRANCH 1
General energy policy and organisational aspects of the electricity supply industry. Industrial relations. Emergency planning. Board appointments. Consumer questions. Code of Practice for payment of electricity bills. International matters. Private generation and combined heat and power. Consents for power stations and overhead lines.
Grade 5
Dr F R Heathcote

BRANCH 2
Electricity investment programmes (England & Wales). Financial aspects
Cont.

30 Government – the components of power

Box 10 (*Cont.*)

of the electricity industry, including corporate planning, prices, tariff policy, financial regimes and auditors. Divisional financial interest in nuclear matters.
Grade 5
P G P D Fullerton

ENGINEERING INSPECTORATE
Public inquiries on power stations and overhead line proposals. All aspects of safety. Representation on committee for preparation of standards relating to supply and use of electricity.
Chief Engineering Inspector (Grade 5)
A T Baldock

ELECTRICITY METER EXAMINING SERVICE
Meter approvals, certification and disputes. Representation on committees for preparation of standards relating to electrical measuring instruments, including electricity meters and their ancillary equipment.
Chief Electricity Meter Examiner
A C J Kirkham

ATOMIC ENERGY DIVISION
Grade 3
C E Henderson
Enquiries: 01-211 6248
GTN 211 6248

BRANCH 1
British Nuclear Fuels PLC, Centrifuge enrichment project and policy. Uranium procurement policy. Energy aspects of Nuclear Installation Act 1965. Relations with Health and Safety Executive. Environmental questions. Physical security. Nuclear insurance, wages and conditions of service; BNF PLC
Grade 5
N A C Hirst

BRANCH 2
Overseas aspects of atomic energy policy, including EURATOM, International Atomic Energy Agency, Nuclear Energy Agency and International Energy Agency. Nuclear exports. Nuclear non-proliferation policy.
Grade 5
G H Stevens

BRANCH 3
United Kingdom Atomic Energy Authority and the National Nuclear Corporation. Nuclear reactor policy and monitoring of programmes. Public Debate on Nuclear Energy. Nuclear aspects of energy policy. Pay and Conditions of Service; AEA. General finance.
Grade 5
J R Bretherton

SAFEGUARDS OFFICE
International Atomic Energy Agency safeguards policy and implementation in the UK. Euratom Safeguards. Safeguards aspects of nuclear trade.
Senior Principal Scientific Officer (Grade 6)
Dr F Brown

Note: This is only illustrative. The Department's responsibilities will have changed by the date of publication.
Source: Civil Service Yearbook 1985 HMSO.

committees, officials advise their Ministers on the feasibility, political and logistic, of any changes he may wish to make. It is usual for a new Minister, particularly following a change of Government after a General Election, to find himself presented with a dossier analysing his Party's manifesto commitments and setting out the Department's arguments for and against their progression. The extent to which Ministers rely on the advice of their officials to defend them in Parliament or against hostile or inconvenient lobbies should not be underestimated. The career of a Minister has often been heavily influenced by his ability to inspire allegiance in his staff and to look good through good advice.

Departments also handle a considerable amount of advisory work for the public, with sponsoring officials being available for consultation on matters relating to their responsibilities and a large number of offices and sub-Departments established specifically to provide information. Among the Department of Trade and Industry's advisory units, to take one Department's example, are the 1992 Information Unit, R&D Requirements Boards, and the British Overseas Trade Board.

Formulation of policy is an area greatly misunderstood by outsiders. Policy decision-making in Government arises from four sources: from ministerial instruction, either implementing the Government's programme or in response to new circumstances or individual cases; from the need to maintain ongoing policy commitments, such as the running of the National Health Service; from delegated legislation (see page 58); and on minor matters where Ministers only need endorse technical Orders and Regulations. Even in the first of these cases, ministerial involvement is relatively limited. It is their officials who assemble information, conduct consultations, draft legislation and present Ministers with a consensus view either for consideration or for simple endorsement. Ministers can and do interfere where they feel that their staff are blocking policy initiatives, have failed to consider views or where parliamentary and public pressure has forced amendment of policy; but the advantage is very firmly in favour of the civil servants since they control a Minister's diary, and with it the bulk of access to him, and because the volume of work carried out by the departmental areas under just one Minister's brief is enormous. No Minister could ever attempt to grasp all the issues and, in the same way that he relies on his officials to draft speeches and answers to Parliamentary Questions addressed to him, he expects the framework of policy to be filled in by them under their own initiative.

Policy is therefore initiated or substantially swayed by the work of officials, mainly between Principal and Under Secretary level, and has usually crystallized some time before it reaches the public domain of Parliament. Although the days are long gone when Canning was able to write or

32 Government – the components of power

Box 11 Government as regulator

Study these examples of the power of just one Department to influence business and industry

DTI inspectors step up insider trading probe

DTI starts investigation of Milbury property group

DTI attacks oil giants for petrol price rises

McCorquodale bid to go to Monopolies

Report on brewing goes to Young

Brittan threatens bar to Tokyo finance firms

DTI expected to clear new type of unit trust

DTI to contain adverts

Further DTI probe at County NatWest

Whitehall blow to hopes of fibre-optic cable network

dictate almost every Foreign Office dispatch, it is still an accepted fiction that all departmental actions are sanctioned personally by Ministers.

Box 12

> British government is anthropomorphic. Everything is done by the Minister and not by the Ministry. The eight or 10,000 planning appeals each year are, theoretically, decided by the Minister of Housing and not by his Ministry. Civil Servants advise the Minister and they execute his decisions, but the decisions are his, not theirs (Ian Gilmour, *The Body Politic*, 1969).
>
> 'As a rule', Gilmour commented, 'only about one Minister in three runs his Department'.

Implementation of policy combines with sponsorship and formulation for a great part of this role consists of administering the sponsoring responsibilities that have been delegated to them. In broad terms, that can mean running the Health Service or defence procurement, ensuring that ministerial powers derived from particular items of legislation are properly exercised and that the vast network of Government grants, subsidies, lines of credit and export insurance arrangements are operated efficiently.

Quasi-departments

We use this term to cover two groups of agency:

(a) *Within Departments*: units administering largely self-contained areas of work and with some autonomy. Their responsibilities may be technical or highly specific, involving a degree of knowledge not possessed by ordinary officials. While the degree of their separation from their parent Department may differ, they are all accountable to Parliament. The larger departmental quasi-Departments may have a Minister with specific responsibility for them and be led by an official of Permanent Secretary grade.

Examples of quasi-Departments are the Inland Revenue, falling within the Treasury, the Export Credits Guarantee Department and OFTEL, which report to the Department of Trade and Industry, and the Property Services Administration, within the Department of the Environment.

(b) *Outside Departments*: agencies linked to or established by Government are sometimes called 'Quangos' – Quasi Autonomous Non-Governmental Organizations – or Fringe Bodies. Again, their existence is justified on the basis of the unsuitability of their role for incorporation in the direct work of the Department to whom they report or with whom they are linked. They may be *Advisory*, where Government needs to co-opt non-Civil Service outsiders to help it with specialist or technical work. Advisory bodies are very useful to Departments in the preparation of technical Statutory Instruments. In many cases, statutes require Departments to consult specified bodies when drawing up legislation. For example, under the 1975 Social Security Act the DSS must consult the National Insurance Advisory Committee on Regulations concerning National Insurance. Other advisory bodies include the Advisory Committee on Advertising and the Advisory Council for Adult and Continuing Education;

Regulatory, where officials and Ministers prefer political control to be distanced from the conduct that needs to be regulated. Many such agencies are established to supervise statutory responsibilities: the Office of Fair Trading, Registry of Friendly Societies, Securities and Investments Board, Monopolies Commission and Equal Opportunities Commission are examples. They may be empowered to take quasi-judicial action themselves or to recommend to the Secretary of State of their parent Department that action be taken to endorse their decisions;

Executive Agencies, which take work from a Department where issues need to be de-politicized; where central Government wishes to give the impression of reducing manpower; or where it is felt desirable to establish a funding body independent of day-to-day departmental control. The Social Science Research Council, Health Education Council, and Intervention Board for Agricultural Produce are examples. Executive agencies may also have a watchdog function on issues sponsored by Departments or over other public authorities. The Gas Consumer Council and Countryside Commission fall into this category; or they may discharge public functions that are too burdensome for their sponsoring Departments to handle. Water and health authorities are typical of this type of agency.

Lastly, *Quasi-Judicial Agencies*, whose remit falls between departmental and Court control of activities and who may themselves be controlled by both. The social security system includes National Insurance and Supplementary Benefits tribunals to assess appeals from DSS decisions; other agencies in this category include the Advisory Conciliation and Arbitration Service (ACAS); the Parliamentary and Health Service Commissioners and the Commission for local Administration in England. The judicial function itself is assisted by the Director of Public Prosecutions and the Treasury Solicitor's offices.

All Quasi-Departments, despite their differences in function, share a number of common features. They derive their existence from ministerial or statutory authority; most of them produce annual reports to the Secretary of State of their parent Department; these are then laid before Parliament. They are usually financed by Parliament-approved Grants in Aid but may

Box 13 Quasi-departments – number and listing 1989

Department	Executive bodies	Advisory bodies	Tribunals	Nationalized industries	Public corporations	Other
Ministry of Agriculture, Fisheries and Food	34	72	4		1	
Office of Arts and Libraries	9 (plus 14 museums and galleries)	4				
Cabinet Office	1	9				
Central Office of Information		1				
Inland Revenue			2			
Ministry of Defence	8	48				
Department of Education and Science	14	11				
Department of Employment	44	190	4			
Department of Energy	2	5		4 (plus 12 boards)†		
Department of Environment	30	20	3	1 (plus 9 boards)†		
Foreign and Commonwealth Office	13	10	2			
Department of Health and Social Security‡	10	124	7			
Home Office	13	129	9		4	121
Lord Chancellor's Department		197	5			
Northern Ireland Office	58	45	11			6
Scottish Office	69	123	14	3‡		
Department of Trade and Industry	48	34	6	3‡		
Department of Transport	5	6	2	4	1	
Treasury	1	6				
Welsh Office	17	28	14	1†		

† In the process of privatization at the time of revision (1 April 89)
‡ Divided into two Departments during 1988

be given the power to raise their own statutory levies. Lastly, their Chairmen and Boards are appointed by Ministers, increasing the Executive's power of patronage, although they recruit their own staff who are not normally civil servants but whose remuneration and conditions are often geared to Civil Service scales.

1.3 Policy scrutiny and endorsement

Parliament is no longer – except in a few defined circumstances – a decision-maker in the public policy process. Its place in the power structure is that of an institution through which the Executive operates and, as a secondary role, as a check on policy and a channel for concern on local or political issues. Unlike Congress in the United States, it does not lie at the centre of power, capable of providing a real counterbalance to the influence of the President. While it has the same functions as Congress – control over expenditure and scrutiny of legislation – their exercise is more apparent than real since the ability of the Executive to secure consent, through its natural voting majority, for its decisions is almost totally reliable. Cross-Party voting coalitions are no longer seen at Westminster unless the Government's majority is very low or where conscience issues are involved, in which case the Whip may not be underlined anyway. Governments can, of course, lose the allegiance of their MPs, but in practice the Whips, media and PPSs would relay the sensitivities of majority Party backbenchers to the Leadership long before the situation became a matter of mass loss of confidence in the Executive.*

There are other factors that contribute to the current comparative weakness of Parliament. Most MPs on the Government side do not have the financial independence they formerly enjoyed and would be unwilling to risk their parliamentary seat in an election should they vote against the Prime Minister. If the Government did not take them to task, their Constituency Association probably would. Unseated Governments become Oppositions, without the influence or access to patronage of the Party in power.

As the hold of Party organizations over MPs has strengthened, the power of oratory and debate to sway MPs and the nation has diminished. The real decisions are taken and mainly influenced elsewhere, leaving Parliament as

---

* Faced with accusations of poor communication between Ministers and MPs, the Conservative Government in 1985 grouped almost half its backbenchers into departmental panels, to be supplied with information produced by Ministers and their Special Advisers on departmental policy. The move did not seem to quell criticism and it was admitted that a danger existed of MPs becoming drawn into defence of a Department and blurring the distinction between the Executive and Legislature.

the gift-wrapping of Government – its polished visible manifestation. Yet, as we have already noted, the dynamic of power must be reconsidered at intervals and Parliament becomes a major force when Government working majorities are low – nine of the 24 governments this century have had majorities of 30 or less, with five having none at all – or where lobbying persuades sufficient MPs and Peers to support a view contrary to the Government's and the Executive is forced to compromise. The institutions and work of Parliament should realistically be viewed in that light.

The House of Commons

Members of Parliament. There are 650 MPs, each representing constituencies of around 67,000 voters. (Despite the best efforts of the Boundary Commission to produce constituencies with equal numbers of voters, the Western Isles has 23,000 voters in a very large area and the Isle of Wight has 94,000 in a densely populated constituency.) Their official role as it has been for 700 years, is to represent the concerns of their electorate to Government. Those concerns may be expressed:

- in public, through speeches or amendments tabled in debates on legislation, Adjournment Debates, Ten Minute Rule and Private Member's Bills (see page 116), oral Parliamentary Questions (see page 113) and speeches or amendments tabled in Standing and Select Committees;
- still publicly, but on a less visible level, through written Parliamentary Questions; or
- privately, by writing to or meeting Ministers.

Collectively, MPs are linked, through their Party machines, on issues forming the Government's legislative programme. In addition to their constituency role they are therefore generically supporters or opponents of the Government. While mavericks exist on all sides of the Commons, persistently defying their Party's Whip, they are few in number and unusually confident of the support of their constituency Party Association, since it is in practice impossible for an MP to be re-elected without that support and Parties seek solidarity with their policies.

They also have an enormous variety of personal interests ranging from defence and agriculture to monkeys and Namibia. Some MPs are extraordinarily energetic, writing books, running companies and actively supporting a great number of causes in addition to the work dictated to them by their Party and constituency obligations. Others prefer a quieter life, rarely speaking in debate or tabling shoals of Parliamentary Questions. Almost all, however, will be a member of at least one of the following:

- *A Standing Committee* – there are six, designated simply by letters A to F, plus two for Scotland, existing to examine legislation while it passes through Parliament. The composition of these committees will change with each Bill considered but will always include the Minister responsible for that Bill, his PPS and a Government Whip. At any one time, Standing Committees will have between 15 and 20 members (very important measures, such as the Finance Bill, may contain double that), appointed by the *Committee of Selection* on the basis of regional or personal relevance and chaired by a senior MP with a sound understanding of procedure, who is drawn from the *Speaker's Panel*.

  In addition to the main items of legislation in any parliamentary year, Standing Committees are also appointed to consider the mass of Orders and Regulations on items such as the 'Milk Quota Amendment (Miscellaneous Provisions) No. 2 Order', to give formal effect to the administrative necessities of policy.

- *A Select Committee* – contrary to popular belief, Parliament has been appointing them on an *ad hoc* basis to examine issues of public importance for many years, with four that are of particular significance becoming permanent bodies:

  The Public Accounts Committee, which has existed since 1861. By convention, its chairman is an Opposition MP and the Financial Secretary to the Treasury sits on it. The PAC, as it is known, examines Government Expenditure to ensure that no sums have been spent that have not been authorized by Parliament. The Committee acts as more than just an audit check, for it can summon Permanent Secretaries, who are responsible for the accounts of their Departments, and question them on wasteful expenditure and irregular commercial contracts. The PAC has 15 members, mostly with an interest in public finance, and is not generally Party political even though all Select Committees have an inbuilt Government majority.

  The Committee on Privileges, made up of 15 MPs who investigate alleged breaches of parliamentary privilege, such as premature leaking of a Select Committee report by one of its members.

  The Services Committee, which manages the administration of the House of Commons and, in assessing the needs of MPs, can produce reports with important commercial implications – for example, recommending that all MPs should be provided with their own computing facilities.

  The Members' Interests Committee was established in 1974, when the House of Commons first produced an annual register of the financial and other outside interests of MPs, to ensure that the principles of the Register are enforced and to investigate questions of conflict of interest, abuse of position and lobbying ethics.

Government – the components of power 39

In 1979 a further 14 Select Committees were created to investigate the work of Government Departments, plus two to cover scrutiny of EEC legislation and the work of the Parliamentary Commissioner for Administration (see box 14).

Each departmental Select Committee has an average of 12 members, plus one or two clerks and a number of specialist advisers. Although membership can be influenced by Executive pressure, and officers of Conservative backbench committees usually do not sit on the equivalent Select Committee, the committees choose their own subjects for investigation and produce a series of reports in each parliamentary year after taking evidence from Ministers, officials, other MPs and interest groups. A request to appear before, or provide papers to, a Select Committee has the same power as a subpoena: it cannot be refused.

The relationship between the Clerk and his members is similar to that between officials and Ministers. While the MPs must approve, suggestions for investigations and witnesses and the drafting of reports is largely left

Box 14 Departmental Select Committees

Agriculture
Defence
Education, science and the arts
Employment
Environment
European legislation
Foreign affairs
Home affairs (including a sub-committee on race relations and immigration)
Parliamentary Commissioner for Administration
Scottish affairs
Social services
Trade and industry
Transport
Treasury and Civil Service
Welsh affairs

The Foreign and Home Affairs Committees and the Treasury and Civil Service Committee each have the power to appoint one sub-committee. Currently, the Home Affairs Committee has an immigration and race relations sub-committee and the Treasury and Civil Service Committee has a sub-committee bearing the same name. A further sub-committee can be established at any time to consider a matter affecting two or more nationalized industries. Membership would be drawn from the Energy, Environment, Trade and Industry, Scottish, Transport and Treasury Committees.

to the clerks. Some committees allow members one nominated investigation each during a two- or three-year term, but otherwise decisions are often reached by discussion between the Chairman and the Chief Clerk.

Select Committees have not been a complete success. While their reports have often cut across Party divisions and their existence has reinforced parliamentary scrutiny of ministerial and official actions, there are deficiencies: (a) their reports are rarely debated and, while departments occasionally produce published responses, the extent to which they can influence Whitehall depends largely on the forcefulness of the Chairman and the media's own pressure; (b) their reports are usually produced too late to affect policies and actions. They are an ex-post facto comment except in the minority of cases where their recommendations have initiated policy change; and (c) many have suggested that departmental Select Committees were only established as a sop by the Executive to MPs grown restless by having too much time on their hands. Select Committees were seen as a way of keeping them quiet. That aside, there is evidence that their effectiveness, and the vigour of their members and chairmen, is increasing.

- *A backbench committee* – if the MP is Conservative or Labour. Both Parties have a range of subject committees to represent the interests and express the opinions of MPs who are not Ministers, Whips or PPSs, but the term 'committee' is misleading. While Labour committees have chairmen and members, Conservative groups have a chairman, vice-chairman and one or two secretaries but no fixed membership, since all backbenchers may attend their meetings. The Parliamentary Labour Party and 1922 Committee (see box 15) organize elections of officers for their backbench committees every November. The purpose of backbench committees is to canalize the views of MPs toward their Party's leadership. At a time of large Government majorities they are a powerful focus for backbench opinion on the Government side, with privileged access to Ministers and a representative role enhanced by their regular meetings, at which business, industry and other interest groups are given the opportunity to voice their concerns or be questioned by MPs.
- *An All-Party Group* – which may cover a subject or country. As the title suggests, these are multi-partisan, but they are not necessarily run by MPs for MPs like backbench committees. Subject and country groups are many and surprisingly variegated. They have officers and a defined membership, which may also include Peers since they are parliamentary, not Commons, committees. Some, however, are financed and run by interest groups, lobbyists and embassies as an easy way to institutionalize their access to Parliament. All Conservative and Labour MPs are members respectively of the 1922 Committee and the Parliamentary

Box 15 Conservative and Labour backbench committees

Conservative Party committees
Agriculture Fisheries and Food
   Countryside
   Fisheries
   Fish Farming
   Food and Drinks
   Forestry
   Horticulture
Arts and Heritage
Aviation
Constitutional
Defence
Education
Employment
Energy
Environment
European Affairs
Finance
Foreign/Commonwealth
Health and Social Services
Home
Legal
Media
Northern Ireland
Small Businesses
Sports
Trade and Industry
   Shipping/Shipbuilding
   Space
   Tourism
Transport
Urban and New Town

Greater London
North West
Scottish
Welsh
West Country
Yorkshire
Party Organization

Labour Party committees
Agriculture
Defence
Education
Employment
Energy
Environment
Foreign Affairs
Health and Social Security
Home Affairs
Northern Ireland
Parliamentary Affairs
Trade and Industry
Transport
Treasury and Civil Service

East Midlands
Greater London
North Western
Northern
Scotland
Welsh
West Midlands
Yorkshire

Labour Party, both of which meet every Thursday at 6 pm, with the ubiquitous Whips in attendance, to put forward views on issues affecting their Party as a whole. The chairman of either committee is regarded as particularly influential and has a position akin to the senior shop steward of a major trade union, representing the concerns of his members to his bosses and possessing great bargaining power.

The Library. MPs are only as effective as the narrowness of the Government's majority. They also need information to enable them to harry the Executive or scrutinize its policies effectively. While they receive briefs on any range of subjects from their Party's head office research departments, the public, business and industry, and pressure groups, they can also turn to the resources of the Commons Library for objective data on any issue. Library research staff prepare fact sheets on matters of general interest as well as produce material for speeches, replies to correspondence, articles and the other information requirements of Members. Since knowledge is power, the Library must be added to any assessment of the influence on MPs.

The Chamber. As we have already said, the power of oratory to sway opinions and mobilize voting alliances has greatly diminished since the War. Speeches in the Chamber of the House of Commons are increasingly expressions of personal opinion; or are made at the instigation of a PPS as a support for the Government; or are designed to register an MP's presence to his local paper or tied pressure group. While it is important that the Minister leading each debate should properly justify Government policy, the requirement is more that his strength should inspire team spirit than win over Opposition votes.

As we go to press, television is being introduced into the Chamber. It will inevitably make MPs anxious to show their constituents they exist. TV will probably draw them away from their office, where the real work in chasing the system on behalf of their electors is done.

The debating chambers of both the Commons and Lords are designed such that debate and the relationship between the Government and Opposition is adversarial. The public may attend all debates, and most of the proceedings of Select Committees (some witnesses' evidence is heard in camera), but the meetings of backbench and All-Party groups are private. The public and private business that is conducted in the two Chambers and in committees is detailed in section 2 of this book. Despite the amount of work done by Parliament, however, it is undoubtedly true that its power has declined in proportion to the growth of the Civil Service and of Cabinet government.

Box 16 Two views on the power of the Commons

(*a*) *Bagehot in 1867.* The House of Commons is an electoral chamber; it is the assembly which chooses our president... our House of Commons is a real choosing body; it elects the people it likes. And it dismisses whom it likes, too. No matter that a few months since it was chosen to support Lord Aberdeen or Lord Palmerston; upon a sudden occasion it ousts the statesmen to whom it at first adhered, and selects an opposite statesman whom it at first rejected. Doubtless in such cases there is a tacit reference to probable public opinion; but certainly also there is much free will in the judgement of the Commons. The House only goes where it thinks in the end the nation will follow; but it takes the chance of the nation following or not following; it assumes the initiative, and acts upon its discretion or caprice.

... because the House of Commons has the power of dismissal in addition to the power of election, its relations to the Premier are incessant. They guide him and he leads them. He is to them what they are to the nation. He only goes where he believes they will go after him. But he has to take the lead; he must choose his direction and begin the journey... [a minister should say firmly], 'Parliament has maintained ME, and that was its greatest duty; Parliament has carried on what, in the language of traditional respect, we call the Queen's Government; it has maintained what wisely or unwisely it deemed the best executive of the English nation.'

The second function of the House of Commons is what I may call an expressive function. It is its office to express the mind of the English people on all matters which come before it....

The third function of Parliament is what I may call... the teaching function. A great and open council of considerable men cannot be placed in the middle of a society without altering that society. It ought to alter it for the better. It ought to teach the nation what it does not know....

Fourthly, the House of Commons has what may be called an informing function – a function which though in its present form quite modern is singularly analogous to a mediæval function. In old times one office of the House of Commons was to inform the sovereign what was wrong. It laid before the Crown the grievances and complaints of particular interests. Since the publication of the Parliamentary debates a corresponding office of Parliament is to lay these same grievances, these same complaints, before the nation, which is the present sovereign. The nation needs it quite as much as the king ever needed it.

Lastly, there is the function of legislation, of which of course it would be preposterous to deny the great importance, and which I only deny to be as important as the executive management of the whole state, or the political education given by Parliament to the whole nation. There are, as I allow, seasons when legislation is more important than either of these.

(*b*) *Richard Crossman in 1966.* Let me describe the central problem as I see it. The physical conditions under which we work and many of our main procedures are survivals from a period when parties were weak, when the making and unmaking of Ministries still rested with the House of Commons, not with an electorate based on universal suffrage, and when the Cabinet was merely the executive committee

Cont.

Box 16 (*Cont.*)

of the Commons. Procedurally, we still behave as though we were a sovereign which really shared with the Government in the initiation of legislation, which exercised a real control not only of finance, but of the administration of the Departments. But, today, not only the House of Lords has been shorn of most of its authority. The House of Commons too, has surrendered most of its effective powers to the Executive and has become in the main the passive forum in which the struggle is fought between the modern usurpers of parliamentary power, the great political machines.

In this transformation of the parliamentary scene the House of Commons has largely lost the three functions for which its procedures were evolved and to which they are relevant, the making of Ministries, initiation of legislation shared with the Cabinet, and the watchdog control of finance and administration.

The question the reformer has to ask himself is whether we should look backwards in an attempt to restore the pristine powers of this House to which our procedures are relevant or whether we should accept our present limited functions largely as they are and adapt our procedures to them. I know that there are some of my hon. Friends who dream of a time when the secret negotiations of the Government with outside interests which precede all modern legislation and the secret decisions in the Committee Room upstairs which largely determine party attitudes will be rendered insignificant because the House of Commons will once again become sovereign and make decisions for itself. I think they are crying for the moon.

Source: (*a*) The English Constitution 1867, (*b*) Hansard, vol. 38 col. 479–80.

MPs use a range of devices to enforce accountability by the Executive, to raise matters of concern or simply to bait Ministers:

- Adjournment Debates, which allow an MP to exchange comments with a Minister on a specific issue;
- Parliamentary Questions, which are tabled by MPs to Ministers for written or oral answer;
- Private Member's legislation – MPs can introduce Bills where the Government is either unwilling or has insufficient time to support the amendment of existing law;
- Early Day Motions, which are akin to backbench MP petitions to the Government on subjects ranging from the frivolous to major areas of policy.

The Chamber is the focus for all these.

The House of Lords

In theory, the Lords should have more influence over Executive policies than the Commons. In practice it has less, but it still retains a number of features that define its usefulness as a part of our model of power.

There are 1186 members of the House of Lords, although only 888 are working Peers in that they have a declared affiliation to a Party or are Cross-Benchers, meaning that they are not prepared to support any of the four main Parties on a systematic basis but wish to make known their independent status. Of those, no more than one half can be considered as more than occasional attenders.

The Lords, while being referred to as the Upper House, is no longer the Senate to the Commons' House of Representatives. It cannot debate or propose matters relating to public finance or taxation. The Commons has the final say over amendments to legislation proposed by the Lords; and other conflicts customarily result in withdrawal by their Lordships. Yet, despite this, the Lords cannot be ignored:

- Peers are generally more financially independent than MPs and, since there are fewer ministerial positions available to them, are less inclined to vote passively because of the promise of patronage.
- There are a number of cross-Party dynastic ties which may be stronger than the power of the Whips to enforce discipline. The complex web of family relationships in the Lords may ultimately prove more decisive on an issue than the best-argued case.
- It has often been said that the Lords is the consultancy arm of Parliament. In many ways that is true. It contains former Prime Ministers and Cabinet members, experts in a wide range of commercial, international, scientific, social and cultural areas, and Peers are generally able to spend more time on detailed subjects than their more pressured counterparts in the Commons. The Government may therefore rely on the Lords to provide the fine tuning in any consideration of a Bill. The Lords, because of this expertise, also has the most consistently cogent Select Committee, the European Communities Committee, which through seven sub-committees considers and reports on Community proposals.
- The Lords' traditional independence can make it an irritant to the Government and a focus for issues which, once considered, cannot be ignored. Although Government defeats in the Lords can always be remedied in the Commons, Ministers take them seriously since they galvanize opposition among MPs and provide an indication of the general parliamentary strength of feeling on a Bill. The Whips in the Commons have to work that much harder if the Lords fail to toe the Party line. In

place of, and more important than Adjournment Debates (see page 117), the Lords has the device of the Unstarred Question, which allows for a debate of 60–150 minutes on any topic with an official response by the Government. There is no Division. Peers may put down unstarred questions on the Order Page and call for their debate at any time, although in practice the date is negotiated between the Peer and the Whips. If he insists on his question being debated at short notice (at least 24 hours' warning must be given) it will be taken after all other business has been completed and may therefore attract little support. There is usually time for ten Peers and the Minister (or Government spokesman) to speak. Usually the only Peers present will be speakers and they may well have been mobilized by the sponsoring Peer (or the interests behind him) to support his position.

Parliamentary Questions can also be tabled in the Lords in both written and oral form. Oral Questions, as in the Commons, allow the questioner to ask a Supplementary and permit three or four other Peers to do so as well. Oral Questions are, however, limited to four per day.

1.4 **Parties**

Outside the structure of decision-making by central Government, but a powerful influence on the Executive and MPs, is the political Party system. Parties, through their power to select candidates, their liaison committees and conferences, exercise a strong and increasing influence over those they send to Westminster. The days when MPs could disregard their constituency associations, secure in the status their position gave, are largely gone and the power to vet candidates ensures that they cannot stand for election with the endorsement of one of the main Parties unless they fit into the mould – shaping attitudes to national policies as well as constituency service – set for them by those local associations and Party head offices.

The Labour Party differs from the others in that candidates may be proposed by trade unions or local cooperative societies. The pressures on Conservative and Alliance MPs only become publicly apparent when their election leads to offers of consultancies or directorships; with Labour candidates it is plain from the start who can call the shots. A large number of Labour MPs are sponsored in this way.

The two main Parties' conferences, held each autumn before the parliamentary Session begins, also differ sharply. The Conservatives traditionally stage manage the occasion, treating it as an opportunity for the constituency and area associations to endorse the leadership and its policies.

Box 17 Parties and MPs – a strong influence

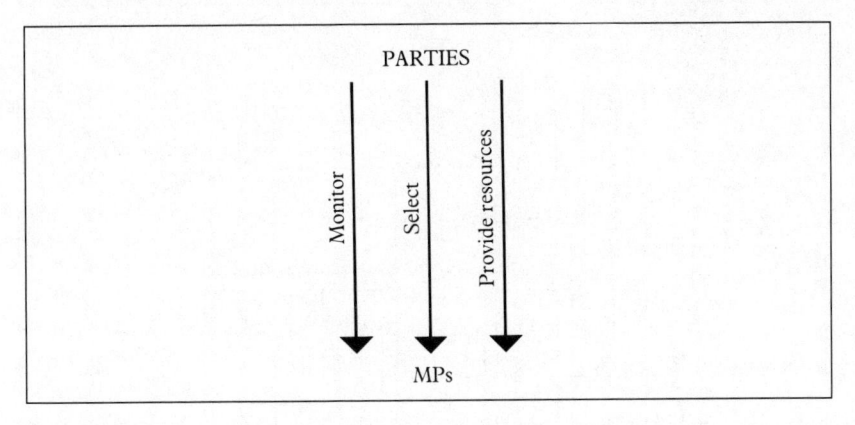

```
                        PARTIES

                    │       │       │
              Monitor  Select   Provide resources
                    │       │       │
                    ▼       ▼       ▼
                           MPs
```

The Labour Party, in contrast, votes on motions that often become official Party policy; chooses the National Executive Committee, the board of the Party that is made up of representatives (MPs and outsiders) elected by trade unions and constituency associations; and elects the Leader and his deputy. While strong leaders and united Cabinets have been able to temper the relative extremism of the decisions passed by a conference membership of activists and trade unions, their Party organization manifests its strength at such occasions and cannot be ignored by existing or potential NEC members and a Labour Cabinet or Shadow Cabinet.

Each Party conference now includes, in addition to the set-piece debates on major policy issues, a large number of fringe meetings and receptions, many of them organized by lobbying groups aware that MPs at their conferences are like fish in a barrel. Party headquarters are a further source of input to MPs. Their research departments provide them with briefs on legislation and Party policies; their international departments link with their overseas counterparts and have the power to make recommendations to the Whips on MPs to travel overseas on political visits; they issue Election campaign guides to MPs and candidates detailing Party policy; and they organize speakers, some of them MPs, to spread the message around the country.

Lastly, Parties produce manifestos before each Election to set out the promises they intend to fulfil if voted into power. Input to the production of the manifesto takes various forms:

The Conservatives. Prior to an Election, a number of policy groups are formed under the leadership of MPs or Peers and staffed by Party officials

48 Government – the components of power

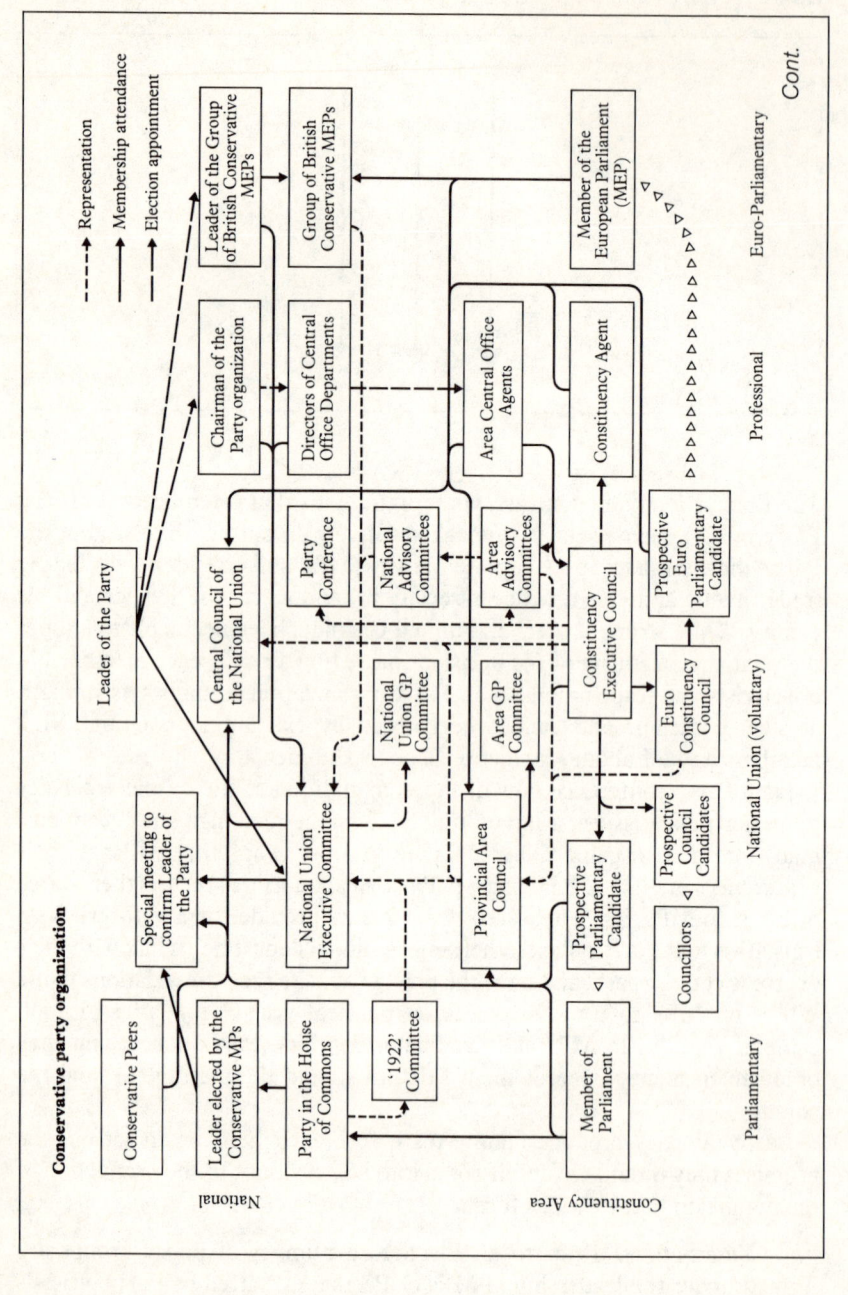

Box 18 Organization of the three main Parties

Conservative party organization

Cont.

Government – the components of power   49

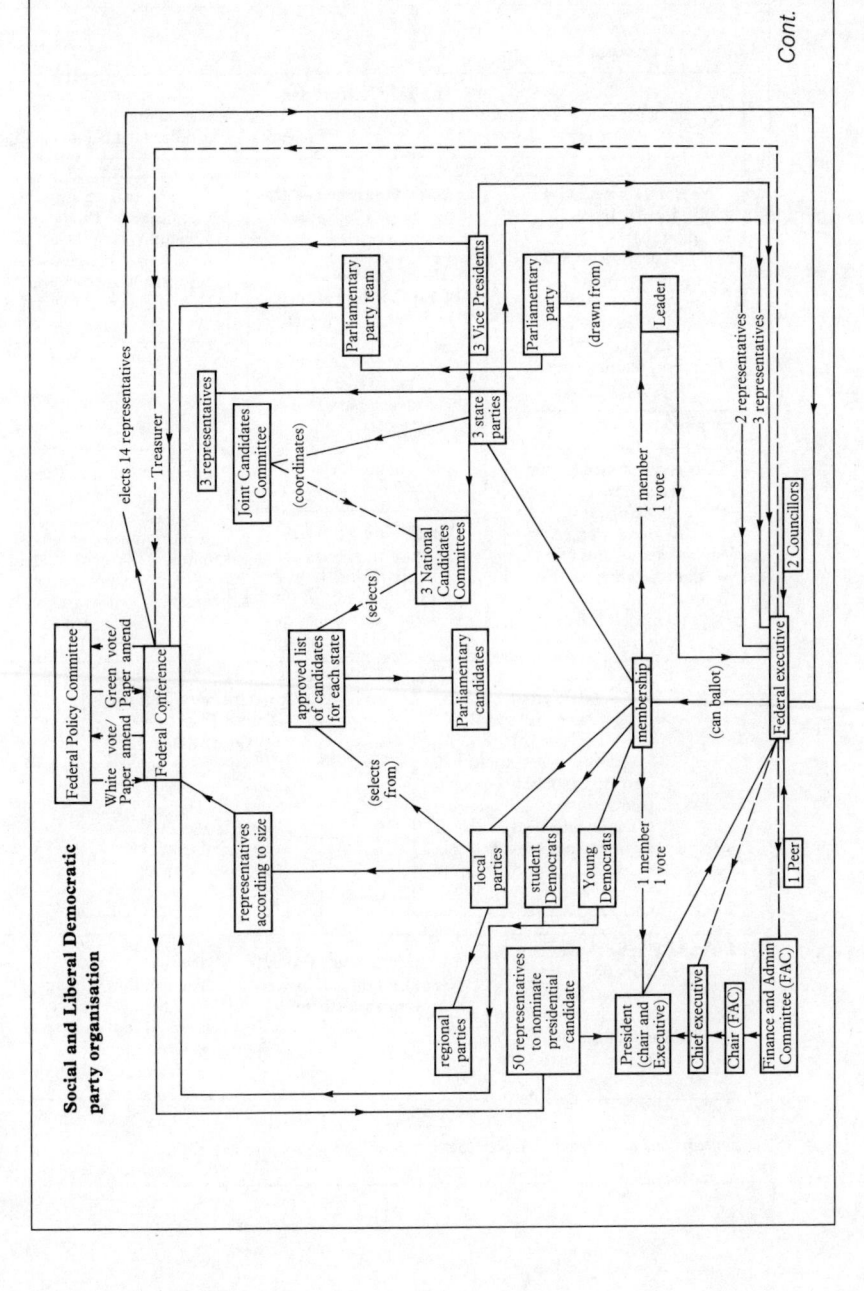

Box 18 (*Cont.*)

Social and Liberal Democratic party organisation

Government – the components of power

Box 18 (*Cont.*)

Labour party organization

Annual Conference
Elected delegates from Constituency Labour Parties, national trade unions and affiliated organizations; ex-officio Labour MPs, peers and European MPs; endorsed candidates; NEC

National Executive Committee
12 union representitives, 7 from constituencies, 5 women, 1 from Socialist Societies, Treasurer, Leader and Deputy Leader – all elected by Conference; plus LPYS representative

Labour Members of the European Parliament

Regional Council of the Labour Party
These are 11 regional areas. Each holds an annual conference, with representative from constituency parties. The conference elects a regional executive committee.

Parliamentary Labour Party
Labour MPs and Labour members of the House of Lords; headed by the Party Leader and Deputy Leader.

County Labour Party Management Committe
(Regional Party Management Committee in Scotland). Representatives from constituency parties and other organizations in the counties

Local Government Committee
In Greater London only: representatives from the General Committees of every CLP in the borough.

District Labour Party Management Committee
Representative of CLPs, unions and other affiliated groups – where two or more constituencies are involved.

Constituency Labour Party General Committee
Elected representatives from branches, women's organizations. Labour Party Young Socialists branches, workplace branches and affiliated organizations in the constituency.

Constituency Labour Party Executive Committee
The General Committee elects officers and an Executive Committee to look after the detailed organization of the Constituency party.

Labour Party Branches
Every Labour Party member belongs first to her or his branch, which is based on boundaries as decided by the General Committee.

Other Labour Party Groups and Affiliated Organizations

Labour Party women's organizations, Young Socialists, workplace branches, trade unions and socialist societies which affiliate locally.

Source: *Mastering British Politics* (Macmillan, 1985)

or close supporters. Initially the Conservative Research Department drafts policy proposals, which are then considered by each group and revised if necessary. The relevant Minister or Shadow Minister, depending on whether the Party is in power or not, considers the group's proposal and, if the matter is a major item, the Prime Minister or Leader will vet it before it is included in the Manifesto.

The Labour Party. Although the two main Parties' research departments are similar, Labour researchers must work within the structure of permanent policy committees and sub-committees of the National Executive Committee which, because it is separated from control by a Labour Cabinet or Shadow Cabinet, may find that its proposals are largely rejected when the Parliamentary Labour Party considers manifesto drafts.

1.5 The power structure: influence, strengths, weaknesses

Having described the components of power in central Government today, we must now compare the influence and power of its main parts. Although we have already said that power centres change depending on the issue involved, certain general assumptions about the system are always true:

- That the power of Parliament depends on the size of the Government's majority.
- That individual MPs are usually only able to sway the Executive on personal constituency issues unless, like the Chairman of the 1922 Committee, they represent a powerful block of opinion.
- That real power rests far further down the Civil Service hierarchy than is often believed. The crucial grades are Principal – Under Secretary.
- That ministerial decisions often do no more than endorse the letters, briefs and draft legislation produced for them by their officials. Far less policy is initiated from the top down than is believed.
- That Cabinet Committees are more influential than Cabinet itself.
- That decisions in Government are rarely single-facet: they are the product of a complex coalition of forces, with two or more Departments, Cabinet Committees, Parliament, public and media opinion, the Policy Unit, Prime Minister and declared Party policy all acting as pressures on the lead Minister in each case.

These assumptions produce a triangle of power (see box 19). If each corner of the triangle of power is pitted against the other the points count in the table on pages 53–6 would be seen. The same treatment can be applied to the components of the Executive and Legislature.

52 Government – the components of power

Box 19 The triangle of power

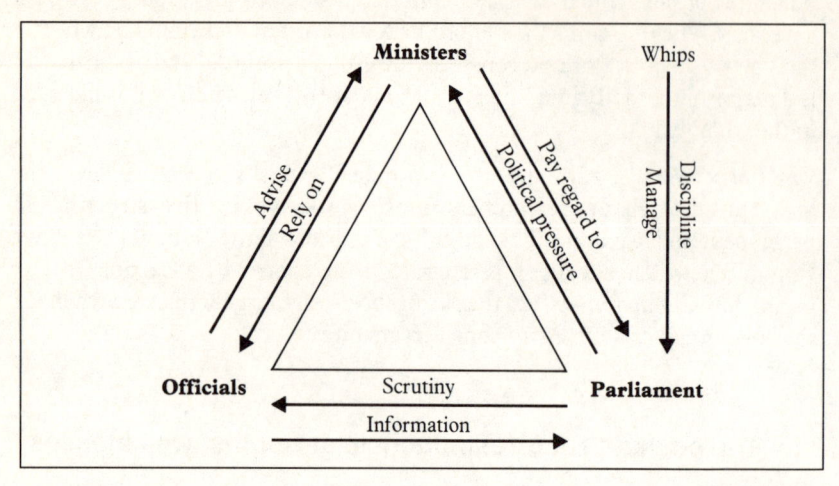

```
                        Ministers                Whips
                          ▲  ▲
                         ╱    ╲                    │
                    Advise    Pay regard to     Discipline
                    Rely on   Political pressure  Manage
                       ╱        ╲                  │
                      ▼          ▼                 ▼
                 Officials    ◄── Scrutiny ──   Parliament
                              ── Information ──►
```

There is no strict order of strength between individual Departments, although most decisions involve the Treasury's control over the Civil Service, departmental budgets and public expenditure priorities. Officials and Ministers therefore often find that policy formulation is a battle between them and the Treasury which may overshadow other interdepartmental considerations. In view of its size and scope, the Department of Trade and Industry is involved in a large proportion of interdepartmental negotiations. Two Departments, the Foreign Office and Ministry of Defence, although falling within the Treasury's net, are worlds of their own because of the structure and functions of the Diplomatic Service and the extensive cross-fertilization of MoD officials and Services staff.

The key components of power have been identified. The next section explains how they work together to reach decisions, formulate policy and produce legislation.

	Influence (/10)	Strengths	Weaknesses
MPs/Peers as a group	4 (but rises to 6 if small majority or obvious public/political issue)	• Public debate • Ability to embarrass Ministers • Privileged access to Ministers • Representation on individual's problems	• Easily overridden by Executive • All talk, no action • Manifestation of democracy rather than a democratic force
Officials	8	• Command of facts • Advice to Ministers often conclusive • Ministers can't survive without them • Draft and formulate legislation • Control consultative processes • Put words into Ministers' mouths	• Usually defensive • Often poor commercial understanding • Must work within overall manifesto/ministerial brief
Ministers	7	• Ultimate decision-makers • Can expedite official action • Can overturn official advice	• Have to depend on officials • Room for manoeuvre limited by ongoing policies and pragmatic constraints • May be moved regularly between Departments

54 Government – the components of power

	Influence (/10)	Strengths	Weaknesses
Prime Minister	10	• Total control	• Too broad an area of responsibility to cover small issues
Whips	9	• Power to persuade • Patronage	• Can't stop occasional revolts • Must bargain when majority low
PPSs	3	• Direct line to Ministers	• Influence depends on the Ministers they serve
Special Advisers	3	• Write speeches • May have close and regular contact with Ministers	• May just be speechwriters
Policy Unit	3 (but can be much greater)	• Direct advice to the Prime Minister • Ability to re-evaluate issues and resolve interdepartmental conflicts	• Not like the Think Tank: must be asked to review issues by the Prime Minister. Cannot operate independently
Individual MPs	1 (unless head of 1922/PLP chairman of backbench committee or purely constituency issue)	• Can take action on problems of the individual • Can draw attention to issues • May become Ministers • Some power if majority small	• Whipped; ignored by the Executive • Harassed; poorly serviced and briefed

Government – the components of power

Select Committees	3 (6 if they can attract public attention to their reports)	• Examination of specific issues • Expertise improving now that more specialists being appointed to advise them • Useful scrutiny of public bodies	• Executive may ignore their work • Unlike Congressional committees: they don't handle consultation processes as a tribunal • Usually work too late to influence policy
Backbench committees	6	• Particularly useful in representing MPs views to Leadership • Direct access to Ministers • Can take up individual cases	• Don't examine issues in depth • Secretaries control access and may use position for their own purposes • Quality of chairmen variable
All-Party committees	2	• Can mobilize support on occasions (e.g. VAT on books)	• Too influenced by pressure groups • Country groups seen as 'beano hunters'
Commons Chamber	2	• Chance for MPs to make Government accountable	• Facade of democracy

	Influence (/10)	Strengths	Weaknesses
Individual Peers	2	• More time to devote to issues • Less inclined to be Lobby fodder • Easier to get debate time than MPs	• Can't deal with money matters
Lords EEC Select Committee	6	• Real expertise • Government takes account of its reports • Works in advance of policies coming into effect	• Can only recommend; can't tell Government what to do
Lords Chamber	3	• Agenda less dominated by the Executive • Cross-party voting potential can embarrass Government • Can delay bills to force concessions	• Amendments usually negatived by the Commons • Despite strengths, Executive usually gets its way

2
Decision-makers – how do they work?

Government – the function of directing and controlling or regulating the actions and affairs of citizens.

Government in Britain, as elsewhere, exists to maintain stability in society. Commercial and economic stability; fair treatment under the law; redressing disadvantage; ensuring that the State's resources are used to best common advantage; defending the State and its citizens against attack; and many other functions that are expected of it. Now that we have examined the main institutions that make the decisions in Government, we must move on to see how those decisions are made: how does the process of policy formulation work? What are the influences on that process? How do the components of power combine or provide a balance to each other.

2.1 Legislation

In the eyes of most people, the making of laws – legislation – is the main manifestation of Government's function. In fact, although the classical model of the Constitution tells us that the courts interpret the laws made by Government, officials constantly re-evaluate existing statutes rather than impose new legislation to suit changed circumstances. The Department of Environment, for example, issues a great number of Circulars, as they are called, to local authorities each year on the interpretation of local government, housing and planning law. Wherever possible, if issues can be decided other than by legislative means, Government will do so. The making of law is an expensive, difficult and time-consuming business with only the tip – parliamentary scrutiny – of a large iceberg being visible to the public. It is also increasingly pressured: while the proportion of parliamentary time spent on legislation has remained level at about 50 per cent, the volume of primary legislation has increased from around 200 pages in 1900 to over 2000 pages a year today.

58   Decision-makers – how do they work?

The need to legislate arises from a number of sources:

- commitments decided by, or forced upon Parties while in opposition;
- other manifesto commitments;
- major political positions taken by the Cabinet;
- from Departments when they find their existing powers to be insufficient or inappropriate for the conduct of administration;
- through pressure by special interest groups; and
- ongoing programmes or unexpected issues such as an epidemic of rabies, or war.

Legislation does not just mean Statutes. There are many ways in which laws can be promulgated:

- *Through Public Bills* – or the Statutes we associate with the Government's programme. They may be introduced either by the Executive, or by individual MPs, in which case they are known as Private Member's or Ten-Minute Rule Bills (but are still Public Bills). Public Bills are so called because they concern the whole community. Between 40 and 70 per cent may be passed in a normal year.
- *Through Private Bills* – which affect only a section of the community such as local authorities and nationalized industries or individuals. Between 30 and 70 may be passed in a normal year.
- *Through Hybrid Bills* – which are Public Bills that have a particular effect on one section of the community.
- *Through Provisional Order Confirmation Bills* – which confirm the granting of land or delegation of power to a local authority. Thirty may be passed in any one year.
- *Through delegated, or secondary legislation* – where a statute gives Ministers the power to make such rules as are necessary to implement it. Most of these, collectively known as Statutory Instruments (some 2000 are issued each year), are administrative Orders or Regulations and are usually very specific, dealing for example with the layout of a form or allocation of agricultural subsidies. The increased need for such flexibility and the inability of Parliament to deal satisfactorily with very detailed matters has led to the growth of Enabling Legislation, which outlines the parameters of a Statute's authority and delegates to Ministers the power to pass Regulations on specific matters within that authority. This device has further transferred power from Parliament to the Executive but makes it easier for fees, penalties and borrowing limits, for example, to be varied in line with inflation or other changed circumstances.
- *Through direct applicability of EEC legislation* – to implement the mass of Regulations and Directives issued by the EEC. This last source is

increasingly important: in some sectors the bulk of new regulatory activity now takes place not in Whitehall but Brussels.

Of all these forms of legislation, by far the most important to the citizen are Public Bills and Statutory Instruments.

Public Bills – procedure

The life of a Bill begins many months – often years – before the public is aware of its existence. A Government's programme is drawn up with a view to implementation over the five years allowed to it. A measure, such as repeal of existing legislation, may become a Party commitment while it is still in opposition. When it is returned to power, it may well find departmental officials placing before Ministers draft legislation put forward by them and ignored or passed over for lack of time by the previous administration.

Irrespective of the source of legislation, all proposed Government Bills must be sanctioned by Cabinet since there is only finite time in a parliamentary year – although about 110 days are allocated for Public Legislation and all but ten are appropriated by the Government, there are certain Bills that take an automatic place in the programme (the Finance Bill for example) and unforeseen events may require legislation, leaving only about 60 days for new Bills.

Before Bills jostle for position to be placed before Parliament, however, they must be created. We shall take a fictitious but feasible case-study to outline a Bill's conception, growth, scrutiny and endorsement.

The Civil Aviation Bill – a case study

Following the privatization of British Airways, a number of changes in the international aviation regime and widespread opposition to flagship carrier rights, airport and route allocation by other airlines has led to pressure on officials, MPs and Ministers to make changes. The media has been skilfully briefed and comment orchestrated. There have been meetings of the rival airlines with the Secretary of State for Transport, the junior Aviation Minister and officials in both the Civil and International Aviation Directorates of the Department of Transport. Attempts at reconciling the positions of BA and its opponents make it clear to Ministers and officials that a voluntary agreement would be inappropriate and, in order to codify a new balance of interests and formalize international agreements in UK law, a new Civil Aviation Act is needed.

In view of the intense lobbying for change and the contact that exists between the chairmen of a number of the airlines and the Prime Minister, it is he who tells the Transport Secretary to act. That recommendation may have been supported by one of the Cabinet Committees staffed by officials which shadow ministerial committees and by the Department's Advisory Committee, a group of senior officials and, possibly, outside experts who advise on policy and programmes. At this stage, say in December of the year before the Bill is introduced, a 'bid' will be put in by the Department of Transport to the Cabinet. This is no more than a first indication – the legislative programme is always tight and many bids do not progress further.

The decision having been taken, Department of Transport officials will discuss a range of options conditioned by the outside views they have received and by their different sponsoring responsibilities – British Airways, other airlines, the Civil Aviation and British Airports authorities, other airports and international relations are all represented by different Divisions within the Department. It may be decided to appoint a consultancy firm to produce independent recommendations on a new structure for civil aviation. The Department's lawyers will be consulted on any legal and outline drafting problems. They may in turn refer to their counterparts in the Foreign Office if questions of international law are involved.

Once Department of Transport officials have a reasonable idea of the policy option favoured by the Minister, they will ask for comments from the Treasury, because of the inevitable cost implications, and from the Department of Trade and Industry in case there are complications relating to competition policy and other EEC considerations on freedom of services or dominant positions by commercial enterprises. The relevant Transport Minister will then take his Department's decision to the Future Legislation Cabinet Committee, which is chaired by the Leader of the House of Commons, for approval by Ministers as a whole of the outline basis of the legislation to come, although an *ad hoc* committee may also meet if a Bill is likely to be particularly contentious or if Departments cannot reach accord. The Civil Aviation Bill is discussed and it is decided that it cannot wait more than one year before being tabled in Parliament. It will be among those measures considered for inclusion in the Queen's Speech at the opening of the next Session in November. The Queen's Speech is delivered by her but written by the Government as an outline of its legislative programme.

Since interest in the issue has been confined to airlines, airports and other bodies such as the Civil Aviation Authority and airline users' groups, the Department may not publish a document known as a Green Paper which sets out the Government's views on an issue and asks for public comment. Instead, there may be a call by letter to a series of interested parties inviting them to present their views on form and substance within the guidelines set by the Department. Six months might be allowed for those groups to submit written representations, have several meetings with officials and perhaps two with Ministers. The Whips will also be asked to advise on parliamentary reaction to the outine Bill, for by then the various interest groups will be lobbying the Labour backbench Transport Committee, Conservative backbench Aviation Committee and the All-Party Aviation Group. The Transport Select Committee

Decision-makers – how do they work?

may also have included the subject on its agenda and would call the Minister, his officials and other interested parties to give evidence.

Drafting legislation is a lengthy and frustrating task. Officials will work in teams and may produce half a dozen Green Paper drafts and a dozen or more revisions of the outline Bill before they are happy that they are word perfect. They hand over the task of drafting the Bill in detail, because of its complexity, to Parliamentary Counsel's office, a branch of the Treasury, having been sanctioned to do so by Ministers after approval by the Future Legislation Cabinet Committee, referred to above, of the Bill's principles. Parliamentary Counsel are all extremely able lawyers experienced in the dry art of legislative drafting. Their work may take around two months and in this case will be performed over the summer, before the new parliamentary Session starts, as the culmination of over a year of preparation and consultations. In theory the Minister has the last word on policy and Counsel the last word on form and law, but the dividing line is hazy and the draftsman is often drawn into policy decisions.

Long before Parliamentary Counsel start their work, however, the Government will probably publish a White Paper, as it is called, which puts forward firm proposals on the basis of the Green Paper consultations that have taken place. The White Paper may leave room for changes on a few points but it is generally regarded as the Government's last word. It may be debated in Parliament for, if the Government does not find space for Parliamentary discussion in its planned timetable, the airlines and others will attempt to persuade MPs to press the Leader of the House to grant public discussion of the issue or, more likely, they will try to secure a short or unstarred debate in the Lords.

Moving forward in time, while Parliamentary Counsel draft the Bill a further decision will be taken on when it will be ready for presentation to Parliament. The earlier Counsel finish their work, the greater the chance that the Bill will command a forward position in the timetable and complete its parliamentary stages before the following summer's end of Session.

At last the Bill is ready. It goes before the Legislation Committee of the Cabinet, which is chaired by the Lord Chancellor and which examines its structures and details a final time.

Only then is Parliament brought into the equation.

Parliament's year stretches from early November to the end of July or early August. It also returns at the end of October to complete endorsement of any Bills that had not been fully considered before the Summer Recess. The Civil Aviation Bill is one of the first to be introduced and receives its *First Reading* in the Commons in the middle of November. Depending on the timetable, and on whether the Government feels that contentious issues of detail should be settled, the Bill may be introduced in the Lords instead (although if its main purpose is concerned with public expenditure or taxation, it can only originate in the Commons). First Reading is a formality in which the title is read and a date announced for *Second Reading*. In this case, it is set for ten days later.

Second Reading represents the first opportunity for MPs to debate the broad principles of the Bill. The Minister in charge explains the Government's intentions, the Opposition spokesman responds, and other MPs make their points either as a matter of personal principle, or because their constituency is affected, or because they are representing external interests. Discussion on individual clauses and other points of detail is not allowed.

In advance of the debate, the departmental PPSs and the Whips on both sides will be attempting to gauge backbenchers' reactions to the Bill and ensure that their Members vote for their Party's line. The PPSs will also be briefing Ministers on possible difficult points that could be raised by MPs in order that officials can draft contingency rebuttals as part of the detailed brief and speech that they prepare for the debate. Throughout the passage of the Bill in both Houses, a team of officials from the Department of Transport, and possibly one from the Department of Trade and Industry, will sit in a cramped box close to the Government Front Bench to give Ministers advice on responding to unanticipated issues.

Second reading debates may take from a few minutes to, on rare occasions, over a day. This measure is still contentious, despite the lengthy consultation period, and the debate lasts six hours, ending with a summary by one of the Transport Ministers and a Division, in which MPs file down two corridors which run either side of the Chamber to record their votes. It is very unusual for a Government Bill to be defeated at this stage.

In addition to the mass of information on the Bill that is sent to MPs by lobbying groups (most is immediately consigned to the bin unless those groups have targeted Members who are particularly interested in their cause and have taken the trouble to develop a preemptive relationship with them) the various Party research departments usually prepare briefs for MPs, who may also ask for additional information from the Commons Library.

Several events take place in the two weeks or so between Second Reading and the next, *Committee Stage*. Since drafting is a complex art, the Government often realizes that it should table amendments to a Bill to tighten small inaccuracies of phraseology. It may also have been persuaded by one group or another to make concessions by way of amendment. Once the Committee of Selection has decided on the composition of the Standing Committee (it always includes a Minister and one or two departmental PPSs, the Opposition front-bench spokesman, and a Government and Opposition Whip as well as backbenchers who have specialist experience or have expressed a particular interest during Second Reading or to the Selection Committee) any of the Bill's Committee members may table amendments prior to or during its consideration of the Bill, provided they are put down before the clause to be amended is debated. These are printed each day and are regularly consolidated into a Marshalled List. Officials will also be preparing notes on each clause to be given to all members of the Committee. The Minister will, on contentious legislation, meet the backbenchers on his own side at regular intervals to ensure they are kept informed and that any rebellious discontent is mollified; otherwise they may misunderstand any concessions to the Opposition on policy points.

Committee Stage begins. Initially, the Standing Committee meets twice a week from 10.30–1.00 but if progress is slow, owing to the number of amendments and Divisions or time-wasting speeches by the Opposition, the government and Opposition Whips may agree to extend sittings to afternoons or even evenings. As a last resort, the Government may impose a 'Guillotine', which restricts debate to a precise timetable.

Standing Committees cannot amend the Bill so that its main principles are destroyed since the House has already agreed to them on Second Reading. The Committee's chairman, who is selected from the senior MPs comprising the 'Speakers's Panel' has the power to select for debate amendments tabled by Government backbenchers or the Opposition on the basis of relevance and he will refuse some, combine others where there are close similarities, and announce the order in which they are to be discussed. In many cases amendments are withdrawn after a short explanation by the Minister of his reasons for not accepting it but he may offer to consider some compromise between then and the next hurdle, *Report Stage*. The Government occasionally sustains defeats in Committee, but the reality of power is that it knows it can almost always reverse them when the Bill returns to debate by the House as a whole and that such reversals do not constitute No Confidence votes against the Executive. Indeed, if the Government is at all likely to accept amendments (other than drafting formalities) it will do so in Committee since less publicity is attracted to their giving ground at that time. Committee Stage, like much of the work of Parliament, is nowadays mainly a matter of the Government allowing the public manifestation of democracy to be seen before it imposes its will and tells Parliament how to grant consent. Over three parliamentary sessions studied by Professor John Griffith in 1973, only 171 of the 3510 amendments moved by Government backbenchers and the Opposition were agreed to.

After two months of hard argument, in which the Government has accepted a number of small amendments and has continued to refine its own drafting, the last clause is approved and the Bill moves to Report Stage some two weeks later. If no amendments had been made, this stage would have been bypassed, but in this case (as almost always in practice) Report Stage allows the House as

Box 20 Government defeats in Commons Divisions 1970–88 (floor of the House only)

	Government majority	Number of divisions	Defeats
1970–4	31	1002	6
1974	0	109	17
1974–9	4	1501	42
1979–88	96	1775	2

This compares with 34 defeats in the period 1905–70.

a whole to contribute amendments and for those accepted by the Committee to be re-examined. If the government wishes to overturn setbacks in Committee it will do so at this stage since its whipped majority can usually be counted on to be obedient.

On a very contentious Bill, Report Stage may take two days but usually one is enough. *Third Reading*, the final Commons stage, often follows immediately and may involve a simple vote without any debate. It is possible, however, for amendments to be introduced if they cover matters already included in the Bill. It is even rarer for the Government to concede by this time.

The Civil Aviation Bill has now passed from the Commons and is sent to the Lords, where the process of scrutiny starts all over again. The stages of debate are exactly as in the Lower House except that Committee Stage is taken by all Peers on the floor of the Lords. This is known as a Committee of the Whole House. Once again, the Government may introduce amendments as small concessions to points well made but, if none are tabled, then Committee and Report stages are dispensed with completely.

It has already been explained that the Lords cannot consider measures directly concerning public expenditure or taxation. The Lords therefore automatically agree to any clauses that relate to the exclusive privilege of the Commons over money matters. The Speaker has occasionally been asked to rule on whether individual Lords amendments infringe that privilege.

If the Civil Aviation Bill is in any way amended in the Lords, it must finally return to the Commons for those changes only to be reconsidered – another opportunity for the Government to negate any embarrassing defeats on its legislation. If the Bill had started its life in the Lords, this procedure would work in reverse, with the Lords considering Commons amendments, except that any revision made by the Upper House at this stage would involve further scrutiny by the Commons.

When both Houses have passed the Bill on Third Reading and considered each other's amendments, the Bill is signed with the Queen's consent and becomes law even though its implementation date may be months (or, in the case of some consumer credit legislation, years) hence.

After 18 months planning and consultation, four months in the Commons and two and a half months in the Lords, the Civil Aviation Act becomes one of the statutes passed by Parliament in that year's Session. Several Private Member's Bills (see box 22) almost lasted the course but had to give way to Government legislation near the end of the Session and failed to complete their passage within the time allotted (in 1987–8 only 13 of the 118 Private Member's Bills that were introduced became law). Their promoters will have to try again from scratch. Of 150 Bills receiving First Reading that Session, only 55 became law.

Box 21 The Speaker rules on the Commons' legislative privilege

Films Bill
Lords Amendment considered.
New Clause
LEVY ON FEATURE FILMS, PRE-RECORDED VIDEO CASSETTES OR BLANK VIDEO TAPES

Lords amendment:
After Clause 5, insert the following new clause—
"The Secretary of State, after one year beginning with the day on which this Act is passed, and after consultation with persons considered by him to be representative of the film production industry may by order made by statutory instrument, establish arrangements to supplement the financial assistance provided under secton 5(1) of the Act by funds derived from any or all of the following schemes, that is to say—
  (*a*) a levy from independent television contractors and the BBC or an appropriate sum of money to be determined by him in respect of the showing by them of feature films on television, or
  (*b*) a levy at such rate as he may determine on pre-recorded video cassettes containing feature film material and sold in the United Kingdom, or
  (*c*) the appropriate film proceeds of any levy scheme approved by him in respect of blank video tape sold in the United Kingdom."

9.23 pm

Mr. Speaker: I have to draw the attention of the House to the fact that the Lords amendment involves a major infringement of the financial rights of the Commons. The amendment, in its third paragraph, involves a charge upon the people. Although it is not within my power to withdraw the Lords amendment from consideration by the House, it would in my view go beyond the conventions of the constitution for the house to agree to it. I therefore call upon the Minister to move to disagree with the Lords in the said Amendment.

Mr. Tim Brinton (Gravesend): On a point of order, Mr. Speaker. I fully accept your ruling, but it raises an interesting point. Would you give the House further clarification? As I understand it, the amendment compels private money to pass from one company to another and not through the public purse. Will you enlighten the House, Mr. Speaker, as to whether, in view of your ruling, you would feel the same about the television levy, the BBC licence fee and other compulsory measures ordered by the House which do not pass through the Treasury?

Mr. Speaker: The House has to consider the amendment sent to it by the Lords. If the amendment had consisted of paragraphs (*a*) and (*b*) only it would doubtless not have raised difficulties. The element of tax lies in paragraph (*c*). The sellers of blank video tapes have no community of interest with the production of films and would derive no benefit from the proposal. It is therefore a tax on that group. That is why I ruled as I did.

Motion made, and Question proposed. That this House doth disagree with the Lords in the said Amendment.—[*Mr. Norman Lamont.*]

Source: Hansard, 30 April 1985.

Box 22 See how they fail

Passed   ELECTRICTY (FINANCIAL PROVISIONS) (SCOTLAND)   Mr M. Rifkind/Lord Sanderson of Bowden   (*Government*)
     Commons: (169)   1R: 17.5   SGC: 9.6   Comm, Rep & 3R: 47
     Lords: (112)   1R: 5.7   All Stages 27.7
     Royal Assent (cap 37, 1988): 29.7

   ELIMINATION OF POVERTY IN OLD AGE ETC   Mr J. Corbyn
     Commons: (61)   1R: *1.12*

Passed   EMPLOYMENT   Mr N. Fowler/Lord Trefgarne   (*Government*)
     Commons: (17,90,152)   1R: *22.10*   2R: *3.11*   Comm (SC F): *12.11–28.1*
     Rep & 3R: 8 & 10.2   LA: 24.5
     Lords: (50,63,67)   1R: 12.2   2R: 22.2   Comm: 7, 8 & 14.3   Rep: 28.4   3R: 25.4
     Royal Assent (cap 19, 1988): 26.5

   EMPTY PROPERTY AND COMMUNITY AID   Mr K. Hargreaves
     Commons: (136)   1R: 30.3

   ENGLISH CHURCH   Mr T. Benn
     Commons: (156)   1R: 18.5

Passed   ENVIRONMENT AND SAFETY INFORMATION   Mr Chris Smith/Baroness Ewart-Biggs
     Commons: (28,160, 193)   1R: 28.10   2R: 5.2 (Debate adjourned): *22.4   Comm (SC C): 4.5
     Rep & 3R: *13.5   LA: 8.7
     Lords: (92,107)   1R: 17.5   2R: 15.6   Comm: 22.6   Rep: *1.7   3R: *6.7
     Royal Assent (cap 30, 1988): 29.7

Cont.

Box 22 (*Cont.*)

Passed   EUROPEAN COMMUNITIES (AMENDMENT)   Mr T. Benn
     Commons: (153)   1R: 4.5

Passed   EUROPEAN COMMUNITIES (FINANCE)   Mr N. Lawson/Lord Brabazon of Tara   (*Government*)
     Commons: (185)   1R: 1.7   2R: 11.7   Comm: 24.10   Rep & 3R: 27.10
     Lords: (132)   1R: 31.70   All stages: 10.11
     Royal Assent (cap 46, 1988): 15.11

   EXTENSION OF CIVIL JUSTICE   Mr Q. Davies
     Commons: (219)   1R: 26.10   (*not printed*)

Passed   FARM LAND AND RURAL DEVELOPMENT [HL]   Baroness Trumpington/Mr J. MacGregor   (*Government*)
     Lords: (11,36)   1R: *21.10*   2R: *5.11*   Comm: *1.2*   Rep: *17.12 & 12.1*   3R: 18.1
     CA: 9.5
     Commons: (85)   1R: 18.1   2R: 1.2   Comm (SC B): 15.3–31.3   Rep & 3R: 5.5
     Royal Assent (cap 16, 1988): 10.5

Passed   FINANCE   Mr N. Lamont/Lord Young of Graffham   (*Government*)
     Commons: (17,12)   1R: *1.7*   2R: *8.7*   Comm: *14, 15 & 16.7*   Rep & 3R: *20.7*
     Lords: (*not printed*)   1R: 21.7   All stages: 23.7   Royal Assent (cap 51, 1987): 23.7
     TITLE OF ACT: FINANCE (NO 2) ACT 1987

Passed   FINANCE (No 2)   Mr N. Lamont/Lord Young of Graffham   (*Government*)
     Commons: (127,180)   1R: 21.3   2R: 26.4   Comm: 3, 9 & 10.5   Comm (SC A): 12.5–30.6
     Rep: 13.7   3R: 14.7
     Lords: (120)   1R: 19.7   All stages: 27.7
     Royal Assent (cap 39, 1988): 29.7
     TITLE OF ACT: FINANCE ACT 1988

Cont.

Box 22 (*Cont.*)

Passed   FIREARMS (AMENDMENT)   Mr D. Hurd/Earl Ferrers   (*Government*)
   Commons: (75,118,224)   1R: *17.12*   2R: 21.1   Comm (SC F): 4.2–10.3   MR (No 2): 1.3
   MR (No 3): 2.11   Rep & 3R: 23 & 25.5   GM: 2.11   LA: 2.11
   Lords: (95,122,128)   1R: 26.5   2R: 24.6   Comm: 18 & 20.7   Rep: 19.10   3R: 31.10
   Royal Assent (cap 45, 1988): 15.11

   FOOD AND ENVIRONMENT PROTECTION ACT (AMENDMENT)   Mr D. Clark
   Commons: (179)   1R: 20.6

Passed   FOREIGN MARRIAGE (AMENDMENT) [HL]   Lord Chancellor/Sir P. Mayhew   (*Government*)
   Lords: (56)   1R: 29.2   2R: 14.3   OCD: *31.3   3R: 14.4
   Commons: (144)   1R: 19.4   SRC: 10.5   Comm (SC D): 21.7   Rep & 3R: 31.10
   Royal Assent (cap 44, 1988): 2.11

   FOREIGN NUCLEAR, CHEMICAL AND BIOLOGICAL BASES (PROHIBITION)   Mr T. Benn
   Commons: (138)   1R: 13.4

   FORESTRY COMMISSION ADVISORY COMMITTEES (PUBLIC ACCESS TO INFORMATION)   Mr R. Davies
   Commons: (112)   1R: 2.3

   FUEL AND ENERGY PROVISION   Mr J. Hughes
   Commons: (210)   1R: 27.7

   GAMING MACHINES (PROHIBITION OF USE BY PERSONS UNDER SIXTEEN)   Mr J. Dunnachie
   Commons: (116)   1R: 9.3

Extract from *Weekly Information Bulletin* at the end of the 1987–8 parliamentary session

Regulations – procedure

Although the Civil Aviation Act has been ratified by Parliament, many clauses require secondary legislation in order to set out powers, rights and duties in detail. A considerable proportion of primary legislation now empowers Departments to formulate Regulations that provide this detail in a way that would be inappropriate for inclusion in the body of the Act itself. Statutory Instruments (SIs) are commonly used for the variation of financial limits since the passage of time may outdate those in the main Act. For example, the Gaming Act 1968 provides a limit of £250 over a week's stake money for winnings that can be paid to bingo competitors. Several SIs later, the Gaming Act (Variation of Monetary Limits) Order 1985 increased that limit to £1250.

In this case, the Department of Transport's own lawyers – Parliamentary Counsel are not involved – and the relevant Principals (senior grades are less involved than they were on the Bill itself) as well as, possibly, one of the many advisory committees of experts that are established by Departments, will be working on the drafting of Regulations while the Bill is still passing through Parliament. Since MPs and Peers naturally distrust vague statutory clauses that reserve powers to Ministers to act as they see fit, the Department may produce an explanatory memorandum during parliamentary consideration which outlines to them the Regulations that are likely to follow the Act. The draft Regulations are sent to interested parties once the Act is passed in the form of a consultative document. Any further points arising from response to the document would be dealt with inside, perhaps, three months. From Royal Assent to finalizing the Regulations there might be a total gap of seven months.

All Regulations have to be approved by Parliament. It is agreed during a Bill's passage whether the approval of Regulations is to be by Positive Resolution, meaning that they can only come into force if Parliament agrees (usually within a 28–40 day period); or Negative Resolution, under which they automatically come into force unless MPs or Peers object within a set time limit (usually 40 days). When Regulations are tabled by either method, they must be approved en bloc by each House. This occasionally means a further debate in one House, with more perfunctory treatment in another or in a Standing Committee of 17 members nominated to deal with SI. Parliament has no power to amend SIs except by a separately passed parliamentary initiative – the Civil Aviation (Amendment) Regulations for example. It would be most unlikely that the Department would table an individual amending Regulation for consideration. Defects are normally accumulated, added to other improvements that become necessary, and are then put before Parliament. In such cases, they are rarely debated.

Decision-makers – how do they work?

Box 23 Regulations – their source and form

Section 9(i) of the Telecommunications Act 1984 gives Ministers Order making powers.

Public telecommunication systems.

9.—(1) The Secretary of State may by order designate as a public telecommunication system any telecommunication system the running of which is authorised by a licence to which section 8 above applies; and any reference in this Act to a public telecommunication system is a reference to a telecommunication system which is so designated and the running of which is so authorised.

(2) An order under subsection (1) above shall not come into operation until after the end of the period of 28 days beginning with—

   (a) the day on which copies of the order, and of the licence to which section 8 above applies, are laid before each House of Parliament; or

   (b) if such copies are so laid on different days, the last of those days.

One of the Orders made under the Section.

STATUTORY INSTRUMENTS

1985 No. 1594

TELECOMMUNICATIONS

The Public Telecommunication System Designation (CableTel Communications Limited) Order 1985

Made -	21st October 1985
Laid before Parliament	21st October 1985
Coming into Operation	20th November 1985

Whereas the Secretary of State has granted to CableTel Communications Limited a licence ("the Licence") under section 7 of the Telecommunications Act 1984(**a**) ("the Act"), to which section 8 of the Act applies, for the running of the telecommunication systems specified in Annex A to the Licence ("the Applicable Cabled Systems"):

Now, therefore, the Secretary of State, in exercise of the powers conferred on him by sections 9 and 104 of the Act, hereby makes the following Order:—

   1. This Order may be cited as the Public Telecommunication System Designation (CableTel Communications Limited) Order 1985 and shall come into operation on 20th November 1985.

   2. Each of the Applicable Cabled Systems is hereby designated as a public telecommunication system.

Most Secondary Legislation, however, is longer and more detailed.

Decision-makers – how do they work? 71

In practice, few Regulations are debated and those (requiring Affirmative Resolution) that are will be subject to a time limit of one and a half hours and discussed after 10 pm.

The involvement of Ministers in the drafting and promulgation of Regulations is minimal. Officials are expected to assess views and produce the end product without political guidance.

Statutory Instruments differ from primary legislation in that, like the work of administrative tribunals, they can be challenged through the courts for *ultra vires* through six legal procedures:

- *mandamus*: to compel a public body or Minister to perform a legal duty;
- *certiorari*: to quash an administrative decision already made;
- *prohibition*: to prevent a public authority from considering a matter without statutory authority;
- *injunction*: to prohibit a Minister or public authority from doing something that would be illegal;
- *declaratory judgment*: which is simply a statement by the court to clarify or define the powers and duties of a Minister or public body;
- *a special procedure provided for in the Act itself*, such as appeal to the High Court.

Apart from affirmative or negative acquiescence, Parliamentary control over Statutory Instruments is exercised in two ways: by a Joint Committee of both Houses (known as the Scrutiny Committee) comprising seven each of MPs and Peers and chaired by an Opposition MP. For Instruments subject to Commons approval only, the MPs meet separately. The purpose of the Committee is to undertake technical scrutiny and determine whether or not the attention of the House should be drawn to an Instrument because:

- it is *ultra vires*;
- it makes an unusual or unexpected use of the powers conferred by the Act;
- it is made under an enactment excluding it from challenge in the courts;
- it purports to be retrospective without provision in the Act;
- its publication or laying before Parliament has been unjustifiably delayed;
- its drafting is defective or unclear.

However, there is no requirement on Parliament to take account of the Committee's views – an Instrument may run through its consideration by the House before the Committee sees it. In 1977–8, this happened on more than 20 occasions, prompting the chairman to complain that it often happened 'when the Department concerned is well aware ... that the Committee has queries on the Instrument'. The Committee is also confined to technical scrutiny and cannot consider the merits of, or policy behind, an

Instrument. In any event, there are too many SIs each year for the Committee fully to scrutinize them.

Under Standing Order 79, Standing Committees of the Commons have also been established to consider a Minister's referral of specific SIs or draft SIs where affirmative acquiescence is required or where MPs feel that an SI should be annulled. Over 60 per cent of Affirmative Resolutions are now dealt with in this way. These committees sit for only one and a half hours. Any MP may take part in the proceedings but only the 17 appointed committee members may vote or move amendments. In practice, motions to annul a Statutory Instrument are normally tabled as Early Day Motions (see page 117). If sponsored by the Opposition they will usually be accommodated in the parliamentary timetable, but backbenchers are (as always) less lucky.

Private Bills – procedure

Instead of the entire aviation industry being affected, it may be that only a small part of it needs legislation to create, amend or clarify legal rights. A local authority may wish to have the power to make bye-laws to acquire land compulsorily in order to build a small airport. It would discuss the matter with the Departments of Transport and Environment (the latter being consulted as the Department responsible for local government and land use) and would then brief one of the seven firms of Parliamentary Agents to draft a Private Bill for them.

The local authority is known as the Promoter of the Bill and has to sign a petition, which must be presented with the draft Bill and other supporting documents to the Private Bill Office in the Commons by 27 November. Where works are to be constructed or land to be compulsorily acquired, plans have to be deposited with the Clerk of the County Council or the Town Clerk of the County Borough by 20 November. This would be a formality for the local authority in this case but must be borne in mind by others seeking to promote private legislation. The Bill and its purposes must also be advertised twice in local papers by 11 December and in the *London Gazette*.

By 5 December, owners of the land to be purchased must be notified. If the Bill is opposed on grounds that these requirements have not been fulfilled, complaint must be made by 17 December.

Examination of the Bill begins on or after 18 December and is by two Examiners, who are appointed respectively by the Speaker and the House of Lords to ensure that the above preliminaries have been complied with. By 8 January, Bills are divided between both Houses by the Chairman of Ways and Means, one of the three Deputy Speakers who presides over the House of Commons when it goes into Committee of the Whole House (which sits instead of a Standing Committee if required on matters of crucial interest), and the Lord Chairman of Committees, his counterpart in the Lords. Opponents of the Bill have until 30 January to present their petitions.

If the Examiner endorses the local authority's petition, the Bill is presented, deemed to have been *read a first time*, and ordered to be *read a second time*. This stage is similar to that for Public Bills. If the Bill is unopposed, its Second Reading can be taken at the start of the parliamentary day, 2.30 pm, as Unopposed Private Business. If not, the Chairman of Ways and Means finds a day for it to be debated at 7 pm as Opposed Private Business. Most Bills are not opposed.

The Second Reading of a Private Bill, unlike that for a Public Bill, only affirms its principle conditionally: that it is not objectionable to the Government. The Whips may oppose it if it is felt, after consideration, that it should be a Public Bill. MPs may be briefed by local or other pressure groups to oppose it. Endorsement is subject to the case that has been put forward by the promoters being proved in *Committee Stage*, which is structured on a tribunal basis. Promoters and opposers are represented by Counsel, evidence is given under oath, and the Committee's members balance public and private interests. The Committee itself is appointed by the Selection Committee, either as the Committee for Unopposed Bills (which ensures only that Standing Orders have been complied with and public rights will not be infringed unduly), or a Private Bills Committee consisting of four MPs or five Peers. Departments may offer advice on the Bill to the Committee's members; as a result of that advice and evidence from both sides, the Bill may be amended. This procedure is lengthy and expensive, since the House charges fees to promoters and opponents in addition to the cost of retaining Parliamentary Agents. In view of this, discussions take place in advance of Committee Stage to agree amendments.

If the Bill is amended, it must wait for three days before being considered, but unamended Bills receive their *Third Reading* immediately following Committee Stage. The House can amend a Private Bill provided such an amendment would have been proposed in Committee. Further stages are as for Public Bills. Box 24 lists a selection of the Private Bills passing, or already passed through Parliament near the end of a Session. Only a few are opposed (O).

Hybrid Bills – procedure

The question of whether a Public Bill affects a particular private interest is one for interpretation by the Speaker and his Counsel. An example is legislation to allow the constructors and promoters of a Channel Tunnel property and other rights, including the ability to levy fees on users of a tunnel under the high seas. Only particular people and corporate bodies

Box 24 Private Bills: Commons proceedings as at 7 July 1988

Name of Bill	Bill read 1st time	2R	Bill committed	*	Bill reported	Bill as amended considered	3R	Royal Assent	Cap No.
Associated British Ports[5+]	22 Jan	28 Jan	28 Jan	U	4 Mar		30 Apr	10 Dec	xxvii 87
Associated British Ports (No 2)[5]	22 Jan	11 May# 22 June#	22 June						
Associated British Ports (Barrow) [HL][5]	21 Apr	5 May	5 May	U	18 May	7 June	22 June	28 June	xviii 88
Avon Light Rail Transit [HL][5]	7 June								
Bexley London Borough Council[3+]	22 Jan	12 Feb	12 Feb	U	6 May		2 Jul	16 Nov	xxiii 87
Birmingham City Council[3]	22 Jan	28 Jan	28 Jan	U	2 Mar		10 Mar		
Brighton and Preston Cemetery[3]	12 Feb	18 Feb	3 Mar	U	20 Apr	3 May	10 May	28 June	xvii 88
British Railways[5+]	22 Jan	16 Feb#	26 Feb	U	13 May		7 Jul	17 Dec	xxix 87
British Railways (No 2)[5]	22 Jan	15 Mar# 27 Apr#	27 Apr	U	22 June				

Cont.

Box 24 (*Cont*)

Name of Bill	Bill read 1st time	2R	Bill committed	*	Bill reported	Bill as amended considered	3R	Royal Assent	Cap No.
British Railways (London) [HL]⁵⁺	16 Jul	20 Jan	20 Jan	U	3 Mar		15 Mar #	24 Mar	xi 88
British Waterways⁵⁺	22 Jan	29 Jan	29 Jan	U	6 May		16 Jul	17 Dec	xxviii 87
British Waterways (No 2) [HL]⁵	16 May	7 June	7 June	U	6 Jul				
Cardiff Bay Barrage³	22 Jan								
City of London (Spitalfields Market)⁵	22 Jan	12 May #	12 May	O					
City of Westminster³⁺	22 Jan	7 May #	7 May	U	25 Nov	17 Dec	14 Jan	15 Mar	viii 88
Corn Exchange [HL]⁴⁺	14 Dec	12 Jan	12 Jan	U	2 Mar		8 Mar	15 Mar	x 88
County of South Glamorgan (Taff Crossing)³⁺⁺	22 Jan 1986 Recommitted	1 May # 1986	1 May 1986 12 Mar	O	22 Jul 1986 8 Apr	23 Oct 1986 5 May	9 Jul		
Dartmouth-Kingswear Floating Bridge⁴	22 Jan	28 Jan	15 Feb	U	2 Mar		10 Mar	28 June	xvi 88

Cont.

Box 24 (*Cont*)

Name of Bill	Bill read 1st time	2R	Bill committed	*	Bill reported	Bill as amended considered	3R	Royal Assent	Cap No.
Dyfed [HL]⁵⁺	10 Dec 1986	<u>13 Jan</u>	<u>13 Jan</u>	U	<u>22 Jul</u>	10 Nov	<u>17 Nov</u>	<u>17 Nov</u>	xxiv 87
Eastbourne Harbour [HL]⁴	17 May	7 June	7 June	U	22 June		30 June		
Essex [HL]⁵⁺⁺	30 Jun 1986	10 Jul 1986	10 Jul 1986	O	<u>26 Mar</u>	14 Jul	<u>21 Jul</u>	<u>23 Jul</u>	xx 87
Falmouth Container Terminal⁴	22 Jan								

Source: Weekly Information (PIO)

rather than everyone, would be affected by such a Bill, and the issue would therefore be the subject of hybrid legislation. After Second Reading, a Hybrid Bill would be referred to a Select Committee and then be considered by a Committee of the Whole House, following which Public Bill procedures apply.

Legislation can be barely noticeable in its effect or, as in the case of the Civil Aviation Act, immediately apparent since the Act creates new regulatory bodies, alters the way British airports are run, and establishes machinery for redistributing air routes between airlines and deregulating fare controls. It also creates a new set of relationships between airlines, the new management and regulatory bodies for aviation and airports, and government. We must now examine how those relationships work and see how the legislation is implemented.

2.2 Policy management and administration – the work of Ministers and officials

Masters and advisers

Ministers have an enormous workload in addition to their responsibilities as MPs and it is common for their working day to last from 12 to 18 hours. A ministerial timetable may include, on any one day, a Cabinet Committee meeting; a visit to one of the many organizations, projects or institutions falling within his Department's responsibilities; speaking for the Government in a parliamentary legislative, policy or Adjournment debate or answering Oral Questions; a morning spent in a Standing Committee; meetings with individuals, groups or organizations who wish to make submissions on proposed policy changes or who have developed an established consultation structure with Ministers (for example, the National Farmers' Union and MAFF Ministers); and internal discussions with officials, with consideration of the many briefs, speeches and minutes prepared by them for those meetings, vists and parliamentary duties. At the end of the day, a Minister will still have a lot of homework: he will be given as many as five 'Red Boxes' full of reports, memoranda and other documents for his comment or endorsement (see box 25).

A Minister could not function for more than a few minutes without his Private Office, which will usually contain a Principal Private Secretary – almost always a fast-stream official at HEO(D) level in his mid-to-late twenties but, for most Secretaries of State, a Principal or Assistant Secretary – one or two Assistant Private Secretaries and a more junior official who keeps the Minister's diary. These three or four officials (Cabinet Ministers

78 Decision-makers – how do they work?

Box 25 A day in the life of a Secretary of State

This extract is taken from the 1985 diary of the Secretary of State for Energy

8.30–8.55 am	Daily meeting with ministerial team, PPS and Special Adviser.
8.55 am	Private telephone call to another Minister.
9.00–10.15 am	Meeting with National Coal Board and officials (5 minute briefing by officials from 9.00–9.05 am).
10.15–11.00 am	Meeting with financial advisers on British Gas flotation.
11.00–11.45 am	Meeting with constituency secretary to discuss correspondence from constituents and other matters arising in the Secretary of State's capacity as an MP.
11.45–12.15	Meeting with officials and one of the two Parliamentary Under Secretaries to discuss a major overseas contract.
12.15–1.00 pm	Briefing to journalists.
1.00 pm	Lunch with a group of MPs (organized by his PPS).
2.45–3.15 pm	Meeting with the Minister of State and a leading energy industry representative group.
3.15–3.45 pm	Meeting with officials about the Energy Efficiency Campaign.
3.45–5.00 pm	Deputation from the Coalfields Communities Campaign with the Minister of State, Welsh Office.
5.00–5.30 pm	Meeting with an oil exploration company.
5.30–6.15	Meeting with officials on electricity policy.
8.00 pm	Host dinner for Prime Minister of Trinidad and Tobago.

That night there was also a three-line Whip in the House that meant he had to leave the Dinner to vote in three Divisions.

12.00	Home. Read through three Red Boxes.

The diary of another Cabinet Minister showed that in the course of a year he attended 42 Cabinet meetings and 106 Cabinet Committees; submitted four Cabinet papers and 45 Cabinet Committee papers; received 1750 Cabinet papers himself; was personally concerned with four Bills, 59 Statutory Instruments, and 33 explanatory memoranda; answered 51 Oral Questions; made 19 visits abroad and took part in 140 broadcasts and interviews.

---

have far larger supporting staffs) are the channel for any communication, whether from other officials and Ministers or outsiders, with their Minister. The role is a two-way one, for the large amount of material that by convention is initially addressed to a Minister (Parliamentary Questions; correspondence from outsiders and so on) has to be distributed to the relevant officials for processing. The power of any Principal Private Secretary to control access to, and the flow of information to or from his Minister is thus potentially great. Like other officials, he has to form a judgement on whether to burden a Minister with paperwork or handle meetings and decisions himself.

Box 26 The Private Secretary as seen by a Secretary of State

> The Private Office is the heart of the Ministry... the Private Secretary... really does try to get my ideas across to the Department... I have got to face it that his main job is to get across to me what the Department wants. The Private Office is the Department's way of keeping a watch on me, of making sure I run along the lines they want me to run on, of dividing my time and getting the Department's policies and attitudes brought to my notice.
>
> Richard Crossman, 1975

It is the duty of officials, however, to ensure that Ministers receive all the information they need and that it is presented objectively and in the form he has requested. If there is any inaccuracy or bias in their advice, they will quickly be brought to task since it is usual for sponsoring officials and one of the Private Secretaries to attend ministerial meetings with outsiders. Principal Private Secretaries also generally have the good fortune to accompany their Minister to meetings outside the Department, including most official lunches, gala premieres and overseas visits. Principal or Assistant Private Secretaries also customarily listen in to all telephone conversations between their Minister and outsiders, civil servants and other advisers in case action is needed immediately.

Ministers are further guided, although not consciously, by one of the most powerful influences on the policy-making process – the weekly meetings of all Permanent Secretaries to discuss the business coming before Cabinet and the line they will advise their Ministers to take. While a Cabinet Minister may adopt an independent position on his own Department's policy, he is even more than usually reliant on his Permanent Secretary for advice on the wisdom of supporting other Ministers' policy positions. Rows in the Cabinet Room, which are anyway witnessed by the Secretary to the Cabinet who also presides over the Permanent Secretaries' meeting, may often be initiated by Ministers who conscientiously follow the counsel of their departmental head – the General Manager briefing his board directors on their lines.

The Permanent Secretary in each Department (or Secretaries, since a number of Departments have a Second Permanent Secretary just a quarter of a rung below their colleague right at the top) has a major and crucial role in addition to his power in concert with others. He is the Accounting Officer for his Department and is liable to appear before the financial committees of the Commons to explain departmental expenditure. He directs and supervises most of his Department's work. And he is a key counsel to Ministers on the formulation of policy and the handling of politically or

Box 27 Ministers, officials and Cabinet Committees – a Minister's view

'On complex issues, Cabinet Committees are just about the worst possible way of arriving at sensible decisions. Ministers would come to the meetings with long briefs prepared by officials who had been members of the appropriate Official Committee which "shadowed" the Ministerial Committee. In fact, "shadowed" is an inappropriate term, for the Official Committee, after carrying out the detailed analytical work intended only to set out the options for Ministers, usually left their Ministers in no doubt whatsoever as to which was the best option – the one they recommended.

In most cases, the Ministers not directly involved had either read the brief late the previous night, or started to do so as the argument proceeded. More often than not, as I have said, they would follow the line of the brief. But sometimes, if you could put the issue simply and succinctly enough, you might just persuade one or two Ministers to ignore their briefs and support you – naturally you had a better chance if they had no departmental interest on either side of the argument....

When all the preliminary lobbying has been done, the Cabinet Committee discussion itself rarely changes Ministers' minds. Often, the senior Cabinet Minister cannot attend personally, and sends a junior Minister who is not able to move from his Department's view. Even when senior Ministers attend themselves, as they normally do on major issues, it is not often possible to make them change their position'.

Joel Barnett, *Inside the Treasury*
(Andre Deutsch, 1982)

Box 28 The work of a Permanent Secretary

'He is responsible for the efficient operation of his Department, for instance its division into operational blocks of work, the allocation of sufficient staff (and no more) to different areas of work.... It is his duty as Accounting Officer to keep the Department's activities and expenditure within the bounds set by Parliament ... He is responsible for the management of his Department's staff including their training and career development ... He has to ensure that his Department has satisfactory arrangements for safeguarding confidential information ... On all this kind of work he is directly answerable to Parliament ... He will also be responsible for ensuring that the Minister is provided with the kind of service he wants ... of which the elements most likely to be of interest are the general organisation of the Department, the disposition of senior officials and the arrangements for providing the Minister with support services, including briefing him on both departmental and general Government matters and handling his correspondence. The Permanent Secretary will also be the Minister's chief policy adviser but by no means the only one ... Official heads of Departments also share in a collective responsibility for the Civil Service ...'

Quoted in Crowther-Hunt and Kellner, *The Civil Servants* (Macdonald, 1980)

administratively difficult issues. Much depends on the Permanent Secretary's own personality: some may prefer Ministers to deal with officials through them and therefore act as a gate-keeper between the political and administrative management areas in their Department. For some Ministers, therefore, the Department *is* the Permanent Secretary, his staff (for Permanent Secretaries also have Private Offices with a similar structure to that of a junior Minister) and the Minister's own Private Office.

Second to the Permanent Secretaries' meeting – the real Shadow Cabinet – is the gathering (also weekly) of the 'Dep Secs' – the Deputy Secretaries in the Cabinet Office, plus the Prime Minister's Principal Private Secretary. This meeting, also chaired by the Cabinet Secretary, plans the agenda of each week's Cabinet and Cabinet Committee meetings. As Joe Haines, Harold Wilson's Press Secretary at 10 Downing Street, commented in *The Politics of Power*, 'This is a power function as well as a planning one. The timing of the presentation to Cabinet or (Cabinet) Committee of an issue can be decisive in its acceptance or not. Where it is placed on the agenda is crucial, too. The Prime Minister may occasionally grumble at the timing of a committee – even, but rarely, veto a proposal because it was inconvenient – but he is far less likely to reject the proposed order of business put forward by the Cabinet Office'.

As an example of the interdependence of Ministers and their officials, we may take a case study that would almost certainly take place as part of the Department of Transport's role in sponsoring the bodies covered by the Civil Aviation Act.

A visit to Associated British Airports – a case study

The Civil Aviation Act establishes a new body to supervise the commercial management of all UK airports. The new Associated British Airports (ABA) is part of the private sector, although the Government keeps a 'Golden Share' to enable it to insist on operational safeguards for emergency defence and other reasons. Liaison between ABA and Department of Transport sponsoring officials is constant in the first few months of its existence and Ministers will have received a number of minutes from the Assistant Secretary in charge of the Branch simply redesignated Airports Policy following the passing of the Act.

Eventually, ABA decides that it is properly structured and staffed and it invites the Secretary of State to open its head office at Heathrow. Having contacted the Diary Secretary in the Minister's Private Office to ensure that he is free on the day, ABA writes direct to him.

The ABA's letter is seen by the Minister's Principal Private Secretary, who will read all correspondence not marked 'personal' (and possibly some that is). He asks the Minister whether he wishes to accept. In this instance his approval is a formality but in a fair proportion of cases officials will produce a note on the advisability or otherwise of a Minister committing himself to a visit or meeting. For example, it may be regarded as a bad idea for there to be ministerial contact with a company tendering for a contract supervised by the Minister's Department – *sub judice* rules of a sort apply when Government acts as a commerical operator. In other cases, if the date is specific and a senior Minister is unable to avoid a clash of commitments but departmental approval is recommended, the invitation may be passed to a more junior deputy.

In the six weeks or so before the Secretary of State travels to Heathrow, his officials will prepare a full brief on ABA; progress since the Act became law; liaison between them and ABA; contentious issues that may arise; and, if ABA has been considerate and notified Private Office of the people the Minister will meet, potted details on the guest list. By the time he visits ABA he will have all the information he needs. Most of the time he would be briefed by his Principal Private Secretary in the car only a short time before arriving but, since it has been decided to make a major policy review speech at the opening, the Minister will be briefed in advance and will concentrate on reading his script, which may have been written by officials, his Special Adviser, or both, on the way.

At an early stage the constituency MP for Heathrow will have been informed of the vist since it is regarded as discourteous for one MP to undertake official business in another's constituency without prior notice.

We have already mentioned that the Minister is often accompanied by one of his Private Secretaries. He may also bring one of the sponsoring Division's desk officers at HEO, Principal or Assistant Secretary grade.

Lastly, the Department's Press Office is told of the visit. It advises that there is likely to be considerable media interest in the visit and in turn is advised by Private Office of the significance of the Minister's speech in order that, at the weekly meeting of departmental information officers, the Department of Transport can try to ensure that no other major speeches or Government media events clash with the opportunity to obtain coverage for a statement of the Government's success in bringing order to civil aviation. The Department will liaise with ABA's public relations department to ensure that the same members of the press are not invited twice and may even produce a joint press release if ABA also wishes to obtain publicity. The Central Office of Information, which distributes departmental press notices to the media and others, would be briefed to expect the announcement on the day of the visit.

Compared with the organization behind it, the visit itself is simple. The only role performed by the Minister alone is delivering his speech.

Contrary to the popular image of Whitehall, officials have to work very hard; even more so today since staff levels are falling (from 732,000 in 1979 to 578,000 in 1988). Every letter, Parliamentary Question, debate, visit and meeting requires extensive research and briefing through a well-established vetting system to ensure that any statement made to the public is an agreed reflection of departmental policy and could not embarrass Ministers by being used against them. Officials form the often unnoticed bulk of the iceberg of Government, supporting their more visible political masters and adding solidity to policy formulation and implementation.

The balance of decision-making between Ministers and officials shifts even further to the latter after policy had been formulated or legislation passed. Implementation of legislative provisions or of ministerial policy decisions, in which officials will have had a crucial advisory role, is essentially an administrative task with occasional involvement by Ministers. The day-to-day liaison with the industries, companies, bodies or groups of people within a Department's sponsoring responsibilities falls to HEOs, Principals and Assistant Secretaries, who may be regarded by those they sponsor as members of an advice bureau. They give guidance on interpretation of legislation and access to financial assistance and will normally be prepared both to indicate the degree of flexibility of departmental policy in adapting to individual problems (moving the parameters of policy is discussed in section 3 of this book) and to assist in cases where illegality, inefficiency, abuse of power or anti-competitive activities on the part of a sponsored body or issue are alleged. Thus OFTEL handles public and commercial complaints about British Telecom; Steel Division of the Department of Trade and Industry deals with questions of production quota allocation between British Steel and its competitors (within the limits, however, of agreed EEC steel policy) and OFGAS supervises the pricing policies of British Gas.

Officials administer all Government contractual tendering subject to initial political guidance – on buying British, for example – or occasional strong parliamentary or direct pressure on Ministers once the purely commercial aspects of the tender have been settled. An example of the interface between the commercial role of civil servants and the political considerations that may influence their work can be seen in the case of a fictional contract for the replacement of helicopters for the Navy.

The Navy helicopter contract – a case study

The Royal Navy has decided that one of its current types of helicopter is reaching the end of its service life and that a more modern replacement is needed. A series of papers detailing requirements and costs options are prepared for discussion by the Directors of Operational Requirements, Fleet Support Coordination and the Naval Air Staff, in conjunction with the Air Secretariat and the Director of Future Aircraft Systems before a coordinated proposal is prepared for the Minister for Defence Procurement and the Chiefs of Staff. At this stage, only two considerations are important: are the new helicopters needed; and can the defence budget afford them? Although the defence estimates of expenditure are presented to Parliament each year in the form of a White Paper for debate, requirements need to be assessed many years in advance in view of the long R&D, construction and testing period involved in producing new warships, aircraft or armaments. In this case, it may be four years from tendering to supply.

The helicopter contract is relatively small – £150 million – in Ministry of Defence terms and non-controversial compared to nuclear submarines or missiles, so there is unlikely to be any interdepartmental discussion, other than with the Treasury, at this stage. If they Navy's request is agreed, it will be written into future defence estimates after very detailed drafting of construction and performance parameters by the Air Contracts Directorate and others, and an assessment of the total cost ceiling within which tenderers would have to operate. At this stage, the Aerospace Division of the Department of Trade and Industry would be contacted for its views about the state of the British helicopter industry. It may advise that the industry is not healthy and that departmental policy is to give every possible assistance to British manufacturers since it is considered important for Britain to retain a strong presence in this field. It might also provide an outline assessment of the likely competitors for the contract and the extent to which each company would be likely to receive subsidies from their governments.

While the basic rule of Government procurement is value for money, other considerations would also apply:

- Even if it is decided not to subsidize British manufacturers or restrict the competition to British suppliers only, principles of public procurement such as the Public Purchasing Initiative (which, among other things, allows for Government to insist that main contractors should use particular British sub-contractors in order to develop the size and experience necessary for British companies to become independently competitive) may be embodied in the tendering rules, or the tenderers may take the initiative and aim to achieve as high a UK content as possible.
- The Ministry of Defence will be aware that, since it is seeking a new design of helicopter, this contract may give the lead to other countries to procure the machine it chooses. The nationality of the winner is therefore important.
- All the potential tenderers are aware that policy requirements may override specification and have therefore entered into joint ventures with British companies who will assemble their helicopters in the UK as a means of persuading the Ministry of Defence that employment will be generated at home.

There are four responses to the call for tenders – from the USA, France, Brazil and the UK. All match the performance criteria set by the Ministry; two contenders comfortably exceed them. Two of the helicopters have been sold successfully in different specifications to other armed forces around the world; the British model has achieved a few sales but the company has essentially been established to pitch for, and grow on the basis of, this contract. The US competitor is still on the drawing board and is regarded as an outsider.

Decision-makers – how do they work?

Initially, the three foreign contenders, through their UK partners, and the UK manufacturer, deal with the Ministry's technical experts only. The three helicopters that are in production are rigorously tested by the Royal Aircraft Establishment, which makes up its mind on the model it prefers on a pure speed/handling/weapons capability basis. It is then that an essentially administrative and practical decision might begin to be tempered by political considerations, assuming that few restrictions were imposed in the call for tenders. All four companies begin to lobby the Minister for Defence Procurement, the Secretary of State for Defence, and the Minister of State in the Department of Trade and Industry who is responsible for the aerospace industry. A second set of considerations begin to emerge alongside cost and specification:

- British banks have lent considerable sums to Brazil, a major debtor nation. Strengthening the export prospects of its aerospace industry would improve Brazil's ability to repay those debts.
- The three British partners of foreign manufacturers all claim potential trade-offs of their own aircraft for US, Brazilian and French defence orders if they win the British contract.
- One of the British partners is based in a high unemployment area that is a marginal Government seat and which has also been designated for preferment wherever possible (the two decisions being made independently).
- All four companies make different claims for the extent of UK jobs and investment that would be generated if they were awarded the contract.
- The sole British manufacturer organizes a publicity campaign to impress the Ministry of the sense of supporting a domestic product.
- Two of the British partners are partly owned by the Government.

With constituency MPs and defence-related Peers also being mobilized by each of the contenders to debate the issue, question and write to the Minister for Defence Procurement, it is decided that the Navy's Brazilian favourite should not be selected yet. It must enter a final review with the French helicopter: both British partners will be asked to resubmit prices to see whether economies could be made.

In the end, the contract is decided by two issues that overturn the Navy's practical judgement and bring the Prime Minister and Secretary of State for Trade and Industry into the argument on the side of the French contestant. Firstly, French Government subsidies enable the price to undercut that of the Brazilians; and it is decided to change the engine to a more powerful version manufactured by a Department of Trade and Industry-funded British company which adds its own lobbying resources in the form of direct representations to the two Ministers, both of whom are firm supporters of the company. The French win.

Budget formulation

The preparation that is put into the Budget is similar to that for any White Paper or Bill but with two differences: the Budget is an annual event and its procedures are firmly institutionalized; and it is prepared in conditions of greater secrecy, with no established consultation period or process.

The Budget is in effect one continuing process, not an annual set piece. It exists to maintain the course of a Government's medium-term financial strategy and its formulation starts almost as soon as the previous Budget is announced with discussions within the Treasury about the shape of the following year's public spending and the outlook for the economy. A broad decision is taken about the amount of money Government needs to raise and the Chancellor's freedom of manœuvre in providing fiscal concessions, although there are usually frequent revisions geared to the price of Sterling or North Sea oil, major industrial disputes and other unexpected circumstances. This decision is taken on the advice of Treasury economists and statisticians, who have access to a computerized model of the economy with some 700 options in its program. They are able to ask the model 'What if?' and receive a projection about the effect of changing tax rates, duties and allowances.

Within the limits of the first decision – how much does Government need and what can be given back to taxpayers – a series of detailed option papers are then prepared by the Treasury, Inland Revenue and Customs and Excise to list alternative combinations of measures that would achieve the objective which may also be politically influenced in that the Government may be committed to particular forms of taxation or concessions. At this stage, around September, lobbying by outsiders begins in earnest on two levels, with organizations seeking changes in the Government's broad financial strategy or, more specifically, to obtain relief from taxation or an increase in allowances or welfare benefits. The Institute of Directors would fall into the former category; the Child Poverty Action Group or Scotch Whisky Association into the latter. The very largest permanent lobbies, such as the CBI, meet Treasury officials and Ministers throughout the year to put their case for change or maintenance of the status quo.

In any Budget year the Treasury will receive thousands of representations. The volume varies in direct proportion to the activities of organized lobbies: in 1986, 2000 letters and briefs were received; in the more contentious year of 1985, the Treasury dealt with 12,000 representations. Many may be stimulated by the traditional hints given by Ministers who want to assess likely reactions to their policy options. Others may be generated by the Chancellor's now traditional Autumn Statement, which sets out likely public expenditure and revenue figures for the coming year and may indicate some of the choices open to him. All the representations received are summarized and put to Ministers. In general, they and their officials are more likely to take account of those covering specific rather than macro areas.

As the content of the Budget crystallizes, two lists are produced under the headings of 'minor starts' or inexpensive measures, and 'major things for the Budget' – items affecting the whole economy. There are always too many proposals on the two lists and a sifting process takes place to assess the effect of each measure on the economy and consider the political implications. More than in most policy formulation processes, the Budget is a genuine partnership between officials and Ministers since the planning involved is intensive and expert and the implications to a Chancellor of a Budget poorly received by his own Party can be serious.

From the turn of the year, policies become firmer, although items are dropped and possibly reinstated even at the last minute. Eight weeks before any Budget, the Chancellor, other Treasury Ministers and some senior officials gather at Dorneywood in Buckinghamshire for a weekend planning session and then enter what is known as the Purdah period, in which they have no meetings with outsiders and concentrate on finalizing items and preparing the Budget speech. In that period a series of meetings take place as the culmination of hundreds of hours of liaison between officials and Ministers. They may include the Chancellor and Chief Secretary to the Treasury, the Financial Secretary, the Paymaster General, the three Permanent Secretaries, the Chief Economic Adviser, the chairmen of the Board of Inland Revenue and of Customs and Excise and economic or statistical officials. While Ministers may have had to consider representations on behalf of concerned parties from their sponsoring Department throughout the stages of Budget formulation, all Departments produce a list of their recommendations for the Treasury a few weeks before Budget Day. Although other Ministers are not told of the content of the Budget until a few hours beforehand, these recommendations summarize Departments' views on the effects that likely measures would have on the sectors for which they are responsible.

The burden on the Treasury, Inland Revenue and Customs and Excise increases as Budget Day approaches since they have to prepare explanatory memoranda for public consumption on every measure. Other Departments such as DSS or DTI are involved if, for example, maternity benefits or industrial grants are affected. As soon as the Chancellor's speech, which may last from 90 minutes to three hours, is delivered the memoranda are released with a 'Red Book' of forecasts for the economy.

The Budget is, in effect, an oral White Paper on which five days of debate are allowed, except that a White Paper often leaves room for views to be taken on uncertain policy areas whereas the Budget is an unchangeable statement of fiscal policy for the current year and also, less definitely, for the future since the speech may announce forthcoming Green Papers or taxation reviews. The draftsmen turn the Treasury's proposals into the Finance Bill which, being a Money Bill, does not go to the Lords. It is usual for the Treasury to produce redrafts of clauses to tighten up working during the passage of the Bill, as happens on all other legislation. Some of the provisions of the Budget, such as changes in Excise duties, do not have to be endorsed by the House and can come into force within a few hours of the end of the Chancellor's speech.

We have illustrated three examples of legislative and non-legislative decision-making to illustrate the work of officials and Ministers. Before turning to the mentality of civil servants and their considerations in dealing with outsiders we should examine the way higher-grade officials fit their responsibilities into their daily schedule.

Box 29 A day in the lives of a Deputy Secretary and a Principal

---

We interviewed two Department of Trade and Industry officials – one close to the top of the Department, the other on a lower rung of the senior officials' stratum.

X, a Deputy Secretary
With 900 staff in his command, he sees his role in several ways: as a link between Ministers and the Under or Assistant Secretaries in Divisions; as a focus for the identifying and (hopefully) resolving of conflicting divisional priorities; and as a point of contact for senior business and industry figures (such as directors of major public companies relevant to his areas of responsibility). His working day divides roughly into thirds – policy advice, including coordination of the interests of his Divisions; management of staff and resource allocation; and representation of the Department in meetings and at functions.

8.45 am	Read daily digest of press cuttings on all matters affecting the Department. See if he should speak to a colleague, or to a Minister's Private Office, about any item.
9.00 am	Read correspondence – mainly official papers such as copies of submissions to Ministers notes of meetings.
10.00 am	Monthly meeting of the Department's Resource Management Group (consisting of the Permanent Secretary, all Deputy Secretaries and the Head of Finance Division) to consider papers on internal management, such as allocation of staff resources within the Department. The Permanent Secretary will then put the recommendations agreed by the meeting to Ministers for their consideration.

Cont.

Box 29 (*Cont.*)

11.30–12.45 pm	Meeting with two or three Under Secretaries and some Assistant Secretaries and Principals about, for example, the Departmental approach towards a merger proposal which is to be discussed interdepartmentally shortly. Alternatively, telephone conversations with industrial executives or officials in other Departments. These conversations either inform them of departmental intentions on policy issues or seek information from them.
12.45 pm	Lunch with a trade association or with a senior executive from a major company sponsored by one of his Divisions.
2.34 pm	Briefing meeting with the Secretary of State prior to a meeting with the Chairman of a nationalized industry.
3.00 pm	He attends the Secretary of State's meeting, which lasts until
3.45 pm	The Secretary of State brings him up to date informally with development on one or two current issues.
4.00 pm	Read various minutes; make telephone calls; handle correspondence.
5.00 pm	Meeting with Minister of State about the visit next day of an industrial delegation.
5.30 pm	Telephone conversations with colleagues in Divisions.
6.00 pm	Introductory discussion with an Assistant Secretary who has just moved to one of his Divisions.
7.00 pm	Home or (on two nights a week) attends a function hosted by a company, a trade association or an embassy.

Y, a Principal
He has three specific responsibilities within his Branch: general policy on his subject area, including speeches, coordinating briefings, parliamentary questions, Ministerial enquiries, review and development of policies related to his subject; international policy, particularly involving the EEC and OECD; and performing a sponsorship function in relation to a specific industrial sector. He sees his role as providing policy advice to senior officials and Ministers, administering departmental support schemes, often involving a high degree of financial responsibility, and ensuring that the interests of the industrial sector he sponsors are reflected in decisions taken by Government. In particular he regards himself as the first point of contact between Whitehall and the companies for which he is responsible.

9.00 am	Works on correspondence and papers. Prepares draft replies to parliamentary questions and letters to his Minister.
10.30 am	Weekly meeting with his Under Secretary to review progress and to alert him to developments or problems arising in his sector.
11.15 am	Meeting with company to discuss an application for departmental support
12.15 pm	Prepares brief for an international meeting.
1.00 pm	Lunch with executives from his sponsored industry.
2.15 pm	Meeting with the Minister and a group of local Councillors concerning a local problem involving his industry.

Cont.

Box 29 (*Cont.*)

3.00 pm	Meeting with other DTI officials on international policy coordination in preparation for an overseas meeting.
4.15 pm	Brief his Assistant Secretary on a visit the latter is paying to a major organization. Discuss with him the first draft of a policy paper that will eventually be submitted to Ministers.
4.45 pm	Telephone conversations with a number of companies including a discussion with a company encountering a significant difficulty which the DTI can help resolve.
5.00 pm	Draft notes of these discussions including a minute seeking Departmental agreement to a policy line intended to resolve the company's difficulties.
5.45 pm	Draft letters for the Minister's signature to follow up the meeting with local councillors.
6.45 pm	Leave.

Their advice on dealing with officials
- Clear the ground at Principal or Assistant Secretary level before seeking a meeting with a Deputy Secretary or higher. Those grades always handle the follow-up work, and senior officials rely on them for advice on the quality of the outsiders' representations.
- If you cannot persuade Principals and Assistant Secretaries of the merits of your case, your chances of securing acceptance over their heads may not be good.
- Some organizations presume that a letter to a Minister, either directly or through an MP is enough to win a battle. It is not.
- People underestimate the extent to which their representations may be probed by officials. More than anything else, therefore, develop a good, well-corroborated case.
- Organizations underestimate the readiness of Whitehall to listen. Do not feel that Government is impenetrable and that liaison is a waste of time. Whitehall does listen, but in a questioning way!
- Bring Whitehall in as early as you can.

Our observations
- Liaison between senior officials and outsiders often takes place on a level for level basis: a Deputy Secretary would expect to deal with directors of major organizations unless there is a strong reason for him to meet more junior executives.
- While Deputy Secretaries have a major role in supervising the policy work of the Divisions and Branches under their command, their role may also be seen as that of a resolver of interdivisional issues where no one Under Secretary can tackle the problem. Issues are therefore passed down to the lowest point in the chain of command at which Departments feel they can be satisfactorily handled. Representations to a Deputy Secretary are often passed down unless the advocate is of sufficient status to justify personal attention. If you cannot persuade Principals and Assistant Secretaries on your case, your chances of securing acceptance over their heads may be sharply reduced.

2.3 Can Ministers exercise power?

Ministers, in theory, have absolute power over policy formulation and the other work of their Department. However, the balance between Ministers and officials invariably tilts towards the servants rather than their masters. There are four reasons for this:

Knowledge is power: Ministers rely on their officials to provide them with the information they need to make decisions. The way that information is presented may predicate the Minister's judgement even though it is not biased. However, as we have noted, the ability of outsiders to embarrass poorly briefed or serviced Ministers is a control, although it is quite common for them to rely on the advice of officials, who are expected to be experienced in their work, even where an analysis and summary of conflicting representations is involved.

Ministers are overburdened. Their diaries can easily be filled with appointments by their officials unless they are careful. This reduces the time available for personal deliberation on, and drafting of, policy. Richard Crossman mentioned a Department's ability seemingly to produce limitless Red Boxes full of documents for Ministers to approve, with the result that great stamina is required if official advice and decisions are not to be ratified 'on the nod'. Canning was able personally to see or draft every communication that emanated from the Foreign Office in the 1820s; nowadays the volume of a Department's work necessarily involves Ministers in trusting the judgement of their advisers to a great degree. Gerald Kaufman (*How to be a Minister*, 1980) takes the view that Ministers *can* take most decisions, overturn official advice and marshall support from other Ministers to thwart the Civil Service machine in Cabinet Committees; but Kaufman was an exceptionally energetic Minister, and one look at the diary of a Secretary of State (and those of his junior Ministers are equally full) shows that Ministers have little time in which to do their job. The constraints of time and expertise make Kaufman's dictum of ministerial dominance essentially an example of the exception proving the rule.

The interdepartmental net. If Ministers reject the advice of their officials, the latter will often enlist the support of other Departments connected with the issue. If a disputed policy involved additional public expenditure, the Treasury would be contacted in order that officials there might be persuaded to advise the Chief Secretary against it. The committees of officials shadowing Cabinet Committees are the best examples of this. Most of the time, however, Ministers and officials work in productive harmony – largely, perhaps, because of the first two reasons above.

Access to departmental papers is restricted. Ministers are by convention unable to see the papers of previous administrations and are therefore at a disadvantage compared to their officials, who may have considered ministerial initiatives before under different Ministers and will have been able to carry out detailed work on logistics that is not available to the present incumbent, who will also not know about the strength of outsiders' arguments or of ministerial reaction to earlier consultations on similar policies. Since Ministers are unable, as a result of this convention, to build on the progress made by other Governments on particular issues, Civil Service opposition to policy proposals has more chance of success. Similarly, the promotion of departmental policies by officials can proceed from Administration to Administration without Ministers being aware of their predecessors' reaction to them. Legislation to abolish Retail Price Maintenance in 1963–4 was the result of officials persistently placing their proposals before successive Ministers until one, Edward Heath, decided to adopt them.

2.4 Whitehall: its mentality and its dealings with outsiders

Since Government plays an increasingly active part in influencing the way we live, work and trade, contact between officials and outside interests has expanded. There are few civil servants at Principal grade and above who do not spend some time of every day giving advice to, engaging in consultations or commercial negotiations with, or simply meeting representatives of their sponsoring area of responsibility. Such contact is usually at HEO, Principal or Assistant Secretary level, with more senior grades being involved only if the stature of the issue or outsider merits it. As with most other walks of life, there is a dichotomy between the top three grades, who receive most of the lunch and speaking invitations, and the next two or three that handle the bulk of the work.

In any dealings with outsiders, a number of written and unwritten rules apply:

- Officials must satisfy themselves of the bona fides of those who deal with them. A relationship of trust is essential since information given to outsiders could be used to substantial commercial advantage or to hinder the development of departmental policies.
- While officials receive very small expense allowances (if at all) they do not generally appreciate lunch invitations unless they have already established a working relationship with the host. Their time is short and brief meetings with succinct supporting documentation are more welcome.

Decision-makers – how do they work?

- Officials prefer to deal on legislative issues with representative bodies rather than individuals. Single companies or groups of people will only carry influence if they can be seen to represent a general consensus or if an individual problem illustrates a clear omission from a Bill's drafting.
- Officials are often moved every three to four years from one job to another. This is particularly the case with high fliers. In some instances this may mean that real expertise in their relevant policy area is not acquired, with the result that they come to rely heavily on their departmental files. This militates against creative thinking and in favour of a line of least resistance on many problems. Outsiders must recognize the frequent need for persistence if even the strongest case for change is to be accepted.
- If officials want to prevent an outside group from having access to their Minister, they can usually do so through liaison with the Private Office. Even if they are called on for advice on whether a request for a meeting between the Minister and outsiders should be accepted and they agree, in 95 per cent of cases they would attend the meeting, brief the Minister in writing (and, usually, orally immediately before the meeting starts), and will stay after outsiders have left to give their opinion to the Minister on the points made.
- While outwardly upholding the legislative position of Parliament and the role of Ministers, many officials become understandably biased against those who base their advocacy to Government on MP-geared pressure on Ministers without consulting those to whom those Ministers would normally turn for advice. The answering of Parliamentary Questions and responses to legislative amendments could in many cases be obviated if outsiders consulted with officials in good time. Consultation periods are rarely well publicized but civil servants do not treat ignorance of their existence as any excuse. Officials are now very familiar with lobbying and the politics of pressure. They both fear the potential power of well-mobilized parliamentary support for a case, particularly if it exposes weaknesses in their own advice to Ministers, and are somewhat cynical of the attempts by PR firms to lavish entertainment on MPs even though the real power is held in their hands. Nonetheless, outsiders are expected to initiate contact with Whitehall; it would be comparatively rare for the reverse to happen.
- It has often been commented that Departments predominantly represent single interests: MAFF represents the farmers; the DTI represents the CBI; the Department of Employment the TUC; and so on. While that is a sweeping generalization, it is frequently the case that non-Establishment pressure groups such as Friends of the Earth find it difficult to obtain equal billing with interests sponsored by officials. Pressure groups are

called just that because officials prefer to maintain the status quo rather than involve their Department – and, possibly, a number of others – in the time, expense and disruption of revising policy of initiating legislation unless they feel it to be absolutely necessary. Pressure must be applied to them by such groups through other means – the media, Parliament, the Parties – in order to secure change.
- The top five grades of officials are in the main staffed by very intelligent people. However, only a very small minority has had experience in the areas they sponsor. Their work is therefore approached in the same way as a barrister's in that complex issues must be mastered on the basis of the brief they receive. As a result, officials are often only as good as the information they get and outsiders should not be surprised if there are occasional gaps in understanding of industries or individual problems. An example of this was contained in the 1985 DTI Green Paper proposing a 10 per cent levy on audio recording tape. Without understanding the mechanics of retail pricing and mark-up mechanisms, the officials who drafted the consultation document failed to appreciate the difference between making manufacturers or consumers pay the levy. (The former would be marked up by retailers to produce a far greater price rise than 10 per cent; the latter, once retailers' margins were deducted, would lead to only 5.8 per cent being paid over by manufacturers). Officials expect technical guidance from outsiders in order to prevent such errors.
- Officials are trained not to show bias. When asked to implement a Government's policies or approached with representations by outsiders, they do not ask themselves whether they agree with those ideas but whether they can be made to work. If officials do not feel they can, for whatever reason, they may try very hard to stop them.
- Many officials become closely attached to the issues they sponsor. This may mean that, in addition to conflicts between Departments on legislative or commercial policy issues, Divisions may clash as they support their sponsored interests – see the Channel Tunnel example on page 25.
- In dealing with outsiders, officials always stress that they cannot make decisions themselves: they can only advise the Minister. While this is technically correct, the great proportion of administrative judgements made and communicated to the public are by officials who have been well trained in the largely fictional convention of Ministerial Responsibility.
- There is an increasing tendency for Government to establish supervisory or regulatory bodies linked to, but physically separate from, Whitehall Departments. These bodies, such as OFTEL, which supervises BT's relations with its market and competitors, and the Securities and Investments Board, which supervises the regulation of the financial services industry, perform the functions of sub-Departments and officials

encourage contact to be made with these bodies rather than the Department itself on relevant issues. In many ways they may be seen as buffers to absorb lobbying and other specific representations and lighten the consultative burden on Whitehall. In fact, they are only as strong as the powers and staff delegated to them and may be dependent on the parent Department for support, but they have partially succeeded in making access to key officials more difficult.
- Since it is a Whitehall convention that current Ministers are not told how their predecessors in other administrations have acted on particular issues and that access to the files or papers of previous Governments are also barred to Ministers, outsiders may perform a valuable service by informing them of a history of consultations on a specific policy.
- As Nigel Forman (*Mastering British Politics*, 1985) has pointed out, it is a convention that officials often take instruction only from their superiors in their own Departments or from Ministers. This puts a great burden on Ministers and the Private Offices that have to process their work, and makes it less certain that officials can respond quickly and effectively to events if they do not receive strong leadership.

An example of dealings between a Department and an outside body can be seen in the hypothetical case study involving Intercontinental Parcels, a large courier service, and its desire to run its own flights on secondary and tertiary routes within the EEC instead of paying the airlines to carry its consignments. It seeks the assistance of the British Government in lobbying for deregulation.

Intercontinental Parcels – a case study

The Managing Director of IP has always believed that liaison with Government automatically means working through Parliament. He meets the backbench Transport Committee on the Government side and puts his case to it. It agrees to take the matter up with the Parliamentary Under Secretary responsible for aviation and suggests that IP approaches its constituency MP to write to the Secretary of State. This it does and finds that the local MP is happy to help. He may even ask IP to draft the letter for him.

The backbench Committee's ministerial meeting is three weeks away (each Committee on the Government side has private meetings with its Ministers every two weeks or so on a rotating basis). In the interim, the Minister receives the constituency MP's letter. It is automatically sent to the appropriate Division for a reply to be drafted, invariably by a more senior grade official than would answer letters from the general public.

The length of time it takes a Department to reply to letters from MPs varies from 10 to 30 days. The response to IP's constituency MP's letter to the

Secretary of State embodies departmental policy which is unlikely to take into account IP's views since they have no record of consultation with the Department. Instead, it is based on (a) ministerial declarations supporting deregulation on the one hand; and (b) the views of the airlines, who are in constant contact with officials and who oppose IP's proposal.

The letter is topped and tailed by the Minister, who will usually address his own MPs by their first name and will pay more attention to the letter to be sent if it is to an MP or Peer. IP is not satisfied with the Department's reply, which strikes a balance between (a) and (b) above without offering a solution, and asks the MP whether he would agree to table an Oral Parliamentary Question in order to obtain some ministerial statement in Hansard, the official record of parliamentary proceedings. Transport questions are next due to be answered in just over two weeks and it is advisable to give ten sitting days, (i.e. 14 days) notice if a Question is to have any chance of being placed near the top of the list. Only one Oral in five actually receives an oral answer.

When parliamentary questions are tabled, the House of Commons Order Paper lists them the next day and the Department's Parliamentary Branch ensures that they are distributed to the relevant Assistant Secretaries for answer by their Branches. Officials first check to see why that MP has asked the question. They may examine their books of parliamentary biographies to find special interests or may notice from the Register of Members' Interests that the MP has a commercial relationship with IP. In this case, they remember the letter they recently had to answer and assume that IP has prompted the question. As is common, the formal answer is drafted to be as bland as possible. While it is not always so, the Supplementary Question that will follow from the MP, and of which no notice is given to the Minister, can nonetheless be anticipated with a fair degree of certainty. Officials draft a supplementary answer, with alternative versions in case particular points are stressed by the MP. The Minister's PPS may ask the MP (if they are both of the same Party) in advance of details of his motivation, so that questions which may seem to outsiders to be calculated to floor a Minister in fact do anything but. There is no obligation, however, on the MP to disclose his supplementary to the PPS or even the Minister in advance.

Question Time passes without a hitch for the Minister and his officials, who were sitting in the box reserved for them to the left of the Government benches to provide help if necessasry. Although officials are by this time anticipating IP's next move and may have asked the airlines about them in the course of their normal conversations, it would be considered most unusual for civil servants to initiate contact with them.

International Parcels has prepared a short but precise brief for the Backbench Committee, which persuades the Aviation Minister at its meeting that there are arguments in favour of examining IP's case. He indicates that if IP wants a meeting with him it is welcome to ask for one. IP is delighted and writes formally to confirm its request. Officials prepare the usual brief, having by now received more formal representations from the airlines, who were alerted by the Parliamentary Question. Their advice is that opposition by HMG to the EEC proposal for only limited flying rights would delay and possibly jeopardize other concessions valuable to the interests the Department sponsors and that IP should be deterred by advising it to talk directly to the European Commission and its MEP.

The conclusion of this example depends entirely on the Minister's ultimate judgement. If he decides to overturn his officials' advice he is likely to face pressure from a larger lobby: pressure that may be assisted by the same civil servants since they want their counsel to be vindicated.

Intercontinental Parcels, in failing to take account of the advisory relationship between officials and Ministers and the common (though not universal) caution shown by the Civil Service to unknown outsiders who want to change departmental policy, has approached the procedure of influencing Government decision-making from the wrong direction. The ministerial meeting should, in most cases, have been regarded as the culmination of negotiations at departmental and EEC level that might have conditioned the advice given to British and other Member State Ministers. In this case, parliamentary pressure was always likely to fail unless, as we have already pointed out, the Government's majority is small or IP expends considerable time and money on mobilizing a lobby of MPs or Peers of a sufficient size to embarrass the Minister into giving way, since no Government wishes to face unpleasant publicity or court unpopularity among a large number of its parliamentary supporters unnecessarily.

2.5 Policy scrutiny and endorsement – the work of MPs and Peers: their mentality; pressures on them; their links with outsiders

MPs: common characteristics

There is no such thing as a typical MP. In the present Parliament, they range in age from early twenties to mid-seventies; from crofters to Etonian landowners; from Marxists to Fascists; from overtly ambitious high-fliers to those who simply wish to serve their constituents.

However, the system within which MPs work can lead the observer to ascribe a number of common characteristics to them:

They all work very hard, even though they may not admit it. Once elected, an MP rarely has much time to call his own since, in addition to his work at Westminster, which may last until the early hours, he will be expected to visit his constituency regularly and give advisory 'surgeries', usually on a Saturday, as well as open fetes and speak to Women's Institutes. The average backbench MP works a 62-hour week.

The official sittings of the Commons commence at 2.30 every afternoon except Friday, when the House sits from 9.30 am to 2.30 pm to allow MPs to return to their constituencies. The Lords usually sits on Tuesdays and

98   Decision-makers – how do they work?

Wednesdays at 2.30 p.m. and on Thursdays at 3.00 p.m. As the Session proceeds and more Bills move from the Commons for further consideration, Monday sittings at 2.30 pm and then Friday sittings at 11.00 am are introduced. In fact, there are a large number of Standing or Select Committee meetings each morning, normally starting at 10.30 and lasting until 1.00 pm. They may also sit in the afternoon from around 4.15 and may not rise, in the case of Standing Committees, until late at night. Mornings are also the favoured time for outside visits, attendance at seminars and work in other paid capacities, the last of these because MPs are poorly paid relative to the hours they work and their commitments (they usually have to maintain two homes, one in London and another in or near their constituency), and many either seek consultancy or executive work or are able to maintain their former careers, for example at the Bar.

Members of Parliament are never short of invitations. Since a high proportion of lunches or dinners are organized by commercial concerns, Conservatives fare better than their counterparts, even when in opposition. On most days MPs attend working lunches with the aim either of informing them about an industry or issue, or of eliciting their support in a lobbying campaign. Dinners tend to be more formal matters, since they may be major affairs organized by trade associations or representative bodies at which MPs might be required to address an audience.

Between lunch and dinner, if an MP is not sitting on a committee, showing constituents around the Palace of Westminster or dealing with his post (MPs receive between 40 and 150 letters a day), he may attend one of the All-Party Group meetings, of which at least half a dozen take place each day except Friday. While some start before lunch, particularly if an outside visit is involved, the bulk occur between 4.30 and 7.30 pm. In the case of country groups, this time is ideal for embassy receptions. Alternatively, MPs may miss parliamentary routine completely by travelling abroad on Select Committee business or as the guest of a foreign government either as part of an official parliamentary delegation or on his own.

A typical day in the life of a back-bench MP is detailed in Box 30.

Returning to the House itself, the daily timetable is usually as follows:

2.30   Prayers
2.35   *Preliminary business* (which can include)
- Motions for new writs (for by-elections to fill vacant seats)
- Unopposed Private Bills
- Presentation of Select Committee evidence and reports
- Presentation of public petitions
- Discussion on Statutory Instruments and EEC legislation

3.30 • Questions to Ministers

- 'Private Notice' questions (on urgent matters such as a terrorist attack – very rare)
- Requests to adjourn the House under SO 10 (where an urgent matter of national interest should be debated instead of the day's business – the Speaker almost always refuses such requests).

4.00 *Public Business*
- Presentation of Public Bills
- Motions for leave to bring in Bills
- Debates on legislation, or Government or Opposition motions (29 days a Session are given over to Supply debates, when the subjects for discussion are decided by the Opposition and backbenchers; six days are allocated to debate on the Queen's Speech; five days to debate the Budget; three days to debate the reports of the Public Accounts Committee; and three days to the Consolidated Fund Bill, enabling any MP to speak on matters relating to public expenditure. There are also traditional debates on the armed forces; on White Papers; and before each Recess.

10.00 *Motion for the Adjournment*
- Certain business is exempted. This includes most financial business, on which debate continues without any interruption at 10.00, and opposition to Statutory Instruments, which may be heard up to 11.30. Otherwise, the House votes to decide whether to continue with a debate. When all other business has finished, the day's Adjournment Debate takes place for half an hour.

While the House of Commons customarily only sits during the week, a Saturday sitting to debate very urgent matters, for example the Falklands War, can take place with the concurrence of the Speaker and the Prime Minister.

There is a regularity from week to week as well. The Prime Minister takes the last 15 minutes of Question Time every Tuesday and Thursday. On the latter day the Leader of the House announces the business for the following week. Cabinet meets every Thursday morning; the Shadow Cabinet every Wednesday evening. The 1922 Committee and PLP meets every Thursday; the Whips meet each day.

In short, there are many pressures on an MPs time. As a result, while they generally cope with their work with extraordinary patience, many representations to them are ignored if they are either impersonal, verbose, or irrelevant to their interests. Alf Dubs, a Labour MP until 1987, estimated that he received 20,000 letters a year and sent 10,000. Perhaps half the mail sent to an MP is consigned to the bin by his secretary: in-house magazines, brochures, and mass-produced lobbying letters. One-quarter may come from

100 Decision-makers – how do they work?

Box 30 A day in the life of a backbench MP

The MP concerned is a member of the Government Party and has a particular interest in foreign affairs.

8.00 am	Dictation
9.00–9.30 am	Meeting of the Foreign Affairs Group, including him, a Foreign Office PPS, the appropriate Whip and two Foreign Office officials.
9.30 am	Read some of the morning's post.
10.30–1.00 pm	Select Committee of which he is a member.
1.00–2.45 pm	Lunch with major multinational, together with another MP.
2.45–3.10 pm	Take constituent to Ministry of Defence to discuss a procurement contract.
3.15–3.30 pm	Attend Prime Minister's Question Time in the Chamber.
3.45 pm	Meet secretary to collect telephone messages and check the letters she has written on his behalf.
4.00 pm	Give tea to a constituent, one of his local councillors.
5.00 pm	Meeting on the Terrace of the House with representatives of a foreign embassy.
5.45 pm	Sign correspondence and deal with further messages.
6.00–6.45 pm	1922 Committee.
7.00–7.20 pm	Attendance at debate relevant to his Select Committee, Party or personal interests. He may also have received many letters and briefs on the issue and might therefore put his name down to speak. If so, he should normally be present for the opening speeches and for most of the debate. If he is a Privy Councillor (the honour bestowed on most senior current and former Ministers and Party leaders) he will be given preference in the speaking list.
7.25–7.45 pm	Briefly attend reception in the House by a television company.
7.45–10.00 pm	Return to the debate, breaking briefly for dinner (no invitation tonight). See a Minister in the Members' Lobby and talk to him about a constituency or a lobbying matter.
10.00 pm	Vote.
10.45 pm	Home.

constituents and is usually given priority treatment. The rest may be parliamentary and Party circulars, invitations, requests to table Parliamentary Questions and more precisely targeted lobbying material.

It is a mistake to assume that MPs are idle during the long Summer Recess (which lasts from the end of July until the end of October) and the short (approximately seven to ten days) Christmas and Easter recesses. The mail is forwarded from the House to their constituency or other address and, although they do not have to attend debates or committees or table parliamentary questions they have less excuse for avoiding Constituency

Association meetings or not attending events in the area. It is their opportunity to cement links with their electorate. They will also be expected by their Association to be present, even for only part of the time, at their Party's conference in September or October.

They are badly serviced. Many share a secretary. A significant proportion have no research assistance. Yet the public expect them to be able skilfully to articulate their concerns to Ministers and the House on a vast range of subjects. Their counterparts in Washington each have secretarial and research staffs of between 20 and 150 to ensure that constituency problems and lobbyists' claims are properly handled and that a Congressman does not have to rely on information provided by special interest groups, much of it – understandably – representing only one side of a more complete case. In Parliament, an MP's normal response to a constituency problem or lobbying letter is two-fold:

- It is sent with a short note to the relevant Minister or local authority department, whose staff process the enquiry. If it is a Whitehall Department matter, the Minister then corresponds with the MP who passes the Department's response to his constituent. If he has a small majority he may take a personal interest in the matter and pursue it further; or
- He sends a letter back on the lines of 'I have read your letter with interest. You may rest assured that when this matter comes before the House I will take full account of your concerns.'

Many of the letters sent by an MP may in fact be written by his secretary and simply be signed by him. Either may call on the resources of the Commons Library or their Party research department for information but, in the vast majority of cases, they must be instant judges of the various versions of the truth that are put before them by those who either have grievances or who seek legislative, policy or commercial advantage. It is scarcely surprising that those close to an issue may often regard MPs as foolish amateurs. It is not just a question of a Member being as good as his brief; in many cases the lack of resources means that MPs have no brief at all or are forced to accept such information as they are given, no matter how inaccurate it might ultimately seem to the trained eye.

They are increasingly career politicians. People no longer enter politics because they regard community service as a duty. There is a growing, and possibly regrettable, trend for budding MPs to become dedicated politicians in their mid-teens and structure their career towards a Westminster seat. The dangers of this are three-fold:

- Loyalty to Party will prevail regardless of individual conscience or constituency duty.
- MPs will become less experienced in the world outside politics and will become distanced from the concerns of those they are meant to represent. (However, Pitt became Prime Minister at 24.)
- Parliament will fill with those who see their work only in terms of what may gain advancement to a ministerial post.

They are increasingly resentful of modern lobbying for two reasons: much of it is directed at them when it should be aimed at Whitehall; and the techniques of many lobbyists, seemingly geared to eating their way out of trouble and communicating with legislators through mass-produced, word-processed letters to MPs whose interest may have no relevance to the problem of concern. A common distinction is drawn between members of the public, who cannot be expected to understand the intricacies of the decision-making process and are encouraged to regard their MP as their initial point of contact with Government, and commercial organizations for whom ignorance of the system is no excuse. The current vogue for public relations techniques aimed at parliamentarians, as a substitute for the clear advocacy of a case to MPs on parliamentary matters, has increased the pressure on MPs and may have led to force of numbers rather than of arguments prevailing on more than one occasion.

Their status now exceeds their influence but their real effectiveness – as guardians of the interests of their constituents and as extra-parliamentary negotiators with Ministers – goes largely unnoticed. MPs continue to be feted as part of the system of government whereas, as has been shown, they possess little political power as individuals. Ministers are, however, always more sympathetic to constituency rather than sectional interests and will more readily grant a private audience to an MP – even from the Opposition – where a matter affecting his own electorate is concerned. Since, as we have said, the local MP may be the only access point to Government of the bulk of the population, the MP's most important function – and one where he can still achieve significant successes against Whitehall – is the advocacy of citizen's problems. Since 1967 MPs and the public have had the assistance of the Parliamentary Commissioner for Administration (the Ombudsman) who investigates complaints of personal injustice or of maladministration by central Government, local authorities and the National Health Service on the reference of an MP. (There are in fact four Ombudsmen in all to cover these areas.)

They need publicity. The need to be known is essential for any MP concerned about re-election. His local paper can be his greatest friend or foe and he seeks to cultivate it assiduously. It is important that his electorate knows who he is and perceives that he is representing them properly even if his Party is undergoing a period of unpopularity. One of the many potential dangers implicit in television coverage of the Commons is that the MP, who while at Westminster is shielded from the need to be seen around his constituency, will feel obliged to be seen by his electorate in the Chamber rather than dealing with their problems from his office.

They fear elections. An MP only has security of tenure during the life of a Parliament. At most this is for five years. Labour MPs have to undergo reselection trials during that period but, even for other Parties' MPs, elections involve much hard campaigning work and the uncertainty that surrounds any MP with a seat that could be affected by an electoral swing to another Party. Years of service to an MP's constituents can count for nothing if the image of his Party's leader has become tarnished.

They can be effective mobilizers of support, a view most powerfully advocated by former Labour and SDP MP, George Cunningham, who argues that MPs possess considerable potential power in coalition. While such power – the ability to vote against the Government or their own Party and thereby defeat policies – has been all but eliminated in practice by the counter-balancing power of patronage, Cunningham himself was able to coordinate sufficient opposition to the Labour Government's devolution proposals in 1976 and 1979 to secure their abandonment. And Michael Grylls MP, after a lengthy campaign to secure parliamentary support for official retaliation to the application of United States' Unitary Tax laws to British subsidiaries, was able in 1985 to obtain Government backing for an amendment to the Finance Bill to that effect.

The so-called 'backbench revolt' should not be viewed in the same light as the mobilizing of opposition to a policy. In general, individual MPs vote against their Party because:

- they have a strong constituency reason for doing so; one that has been discussed with the Whips;
- it is an expression of dissatisfaction if their Party has failed to communicate with them;
- it is a signal to their Party's leadership that its policies are unpopular.

Such votes are carefully calculated, however, to make an impression without defeating Party policy. They are often the luxury of a large majority, in which greater individuality of expression is permitted without endangering the Government's position. It is doubtful, therefore, whether George Cunningham could have achieved his coup if he had needed the support of a large number of Labour Members.

Parliamentary scrutiny of policy

Apart from the work of Standing Committees described in our earlier analysis of Public Bill procedure, day-to-day scrutiny of Executive and administrative policies and actions is carried out by backbench committees on the Government side and by the Select Committees in both Commons and Lords.

Backbench committees have no formal procedure. They meet weekly and their agenda is set informally by their officers, either as a result of representations made to them or because of the accepted responsibilities of an individual committee (for example, the Trade and Industry Committee would normally wish to have briefing discussions with British Coal or British Shipbuilders, both of them nationalized industries) or because officers have a particular interest they wish to develop. They meet departmental Ministers regularly to convey views to them in the name of the Party's backbenchers and their opinion on policies can be influential if pressed sufficiently strongly. However, if a Minister is torn between adopting or pursuing a policy and abandoning or modifying it, he would normally canvass the views of his PPS and the Whips to ensure that the weight of opinion that backbench committee officers allege in support of their views really exists. The position of these committees and their power to scrutinize policy to any effect therefore depends on their ability to express a genuine consensus view to ministers and on the political weight attaching to the chairman.

Select Committees have a more defined procedural structure. Departmental and other Select Committees have the power to subpoena any witnesses they wish, including Ministers and civil servants. Once the decision has been taken by a committee and its clerk, it may therefore be impossible for individuals or bodies associated with the investigation to avoid being called to give evidence.

The normal procedure would be for the Clerk or his assistant to telephone potential witnesses and arrange a date for their hearing. They would be asked whether they would wish to submit a written brief in advance; this would usually be printed with the Committee's report. In the course of questioning by the Committee's members, further requests may be made for supplementary memoranda where the witness either does not have sufficient information at the time or where the answer would be too detailed, statistical or graphic to be accommodated in the time available.

An exception to the above rules may be made in the case of some

Ministers and officials where public evidence or the publication of memoranda or briefs would be against the interests of State security. In these circumstances, arrangements to assist with the Select Committee's enquiry are normally agreed privately with the Chairman.

It is usual for the Clerk to inform all witnesses, apart from Ministers, of the broad area of questions that will arise. In many cases, these questions are suggested to the Committee's members by its expert advisers and by the Clerk, who meets regularly with the Chairman to discuss timetables, witnesses, questions and the drafting of reports. Since the Chairman directs proceedings it is important that he is aware in advance of the questions individual members wish to ask or have had assigned to them. There is normally a private meeting of the Committee for a few minutes before each week's session to ensure this. The framework of any one session will usually be determined jointly by the Chairman and the elected leader of the other Parties' members. They agree a number of neutral questions to be put by the Chairman in addition to those that will be asked by the other members.

Select Committee proceedings are public, although sensitive evidence, as mentioned above, may be taken in a different way, for example via in camera hearings. If Departments have not detailed possible points of difficulty in responding to a request to give evidence, they may discuss problem areas privately with the Committee during the brief private negotiations that take place before the public is admitted. An advice note, 'Memorandum of Guidance for Officials Appearing before Select Committees' was produced in 1980 to list the rules for officials giving evidence under such circumstances. It errs very much on the side of caution and implies that questions about relationships with Ministers, for example, should really be answered by politicians, not civil servants. A number of Select Committee chairmen have commented that a common reluctance by officials to give evidence constructively has led to Select Committees favouring the calling of ministerial witnesses wherever possible. (See box 31: Select Committees – rules for officials giving evidence.)

Many witnesses bring others with them to share the burden of answering questions or to provide them with information. Officials will always be present behind, and possibly alongside, any Minister giving evidence. The time taken to examine witnesses varies from no more than twenty minutes to two and a half hours. Copies of the evidence given orally are sent to witnesses in advance of publication of the Committee's report, but that evidence is not allowed to be released verbatim prior to issue of the report. To do so would constitute a breach of parliamentary privilege.

It is for the clerks to draft the Committee's report following an investigation. Three or more versions may be sent to members for their comments before the final report is printed. Following publication, the onus

Box 31 Select Committees – rules for officials giving evidence

10. Officials appearing before Select Committees do so on behalf of their Ministers. It is customary, therefore, for Ministers to decide which officials (including members of the Armed Services) should appear to give evidence. Select Committees have in the past generally accepted this position. Should a Committee invite a named official to appear, the Minister concerned, if he did not wish that official to represent him, might suggest that another official could more appropriately do so, or that he himself should give evidence to the Committee. If a Committee insisted on a particular official appearing before them – whether serving in the UK or overseas – they could issue a formal order for his attendance. In such an event the official would have to appear before the Committee. In all circumstances, the official would remain subject to Ministerial instructions as to how to answer questions.

20. The general principle to be followed is that it is the duty of officials to be as helpful as possible to Committees, and that any withholding of information should be limited to reservations that are necessary in the interests of good government or to safeguard national security. Departments should, therefore, be as forthcoming as they can (within the limits set out in this note) when requested to provide information whether in writing or orally. This will also help to ensure that the reports of Committees are as soundly based on fact as possible. Oral evidence is recorded verbatim. When oral evidence is to be given, it is advisable for Departments to send at least two witnesses so that they can divide between themselves the responsibility for answering questions. Because officials appear on behalf of their Ministers, Departments might want to clear written evidence and briefing with Ministers. It may only be necessary for Ministers to be consulted should there be any doubt among officials on the policy to be explained to the Committee. However, Ministers are ultimately responsible for deciding what information is to be given and for defending their decisions as necessary, and Ministers' views should always be sought if any question arises of withholding information which Committees are known to be seeking. It should be remembered that an extended and unexplained delay in providing the evidence requested by a Committee may be interpreted by them as a refusal. If Departments are asked by Committees to undertake research work or surveys on their behalf, it may be possible to meet such requests by the utilisation of existing information, modified as appropriate. But if the new work involved is likely to be substantial, and the Committee has power to appoint its own specialist advisers (see paragraph 17) it may be appropriate to suggest to the Committee that it considers this alternative, or possibly the employment of private research agencies or universities.

21. Officials appearing before Select Committees are responsible for ensuring that the evidence they give is accurate. They are reminded to take particular care to see that they are fully and correctly briefed on the main facts of the matters on which they expect to be examined. Should it nevertheless be discovered subsequently that the evidence unwittingly contained errors, these should be made known to the Committee at the earliest possible moment.

Cont.

Box 31 (*Cont.*)

29. The Procedure Committee recognised that there may be occasions when Ministers may wish to resist requests for information on grounds of national security. Appendix C, Annex III, of the Committee's First Report (Session 1977–78, HC 588–I) reproduces the text of a letter of 9 May 1967 to the Chairmen of certain Select Committees from the then Lord President of the Council and Leader of the House (see Annex C). This letter refers (among other limitations on the provision of information) to 'information affecting national security, which would normally be withheld from the House in the national interest'. Guidance to Departments on the release of classified information to Committees is given in the manual 'Security in Government Departments'. This manual is the overriding authority; what follows must be read subject to its guidance. Officials must not disclose information which the manual says must be withheld; they should consult their Departmental Security Officers if in doubt.

30. Officials should not give evidence about or discuss the following topics:
    (i) In order to preserve the collective responsibility of Ministers, the advice given to Ministers by their Departments should not be disclosed, nor should information about interdepartmental exchanges on policy issues, about the level at which decisions were taken or the manner in which a Minister has consulted his colleagues. Information should not be given about Cabinet Committees or their decisions (see paragraphs 31–33).
    (ii) Advice given by a Law Officer (see paragraph 36).
    (iii) The private affairs of individuals or institutions on which any information held by Ministers or their officials has been supplied in confidence (including such information about individuals which is available to the Government by virtue of their being engaged in or considered for public employment).

Officials should also, where possible, avoid giving written evidence about or discussing the following matters. Where appropriate further guidance is provided in the succeeding paragraphs:
    (iv) Questions in the field of political controversy (see paragraphs 34–35).
    (v) Sensitive information of a commercial or economic nature, e.g. knowledge which could affect the financial markets, without prior consultation with the Chancellor of the Exchequer, sensitive information relating to the commercial operations of nationalised industries, or to contracts; commercial or economic information which has been given to the Government in confidence, unless the advance consent of the persons concerned has been obtained (see paragraph 53 for the provision of information by Government contractors).
    (vi) Matters which are, or may become, the subject of sensitive negotiations with Governments or othr bodies, including the European Community, without prior consultation with the Foreign and Commonwealth Secretary, (see paragraph 37) or, in relation to domestic matters, with the Ministers concerned.
    (vii) Specific cases where the Minister has or may have a quasi-judicial or appellate function, e.g. in relation to planning applications and appeals, or

Cont.

Box 31 (*Cont.*)

where the subject matter is being considered by the Courts, or the Parliamentary Commissioner (see paragraphs 38–39).
Where, exceptionally, matters such as iv–vii have to be discussed, application may be made for 'sidelining' (see paragraph 51). There is no objection to saying in general terms why information cannot be given and it is very unusual for a Committee to press an official who indicates that he is in difficulty on such grounds in answering a question. If, however, this happens, it may be best to ask for time to consider the request and to promise to report back. Paragraphs 7 and 8 should be referred to.

31. Departmental witnesses, whether in closed or open session, should preserve the collective responsibility of Ministers and also the basis of confidence between Ministers and their advisers. Except in a case involving an Accounting Officer's responsibility (see paragraphs 9 to 11 and 17 of the Accounting Officers Memorandum, reproduced in paragraph C4 of "Government Accounting") the advice given to Ministers, which is given in confidence, should not therefore be disclosed, though Departments may of course need to draw on information submitted to Ministers. It is necessary also to refuse access to documents relating to interdepartmental exchanges on policy issues. Equally the methods by which a current study is being undertaken should not normally be disclosed without the authority of Ministers, unless they have already been made public. Nor should Departments reveal the level at which decisions were taken. It should be borne in mind that decisions taken by Ministers collectively are normally announced and defended by the Minister responsible as his own decisions, and it is important that no indication should be given of the manner in which a Minister has consulted his colleagues (see also paragraph 36 on the special position of the Law Officers).

34. Official witnesses, whether administrative, professional or Services, should as far as possible confine their evidence to questions of fact relating to existing Government policies and actions. Officials should be ready to explain what the existing policies are and the objectives and justification, as the Government sees them, for those policies, and to explain how administrative factors may have affected both the choice of policy measures and the manner of their implementation. It is open to officials to make comments which are not politically contentious but they should as far as possible avoid being drawn, without prior Ministerial authority, into the discussion of alternative policy. If official witnesses are pressed by the Committee to go beyond these limits, they should suggest that the questioning be addressed, or referred, to Ministers. If there is a likelihood of a material issue of policy being raised by a Committee in its questioning of official witnesses, Departments will wish to consult Ministers beforehand. (On appearance by Ministers, also see paragraphs 7–8.)

35. A Select Committee may invite specialist (as opposed to administrative) civil servants to discuss the professional or technical issues underlying controversial policies. This may raise particular problems in the case of, for example, economists, if Committees discuss issues of economic reasoning which bear upon controversial policy questions and which are also matters of technical and professional

Cont.

Box 31 (*Cont.*)

controversy among economists. When this is so, and where Economic Advisers to the Government appear as official witnesses, they may find themselves in the difficulty that their own judgement on the professional issues has, or might easily appear to have, implications critical of the Government's policies. It is not open to them to explain the advice which they have given to the Government on such a matter, or would give if asked by the Government. They cannot therefore go beyond explaining the economic reasoning which, in the Government's view, justifies their policy. This will only be possible where the underlying theory has indeed been explicitly formulated; and the status of what was being presented would have to be made clear. If there is no quotable public evidence of a Government view and the witness is asked for his own professional judgement on the issue, or his judgement of the view that the Government would be likely to take, he should refer to the political nature of the issue and suggest that the questioning be addressed or referred to Ministers. Similar considerations apply in the case of other specialist civil servants.

41. In addition the following considerations may be relevant:
    (i) While Select Committees should not press for internal advice to Ministers to be revealed, they are less likely to accept without argument a refusal to reveal a report from a departmental committee containing outside members, and even less likely to accept a refusal in the case of a wholly external committee. In particular, they will be understandably reluctant to accept a refusal where the establishment of the committee in question has been announced, together with its membership and terms of reference, and where its report is known to exist. These implications need to be taken into account in deciding how much publicity should be given to the establishment of comittees of this kind.
    (ii) In particular cases Departments may consider that, while a report cannot be published, it would be helpful to provide it to a Committee, provided it was treated in confidence (see paragraph 48).
    (iii) In certain cases, where a Select Committee might reasonably expect to receive a certain amount of detailed information, Departments may be able to provide a written memorandum in place of the report itself. If Departments can assist Committees in this way, it is generally desirable to do so.
    (iv) Ministers are responsible for decisions about the release of Rayner scrutiny reports. This was confirmed by the Prime Minister's answer to a PQ on 22 February 1980:

    'The reports referred to are prepared by departmental officials for their Ministers. It is for the responsible Minister to decide how each should be handled'.
    (Official Report, Vol. 979, Col. 351 WA.)

    The general principle is that reports should be released unless their content or classification preclude it.
    (v) Departments should always seek the views of Ministers before refusing a request from a Select Committee for a particular report, since the Minister

Cont.

Box 31 (*Cont.*)

personally might be called on to defend the decision to the Committee, or, indeed, to the House as a whole.

42. The Procedure Committee recommended that:

'Select committees should regard any refusal by government departments to provide information relating to departmental or interdepartmental organisation – unless fully explained and justified to their satisfaction – as a matter of serious concern which should be brought to the attention of the House.'

A considerable amount of information about the internal distribution of business is already available in published form (e.g. in the Civil Service Year Book) and the normal presumption should be that more detailed information about Department's organisational structure, such as directories and organisation charts, should be provided to Committees if it is requested. Where a description of duties of a sensitive nature necessitates the revelation of classified information, the considerations in paragraphs 48–51 apply.

43. Requests for documents which go beyond a description of the existing organisation of a Department and deal with methods of operation (e.g. arrangements for formal and informal co-ordination or for delegation of authority) or with reviews of existing departmental organisation or methods may raise more difficult questions, since these will frequently be internal working papers. Ministers should be consulted about any requests for information of this kind, with the presumption that information on these matters should be provided, in an appropriate form, unless it would conflict with the guidance in paragraph 30 above. Except where particular arrangements have been made public, information about interdepartmental organisation may present more difficulty (see paragraphs 31–32).

44. There are well-established conventions which govern the withholding of policy papers of a previous Administration from an Administration of a different political complexion. Since officials appear before Select Committees as representatives of their Ministers and since Select Committees are themselves composed on a bipartisan basis, it follows that officials should not provide a Select Committee with papers of a previous Administration which they are not in a position to show to present Ministers. If such papers are sought, Ministers should be consulted about the request. The general rule is that documents of a former Administration which have not been released or published during the period of that Administration should not be released or published by a subsequent Government. Where Ministers propose to make an exception, it would be necessary to consult a representative of the previous Administration before showing the papers either to present Ministers or, with Ministers' agreement, releasing them to a Select Committee.

Source: Memorandum of Guidance for Officials Appearing before Select Committees, Cabinet Office, March 1988.

is normally on the Department concerned to produce a response which, if the Committee considers it unsatisfactory, may lead to what is known as a second-stage enquiry.

The House of Lords has three major Select Committees. The European Communities Committee is divided into seven sub-committees covering Finance and External Relations; Trade and Industry; Energy, Transport and Technology; Social and Consumer Affairs; Agriculture and Food; Law and Institutions; and Environment. They consider Community proposals and take evidence in the same way as their counterparts in the Commons. Although the European Legislation Committee in the Lower House deals with the legal and political implications of Commission draft proposals and recommends, without any comment on their merits, whether any EEC documents should be debated, the Lords Committees tend to work on subjects rather than documents and can therefore work in advance of the Commission finalizing decisions.

The European Communities Committee has 24 members, with another 60 co-opted to serve on the sub-committees. Its chairman is a salaried officer of the House. It meets every two weeks.

When Commission proposals are published they are sent by the Government to both Houses, with an explanatory memorandum. The Chairman of the Lords EEC Committee then decides whether the proposals are 'A-type' (unimportant) or 'B-type' (worthy of consideration by one of the sub-committees). All proposals are considered by two sub-committees since the Law Committee considers the legal implications of all 'B-type' documents. Around one quarter of proposals are designated 'B-type', although sub-committees may not consider such documents once submitted to them: only one-tenth of the documents published by the EEC are reported upon by the Lords, but the sub-committees often group proposals together into a report on a major subject such as Competition Policy. About half the reports recommend a debate, and the Government has undertaken that it will not agree to any proposal in the Council of Ministers while it awaits such a debate in either House. Discussion of reports is usually lengthier in the Lords than in the Commons.

The Lords Committee on Overseas Trade, which has 11 members, considers the causes and implications of the UK's balance of trade in manufactured goods and makes recommendations to the Treasury and Department of Trade and Industry on improvements. Like Select Committees in the Commons it has the power to call witnesses, including Ministers.

The Science and Technology Committee, which has two *ad hoc* sub-committees, selects the subject of its investigations from a wide field. Its membership is 16, but other Peers are co-opted onto those sub-committees

112 Decision-makers – how do they work?

Box 32 Select Committee investigations – three typical days

	Time	*Room/Place*
Monday 11 July		
Televising of Proceedings of the House	6.00	8
Witnesses: Broadcast Debates Ltd; Broadcast Communications plc (6.30 pm approx)		
Tuesday 12 July		
Employment	3.35	20
Subject: Legionnaire's disease in the working environment		
Witnesses: Broadcasting and Entertainments Trades Alliance; Cogent Limited		
Members' Interests	4.15	15
Subject: Parliamentary lobbying		
Witnesses: (1) Public Relations Consultants Association (4.25 pm)		
(2) Institute of Public Relations (5.20 pm)		
Transport	4.15	17
Subject: Air traffic control safety		
Witnesses: Joint Airmiss Working Group; Department of Transport		
Wednesday 13 July		
Environment	10.30	21
Subject: Toxic waste		
Witness: South Yorkshire Hazardous Waste Unit		
Education, Science and Arts	3.00	16
Subject: Scrutiny Session		
Witnesses: Rt Hon Kenneth Baker MP, Secretary of State for Education and Science and officials from the Department		
Transport	3.30	17
Subject: Airline competition: CRS		
Witnesses: Civil Aviation Authority; Department of Transport		
Home Affairs	4.15	20
Subject: Police Complaints Authority		
Witness: Home Office		

Source: House of Commons *Weekly Information*.

only for the duration of an enquiry. Like the other two main Lords Select Committees it has a number of specialist advisers to assist it but its reports are both produced less frequently and with less impact than those of the EEC Committee.

Although it is normal for Select Committees in both Houses to select their own agendas for investigations, there are two exceptions.

- Some committees' work is largely dictated by their remit. The EEC and Statutory Instruments committees of both Houses deal with specific items submitted to them even though the Lords EEC Committee enjoys some freedom of choice.
- Any individual can recommend subjects for investigation to the Chairman and members of a Select Committee. Agendas of departmental Select Committees are often, however, decided upon several months in advance.

The Public Accounts Committee in the Commons is assisted by the Comptroller and Auditor General, an officer of the House who has two main functions:

- To control the issue of money from the Consolidated Fund (a Bank of England account covering current receipts and expenditure), by ensuring that the Treasury's requests match the sums authorized by Parliament in the annual Appropriation Act.
- To audit the accounts of Departments and some public bodies to ensure that money has been properly spent.

The Comptroller and Auditor General heads the National Audit Office, which performs the accountancy function for Government Departments.

Although the PAC in theory only examines sums already spent by Departments, it concerns itself more generally to see that money has been spent efficiently and it produces recommendations on future expenditure practices. Its reports are sent to the Treasury (an official from which sits in on all PAC meetings) and the Departments being scrutinized. The Treasury comments on the Committee's recommendations in a formal Annual Treasury Minute and, as with other Select Committee reports, the PAC's views may be debated in the Commons (box 33). Apart from the scrutiny powers of MPs acting collectively in committees, as individuals they can use a range of devices to enforce accountability by the Executive, to raise matters of concern or simply to bait Ministers and remind them that they must not ignore the potential checking power of the Commons:

Parliamentary Questions, which may be oral or written. Oral Questions are answered for an hour each day except Friday by Ministers in the Chamber, with the questioner being allowed a supplementary question, without notice,

Box 33 Scrutiny of departmental financial dealings by the Public Accounts Committee

Commons committee attacks handling of BT privatisation

By Lucy Kellaway

THE Government's £3.9bn sale of shares in British Telecom did not raise as much money for the taxpayer as it might have done, the all-party Commons Public-Accounts Committee has concluded.

Its report on the sale, published yesterday, is broadly critical of the handling of the privatisation of British Telecom. It recommends that, with further Government share sales planned, the Government "should thoroughly review the arrangements for and results of this sale."

Its finding comes ahead of next year's planned sales to the private sector of British Gas and British Airways.

One of the report's central complaints is that the British Telecom issue was underpriced. It argues that the 130p selling price of the shares was "over-cautious, and a modest further increase in the price would have brought in a higher return without risk."

The pricing of the BT issue, which resulted in a 33 per cent appreciation over the full offer price on the first day of dealing has already been widely criticised. This week, the independent Institute for Fiscal Studies estimated that the privatisation of BT resulted in what it called a net loss to the public of £3.34bn.

The committee also attacks the size of the commission paid to underwriters of the issue and urges that in future a "careful assessment be made ... of the need for underwriting." In the case of British Telecom the committee says it was "not convinced that the extent of the risk justified the rates agreed for placing commission."

It also questions whether all the special selling methods used in the flotation were justified. The total costs of the issues were £263m, 6.8 per cent of the issue proceeds, compared with an average of 3.3 per cent in previous privatisations. "It seems questionable whether the whole package of measures was necessary to meet the Government's objectives," the report says.

The costly technique of selling shares overseas comes in for particularly heavy criticism. The report claims that shares sold in the US quickly found their way back to the UK market. "We recommend that a thorough review of the method, desirability and value of overseas sales should be carried out by the department and the Treasury," it says.

The BT privatisation also raises questions about the way the nationalised industries prepare their accounts, the committee says.

Commons Committee of Public Accounts; sale of Government shareholding in British Telecommunications. Commons paper 35, HMSO, £3.50.

Source: *Financial Times* (18 December 1985)

following the Minister's reply. Each Department answers questions on a rota basis, so that each takes it turn roughly every three weeks. Officials spend many hours anticipating possible supplementaries and drafting alternative responses for Ministers, although many Oral Questions are not answered by the end of the hour and only receive written replies without the opportunity of asking the all-important additional question to which the first will have led. To have any chance of being answered in the Chamber, Oral Questions must be tabled two weeks in advance of the day on which they will be answered, but the chances of an answer are random since the order in which they are called at Question Time is determined by ballot.

Prime Minister's Question Time, which lasts for 15 minutes every Tuesday and Thursday, is the apotheosis of the supplementary question game of battleships that is fought between questioner, Minister and officials since questions to the Prime Minister are traditionally of the 'Whether she will list her engagements for the 23 May' type, with no possible indication of the supplementary unless the questioner is a sympathetic backbench MP who has been primed with a helpful question by the Prime Minister's PPS. Otherwise, the supplementary question, which would normally begin 'In the course of her busy day, will she take the time to consider . . .', would continue with any subject that may concern the questioner – unemployment, industrial decline, lost export orders, and so on. The result of these brief twice-weekly sessions is more a test of nerve than an exposition of facts.

Written Questions are designed to elicit information on specific points and partly stem from the convention that MPs should not deal direct with civil servants. All written Parliamentary Questions are therefore addressed to the

Box 34 Typical written Parliamentary Question and Answer

Passenger Transport Authorities

Mr Brandon-Bravo asked the Secretary of State for Transport what expenditure levels he proposes to determine in respect of 1986–7 for the new passenger transport authorities.

Mr Ridley: I expect to receive shortly the financial plans of the passenger transport executives which are submitted to me under the provisions of the Transport Act 1983. My advice under section 3(5) of that Act was issued to the PTEs in May this year, and I expect the plans to include projections based on that advice. Expenditure levels determined for the new authorities will need to take into account the best available information from the PTEs, and I do not therefore propose to announce figures until the new authorities are established.

Source: *Hansard* (25 July 1985).

senior Minister in the Department concerned, with the answers being drafted by his officials and published in Hansard, the official record of parliamentary debates and answers. Some 50,000 questions are tabled each year.

Before leaving the subject of Parliamentary Questions, the observer should be aware of two points: answers tend to be cautious and often aim to give away as little as possible. The usefulness of each answer is therefore often related to the MP's skill in drafting his question and his ability to obtain advice from the Table Office, through which all questions pass and which ensures that they observe well-defined procedures, some of which are detailed on page 155. And questions may occasionally be 'planted', with Ministers or their PPSs asking their backbenchers to table an arranged question as an opportunity for the Government to make a policy statement to the House.

Privy Councillors and Opposition spokesmen are more likely to be called at Question Time than other backbenchers (once an MP's supplementary has been answered, it is possible for others to question the Minister on his response). This privilege also extends to debates (see A Day in the Life of an MP, page 100).

Adjournment Debates. Each day at the close of business there is an Adjournment Debate, allowing an MP the opportunity to raise a specific subject in the Chamber and receive a detailed response from a Minister. The debate lasts half an hour and usually comprises four speeches: the MP's statement of concern; the Minister's answer; the MP's comment; and a conclusion by the Minister. No vote is taken and there may on occasion only be the two protagonists present. However, for many MPs (there is always competition for Adjournment Debate slots and Members enter a ballot or, on Friday, are chosen by the Speaker) this device gives them the opportunity to raise a constituency issue or matter on behalf of an outside interest and receive an official response on the record so that his constituents and others can see that he is playing his part in representing them.

Ten-Minute Rule Bills. It is possible for MPs to bring a matter to the notice of the House by introducing a Ten-Minute Rule Bill, allowing him to speak on his chosen subject for ten minutes immediately after Question Time on Tuesdays and Wednesdays, with the intention of introducing a Bill on that subject. Any MP who objects can speak against the Bill for the same length of time. This device is almost always used to publicize an issue without any hope of the Bill proceeding, although some Ten-Minute Rule Bills are considered to be generally worthy and receive the essential support of the

Box 35 Adjournment debates – a typical week

Notices of Questions and Motions: 28 November 1980

MEMORANDA

Subjects proposed to be raised on the Motion for the Adjournment of the House up to Monday 28th November:

Tuesday 22nd November	Mr Michael Shersby	The pay and conditions of physiological measurement technicians (Cardiology)
Wednesday 23rd November	Mr Chris Mullin	The future of North East Shipbuilders Ltd.
Thursday 24th November	Mr Conal Gregory	The British Rail pension fund.
Friday 25th November	Mr John Battle	Asbestos pollution and mesothelioma in Arnley, West Leeds.
Monday 28th November	Sir Anthony Grant	The Cambridgeshire structure plan.

Source: House of Commons Order Paper

Government Whips, in which case they may become law without even being debated. Only about 15 Acts have been passed in this way since the War.

Although competition for Ten-Minute Rule Bill time is more intense than that for Adjournment debates, with MPs having to queue from dawn to have any chance of winning a place when the Public Bill Office opens at 10 am on any Tuesday or Wednesday (exactly three-weeks' notice must be given), it is regarded as a unique opportunity to address the House in Prime Time. The three-week cycle is broken by recesses, when a number of Ten-Minute slots become available after the usual Thursday announcement of the following week's business, which includes the Recess dates.

Early Day Motions. These are also publicity devices. Although they are tabled for debate on 'an early day', their sponsors (usually six backbenchers but sometimes only one or two) only intend that as many MPs as possible will sign them as an indication to the Government of parliamentary interest in an issue, although the Department affected by the subject of the Motion will always prepare a brief for its Ministers and for the Leader of the House in case it is mentioned in debate or during Oral Questions. They are, in practice, never debated and the Whips know that such safe declarations of demands or concerns by MPs on the Government side are rarely translated into votes against their Party. Nonetheless, several hundred EDMs, as they

Box 36 A typical early day motion

662 RENEWAL OF THE MULTI-FIBRE ARRANGEMENT
Sir John Farr
Mr Frank Haynes
Mr Peter Rost
Mr J. D. Concannon
Mrs Elaine Kellett-Bowman
Mr Joe Ashton

[New signatory the previous day] Mr Ted Leadbitter ★ 128
[Number of signatories to date]

That this House notes that the textile and clothing industries in the United Kingdom provide employment for 500,000 people, largely in areas of already very high unemployment, contribute an annual value added of £4,000 million to national wealth, achieved exports of over £2,700 million in 1984, and have increased output per head by 33 per cent, since 1980; calls attention to the heavy unemployment and severe disruption that would be caused by an unrestrained upsurge of imports from low-wage suppliers, and from China and other state-trading countries; and, believing that the prospect of a stable international trading environment is essential for growing investment to improve further the industries' competitiveness, calls on Her Majesty's Government to work for an effective renewal of the Multi-Fibre Arrangement which provides developing countries with guaranteed and growing access to the markets of the European Community and ensures a framework of order in international textile and clothing trade which would not otherwise exist.

As an Amendment to Sir John Farr's proposed Motion (Renewal of the Multi-Fibre Arrangement).

Mr Peter Thurnham
Mr Bowen Wells
★ 2

Line **12**, at end add 'while recognising that the Multi-Fibre arrangement was introduced as a temporary measure in 1974, with the objective of seeking a greater liberalisation of trade, to the benefit of all consumers.'

Source: House of Commons Order Paper (5 June 1985)

are known, are published in Hansard each year. Many receive little support but the occasional few, usually because of persistent pressure-group lobbying, attract over 100 signatures.

Private Members' Bills. Any MP may attempt to influence public policy by promoting a Bill himself through the Ten-Minute Rule procedure or by winning a place near the top of the ballot held each November for preference in the tabling of Bills by MPs. About half of the Commons enters the ballot, so the chances of finishing in the top 20, which gives an MP some chance of pursuing his Bill past Second Reading, are slim. Many MPs do not enter the ballot with a specific measure in mind. As soon as the result of the draw is known, they will be assailed by hordes of lobbyists, pressure groups and even the Whips, since the lucky few MPs may decide either to espouse the most worthy of the cases put to him or 'sell' his time to the Government, volunteering to introduce minor legislation to ease the pressure on Government time in return for preferment or a promise that the Executive might consider the subject as part of its own legislative programme.

If he decides to proceed, whether with his own or an outside body's Bill, he must do so within three weeks and he will have only ten days in the year's Session (six for Second Reading and four for later stages) to push through his measure. Since the Second Reading of each Private Members' Bill takes up most of the time allotted to Public Business on the day in question, Bills outside the top six on the list have a greatly diminished chance of proceeding. The odds against a Private Members' Bill becoming an Act are great: if it offends Government policy, the Whips will ensure that a majority oppose it; opposing interests may try to debate the previous item of business at great length to deny parliamentary time to the Bill; and, since Private Members' Bills are only debated on Fridays, when most MPs normally travel to their constituencies, finding support is not easy.

There are occasions, however, when a Private Members' Bill introduces legislation supported by the Government but not included, for lack of space, in its own programme. In this case the Whips may help the MP to find support for his Bill and may make the facility of Parliamentary Counsel's Office available to him to draft the measure. Otherwise, the ten leading MPs in the November ballot are allowed £200 towards the cost of drafting, which would normally be undertaken by Parliamentary Agents; or the cost would be borne by the group on whose behalf the Member is acting.

The rules of the House of Commons also allow MPs to introduce Bills under the Standing Order 39 procedure, although they have to take their place on Fridays behind balloted Bills and may not, therefore, be debated. Standing Order 39 is often used for non-controversial legislation; for keeping before the House a Bill introduced in a previous Session; and for similar backbench Bills introduced in the Lords. Private Members' Bills may be introduced in the Lords at any time after consultation with the Public Bill Office, and those measures contemplated too late for the November ballot may find that the simpler procedure in the Upper House may make it easier for Private Members' Bills to proceed further faster than might be the case in the Commons.

In view of the restricted time allocation for Private Members' Bills, some aspects of procedure may appear more complex than for Government legislation. Once the measure is decided upon, the sponsoring MP can nominate a day for Second Reading. The MP drawn at the top of the Ballot will nominate the first Friday available (this is known following a decision of the House about two weeks after the beginning of each Session); the second-placed MP will take the second Friday, and so on. Once the first six Fridays have been taken, precedence is given to later stages and to measures that have originated in the Lords.

The MPs outside the first six can hope that debate on any of the first six Bills is short, or that his Bill is felt to be so non-controversial that it is given a Second Reading without debate at 2.30 pm, the close of proceedings on Fridays. However, if a single MP shouts 'object', the Bill cannot receive a Second Reading even if the rest of the House supports it. If there is an objection, the sponsor can nominate another Friday and try to persuade the objectors that a compromise could be reached. If it is a Whip who objects in the name of the Government, it is unlikely that the Bill will move further.

A Bill given a Second Reading without debate will usually be committed to a Standing Committee, but it could go to a Committee of the Whole House if the sponsoring MP moved for it after Second Reading. Its Committee and other stages would then be negotiated without debate on a subsequent Friday, with the right of objection still existing at any time. Some non-controversial Bills have been passed completely in a day under this procedure, with the modification that instead of agreeing on a date for Committee Stage, the sponsor calls for it to take place immediately after Second Reading. Amendments can still be made under this procedure, but they cannot be deleted and any attempt at debate would constitute an objection.

After the sixth Private Members' Friday, a sponsoring MP (whether his Bill was introduced under the Ballot, the Ten-Minute Rule or Standing Order 39) may give ten days' notice of his intention to move that the Bill be referred to a Second Reading Committee if it has not yet received its Second Reading. Standing Order 39 has the power to recommend that a Bill proceeds to Second Reading. Again, the objection of a single MP is enough to prevent this procedural ploy from working.

A further barrier to a Bill receiving a Second Reading is the necessity to secure the Closure. If the Bill's opponents are still speaking just before 2.30 pm, its sponsor or another MP sympathetic to the Bill must seek to move 'that the Question be now put', otherwise the debate would stand adjourned without any vote taking place to decide whether a Second Reading should be given. The Speaker will not allow the Closure to be moved if insufficient debate has taken place or if there are fewer than 100

MPs present to vote for the Closure. Sponsoring MPs must therefore be energetic publicists and mobilizers of support for their cause.

There is a single Standing Committee for all Private Members' Bills which have been given a Second Reading.

In addition to the ten Fridays exclusively allocated to Private Members' Bills, there are another nine Fridays when Private Members' Motions may be discussed. On these days, Bills may be summarily dealt with at 2.30 pm. Normally, this slot is taken by Bills that have had objections lodged against them on an earlier date.

Since Private Members' Bills, like all other legislation, must pass through both Houses, a sponsoring MP must find a counterpart to pilot his measure through the Lords, and vice-versa. If he introduces any measure which affects the spending of public money, he must approach the relevant Minister to seek his willingness to introduce the Financial Resolution necessary to approve any expenditure increase.

Roughly one Private Members' Bill in eight successfully passes through all its stages and becomes law.

The reader should by now have a feel for the working practices, motivations, pressures and procedures of Government and those who play a part in it. In the final section this book becomes, as its title suggests, a users' manual, explaining how to obtain positive and cost-effective results when finding out about or advocating a case to the public policy planning system.

3
Dealing with Government

The four most common mistakes made by organizations in their dealings with Government

- *The Friends In High Places syndrome*
  The most common misconception. Those who think they can get their way because they 'know' Ministers, MPs or senior officials are sadly mistaken. Before using your contacts, you need a sound case and an understanding of the way decisions are taken on the issues of concern to you.

- *The Eat Your Way Out of Trouble syndrome*
  This is the PR firms' stock in trade. In most cases, you can save your money and your time by concentrating on well-researched advocacy, conveyed without largesse. Would you lunch a judge and jury?

- *The Congressional syndrome*
  The tendency to treat Parliament like the US Congress, which sits at the centre of the power structure. It is a mistake to divorce one institution of Government from the others. Think Government, not Parliament, and view decision-making globally. Many decisions have only a minimal political or public interest element and Parliament's influence varies with the issue and with the Government's majority. If you intend to enlist the support of MPs and Peers, ensure that you also square your case with those who advise the Minister you may wish to influence.

- *The Act Now, Think Later syndrome*
  Always do your research thoroughly first. If you do not know how Government will react to your case *before* you advocate it, you have not worked hard enough.

3.1 **Fundamentals**

Those who consistently succeed in their dealings with Government are those who understand the dynamics of decision making on public policy issues. Seeking information from, or making representations to any of the components of power without that understanding is as haphazard as cold selling. We commented earlier that gathering intelligence before lobbying is much like a game of Battleships: the advantage of being able to ascertain the other player's position is obvious. We now move on to explaining how you can ally your knowledge of Government to the techniques that satisfy the Need to Know; the Need to Inform; the Need to Negotiate; and, lastly, the Need to Lobby.

Prime considerations

Any individual or organization should ask two simple questions of themselves: do the activities of Government, or could they in the future, affect our interests to our detriment? Could Government benefit us if the right case was put to it?

The answers to both questions will be uncertain for most people since there is little understanding by the citizens of any State of the workings of Governments or their policy intentions. Yet Government impinges on our lives every day:

- by taxing us;
- by allocating those taxes to policy priorities such as defence and education;
- by providing subsidies, grants, allowances, export credits and reliefs to individuals and companies;
- by regulating the manufacture, marketing, distribution and use of tens of thousands of items;
- by controlling the way people do business and employ staff;
- by regulating human relationships generally through its legislative control over the law; and
- by controlling the environment

So you cannot always build your house as you would like to; or run your company as you would wish; or enjoy unrestricted use of your property. Decisions affecting individual and corporate affairs are being made in their hundreds every day by those you elect and whose salaries are funded by your taxes.

This final chapter deals with the user's end of the decision-making processes of Government. It explains how the four fundamental requirements of citizens in dealing with Government – the Need to Know, Inform, Negotiate and Lobby – can be satisfied and how an approach can be taken by the governed that enables them to exercise their democratic rights professionally, cost-effectively, without undue disruption to our political and administrative processes and, in many cases, to the benefit of both sides. It is that approach that should be analysed first.

The four basic needs outlined in the introduction to this book are stated in order of precedence. Whether the user of Government is a local ratepayer or a major multinational, *the primary rule of working with Government* is:

- monitor   first;
- talk   second;
- argue   third;
- apply pressure last.

In greater detail, this means that any approach to averting or resolving issues that could affect relations between citizens and Government must begin with, ideally, advance warning of opportunities or problems or, if that is not possible, the collation of all relevant data enabling the citizen to decide whether he need be concerned and, if so, whether he should take action to secure an advantage or defend himself against the State. Every hour spent on research and monitoring is worth ten spent on lobbying.

In many cases, reliable monitoring pre-empts the need to take drastic action by giving the governed time to correct misinformation or other distortions of the policy process through quiet and welcome input to the components of Government. This is no different from normal commercial practice in which sound market intelligence allows organizations to adapt their corporate strategies at their own pace, without dislocation to their workforce or share price, and on their own terms.

The most obvious example of disregarding monitoring as the prime rule is being unprepared when The Bomb drops, but there are others that illustrate the importance of observing the above sequence of events in a more normal context:

- A group of householders who have heard that the construction of a bypass could destroy the common land adjoining their houses are clearly in a stronger position if they can understand the intentions and planning of the Departments of Transport and Environment at an early stage than if they ignore the matter until the issue is made public, by which time expensive studies and many hours of detailed administrative thinking may have led to the formation of a conclusive opinion that could be antagonistic to that group's interests.

- A successful manufacturing company, part of a publicly owned industrial group, was unable to understand why attempts to obtain ministerial consent for its privatization were consistently being met with refusals. It had tried to negotiate before doing its homework or establishing a working relationship with decision-makers. Research revealed that officials in its sponsoring Division in the Department of Trade and Industry had misunderstood a number of factors relating to the company's interdependence with its parent and had advised the Minister to veto the privatization plan in the absence of the real facts. Having learnt the reasons behind the Minister's decision, the company was able to correct official misconceptions and secure the privatization pledge it wanted.

This primary rule – that information is the most important requirement of any user of Government – is supplemented by three others: The technique of dealing with Government can be summarized in three words: WHO?; HOW?; and WHEN?

- WHO makes the decisions?
- WHO can influence the decision-makers?
- WHO do you make your case to?

- HOW do you make your case?
- HOW do you obtain access to Government?
- HOW do you monitor Government?

- WHEN is the right time to monitor, talk, argue or lobby?

Who. Whether the needs of users of Government are merely for passive monitoring or, at the other extreme, for the organization of a major campaign to secure legislative or policy change, it is important that they appreciate the power structure behind issues that concern them. An essential element of any working strategy is therefore to identify the decision-makers connected with those issues. Does real power lie with officials, Ministers or Parliament in each case? Remember that it changes in relation to the Government's majority in the Commons, the strength of the Ministers involved, the views and sponsoring links of officials, and whether the matter is a political commitment or an administrative necessity. Within each component of the power structure, where is the power centre on a particular issue?

Example: On a complex legal or administrative matter in which a new and inexperienced Minister is involved, officials will possess considerable power. However, if the issue is a matter of controversial public interest at a time of small majorities in the Commons, power will be more evenly divided

126 Dealing with Government

Box 37 Power centres and influences

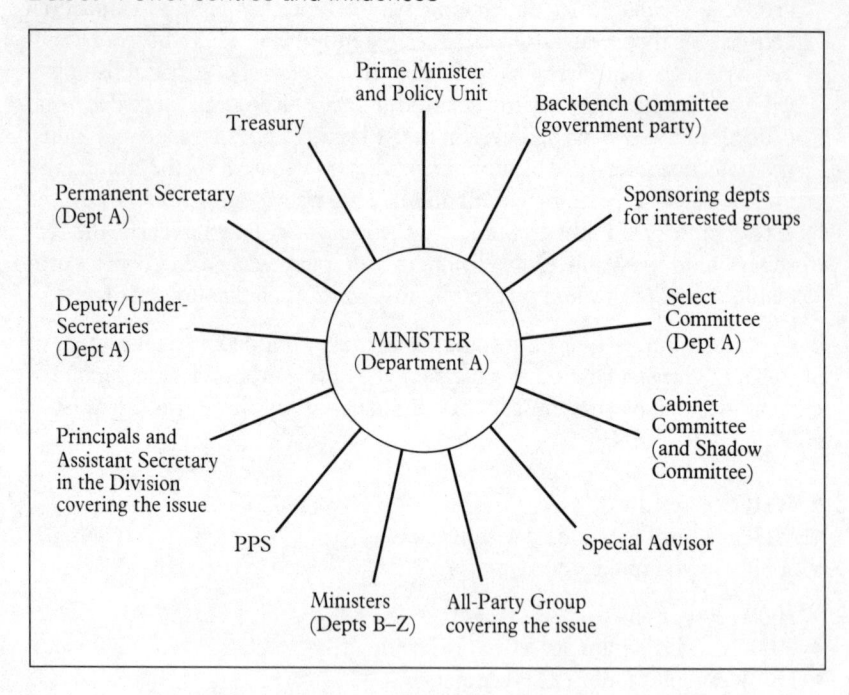

```
                    Prime Minister
                    and Policy Unit
         Treasury                    Backbench Committee
                                     (government party)

Permanent Secretary                           Sponsoring depts
(Dept A)                                      for interested groups

Deputy/Under-                                 Select
Secretaries              MINISTER             Committee
(Dept A)              (Department A)          (Dept A)

Principals and                                Cabinet
Assistant Secretary                           Committee
in the Division                               (and Shadow
covering the issue                            Committee)

              PPS                    Special Advisor

                 Ministers    All-Party Group
                 (Depts B–Z)  covering the issue
```

between officials and Parliament. A particular Cabinet Committee may lie at the heart of the decision-making process in either case.

Wherever power rests on an issue, it should be identified together with the influences on that power centre. It is then possible to know who to inform, negotiate with or lobby.

How. This covers technique. At this point, the conflict between the 'who you know' and 'what you know' lobbies should be resolved if the art and science of policy research and representations is to be seen in perspective.

Working with Government is no longer a matter of a few words in a few Establishment ears. It is essential to understand the infrastructure of decision-making and the mentalities of decision-makers, as would any business in dealing with potential clients. A developed relationship of trust between users of Government and decision-makers helps to obtain both access and a more sympathetic hearing – but access to power is the only real advantage of knowing the right people. If the case is not valid or well put; if the procedure of decision-making is not understood; if the case is advocated too late – then who you know will not help except in ensuring that your lack of knowledge is treated with marginally more lenience than might otherwise be the case.

Effective work with Government is a combination of both elements. It is important to develop contacts and cultivate those who already have them. Even if an individual or organization does not have significant relationships of trust in Parliament or Whitehall, if it can show Government it has a real understanding of the correct method of dealing with it efficiently to the benefit of both sides, it has a greater chance of building respect and a mutually advantageous relationship.

Working with Government as a professional technique falls between the law, the practice of which is based on technical knowledge, and public relations, in which strong contacts are essential. It borrows from both disciplines.

When. Timing is also crucial. An understanding of this facet of work with Government means ensuring that representations are made within consultation periods; that input is made to policy formulation before the publication of the Green Papers that prompt those consultation periods; that wasteful last-ditch lobbying is avoided; and that ongoing or campaign representations are structured to ensure that the components of the wheel of influence (see box 37) are tackled in the right order. Structuring the sequence of activities in dealings with Government is only one element of *When*; timing also involves an understanding of the daily, weekly and yearly cycles of Government – knowing that it is easier to contact MPs in mid-week than on Fridays or Mondays, when they normally travel to and from their constituencies; that it is very difficult to meet Ministers in August since they traditionally take end-of-Session holidays, leaving only one or two of their colleagues on duty in each Department; and that certain events during the week take precedence in the minds of many MPs over contact with the outside world: Prime Minister's Questions, which last from 3.15 to 3.30 pm on Tuesdays and Thursdays, and the 1922 Committee and PLP meetings at 6 pm on Thursdays. Those are three of the many fixed factors of time that circumscribe the ability of the outsider to obtain information from or make representations to the components of power.

Treat Government as a tribunal. In the introduction to this book, Government was described as having to act as a court if it is to take into account the submissions of those concerned by its judgements. It is therefore wise for outsiders to approach any dealings with it as they would approach legal action – through honest, unemotional advocacy backed by research.

Under this interpretation, working with Government can be seen as both structured and adversarial in the way decision-makers are approached and your case is made. Present the case for policy change/legislative amendment/awarding you a contract or subsidy; and set out the reasons for your point of view, taking into account every argument that could be raised against you – in fact, the soundest advocacy technique in negotiation and lobbying is often negative: this is the case against us; these are its weaknesses. Since it is harder to initiate policy change than to stop it, effective advocacy should aim to remove official or political objections to your case before accentuating the positive.

There are, however, important differences between legal work, as it is commonly understood, and what we may call the Government Bar. In working with Government there are a few accepted procedures; no precedent to assist with the organization of representations; and the would-be user is given little guidance as to which court to attend, there being a great number. Even if the right course of action is decided upon, the user may find himself having to present his case to several tribunals at once. Lastly, and most difficult from the advocate's point of view, he cannot assume that the courts in which he needs to plead will wish to listen to his case: he must interest the judges sufficiently to persuade them to grant him access to their court and then argue further to seek acceptance of his ultimate objective.

There is also available to the user of Government an option that would be regarded as highly destructive if allowed in a legal context – pressure, which may be seen as the equivalent of a right of appeal but to a different tribunal, that of public opinion. When pressure is allied to the making of representations to Government, it is called lobbying.

Some bodies have to follow the pressure path first because their access to the system may not immediately be easy. While there are well-established consultation channels between Government and representative bodies such as the National Farmers Union and the Trades Union Congress, it is still up to many lobbying organizations to hack at the system from the outside rather than work within it. It therefore remains easier for those users of Government who may be termed 'Establishment' to work through the 'correct' tribunal method than it is for the Campaign for Nuclear Disarmament or Friends of the Earth (the comments on page 126 about the who you know approach notwithstanding). Attention was drawn to this distinction when Prime Minister Harold Wilson declared in the commons in October 1966 that 'it is our duty to consult with the CBI, the TUC and others'. Yet the imbalance in securing results that this situation suggests is potentially more apparent than real, since many on the Establishment side fail to work with Government properly through a misunderstanding of Government's decision-making system; and public opinion, if properly harnessed, is a powerful weapon in a democracy.

The amount of noise made by advocates is usually in inverse proportion to the strength of their case or their abilities. While there are numerous exceptions to illustrate the importance of battering Government to entertain views widely accepted by the public (the campaigns for abortion law reform in the 1960s and for lead-free petrol in 1981–4 are good examples) the analogy (one that has already been widely used in this book) between Government and a commercial organization applies overwhelmingly. If a clothing manufacturer wishes to sell its products to a chain store it must show them to the potential buyer and persuade him that quality, price and delivery ability are satisfactory. Alternatively, the manufacturer could mount an advertising and PR campaign to influence both consumers and the chain store that its products are both fashionable and desirable. A third option would be to threaten the potential buyer with dire consequences if the manufacturer does not receive an order. Most people would accept that the process of persuasion starts with the first two of these options.

Work with Government is no different. It is a matter of ascertaining Government's intentions and susceptibilities and then selling ideas to those who make the decisions. The best-selling work is persuasive rather than coercive. There can, however, be a sharp distinction between administrative and political issues, with the latter justifying a higher profile of activity. In the example of the Navy Helicopter Contract cited in section 2 (see pages 83–85) an administrative matter both became a political issue because of its implications and was turned into one by the tenderers. Political criteria can often successfully supplant administrative needs. Pragmatism and expediency just as often counter logic and reason.

Myths

Some of the countless misconceptions about the workings of the power structure were dispelled in sections 1 and 2. Arising from that exposition, five lobbying myths should be highlighted and remembered:

Parliament is all-important. Do not be confused by the emphasis of the media on Parliament or by the current vogue for 'Parliamentary Consultants'. Parliament is one component of the power structure with the ability to assert itself only when governments have precarious majorities or where a considerable amount of work is done to persuade large numbers of MPs and Peers to oppose or change Government policy. Individual MPs have more ready access to Ministers than do members of the public and can make representations to them privately, which outsiders will almost never be able to do, but in the end the Government's ability to command Whipped support in the Commons is the only security it needs, provided it maintains reliable lines of communication and feedback to and from its own backbenchers.

It is very rare, therefore, that Parliament would be placed at the hub of the wheel of influence. The VAT on books campaign, referred to on page 24, aimed to secure the support of sufficient Conservative MPs to overturn the Government's majority, but all involved were aware that threats of opposition would be less certain of being translated into votes that could bring down the Administration and force many of the 'rebels' to put their seat and Party endorsements on the line.

If representations to Ministers are made through Parliament, it is vital that full briefing is given to the officials on whom the Ministers rely for the information and arguments that can defend them against attack. Decisions in Government rarely start with Parliament. Late information may place more emphasis than is desirable on the endorsing stage of the policy process, and parliamentary activity may form a valuable part of any programme, but Parliament's power must not be overestimated.

Pressure gets results. Only experience will advise users when to employ high profile pressure to make their point. One pressure tactic, however, is often used but is completely wasted: the mass lobby. Members of Parliament are unimpressed by the prospect of hundreds of people descending on Westminster to lobby them. Many ensure that they are unobtainable when obviously orchestrated groups crowd Central Lobby of the Palace of Westminster to see them. Members of Parliament are more responsive to the same number of people meeting them at their constituency surgeries on Fridays or Saturdays. If mass opinion is to be canalized to Government, legislators are also more responsive to individual letters than to large delegations to the House which may attract short-term publicity but little else.

Start at the top. The common approach to Government relations used to be that any strategy should concentrate on the Prime Minister, Ministers and Permanent Secretaries. While those three grades hold great power, representations made to them are always passed down to the Divisions relating to that issue. Those Divisions will advise Ministers and senior civil servants on the basis of the information they have and it is therefore essential that they are briefed before any approach is made to the top – it helps to have some control over the answer before any question is asked. Since opportunities to obtain access to senior decision-makers are limited, proper groundwork at Principal/Assistant Secretary/Policy Unit level should be laid in advance of advocating a case to senior Ministers or the Prime Minister and certainly before approaching a Department's Permanent Secretary.

MPs and officials should be entertained. This may be termed the 'eat your way out of trouble' philosophy. MPs receive an enormous number of lunch and dinner invitations. While a few are known freeloaders, most are happier for a case to be made to them in 20 minutes rather than in two hours. Officials must also be careful of accepting invitations from individuals or bodies with which they are unfamiliar. Any experienced official or legislator is completely aware of the purpose behind lunches, receptions and dinners for them and it is important that, if entertainment is offered to them, the medium should never obscure the message. No attempt should ever be made to suborn decision-makers with hospitality. No-one would ask their lawyer to wine and dine a jury.

Working with Government is an extension of public relations. Working the system is not just a matter of image-building. Public relations is important as a reinforcement, or even as a lead technique where the mobilization of public opinion or the promotion of an organization's image is important to advocating a case; but PR methods are irrelevant to the *need to know*; to the technique of advocacy; to an understanding of the procedures and processses of decision-making; or to the core of successful commercial negotiation with Government. Public relations is therefore a strong peripheral device but is not a substitute for a knowledge of the way Government works and of legislative and policy case-making. In the United States, where lobbying is both more prevalent and more institutionalized, the business of dealing with Congress and the Administration is divided into two halves: access, involving a combination of PR and understanding of the system; and advocacy, which is reserved almost exclusively to lawyers. The two disciplines work well side by side; both must be learnt by users of Government.

Ethics

At the start of this book, the right to monitor, inform, negotiate with or lobby Government was explained in ethical terms (page xiv). More specifically, there are a number of ethical rules applying to the exercise of those rights. Even though stories abound of deals being done in high places or of MPs being pressured to take a view on issues by an electorate mobilized by propaganda, the right to deal with Government in a democratic society is only endangered if abuses of the policy-making or public sector contract system are taken as examples to be followed.

On the assumption that the above advice will be followed, always heed the following guidelines:

Observe total honesty. Advocacy is about the skill with which the truth is presented. There is therefore a duty on any user of Government to inform policy-makers accurately. That duty is paramount in the case of input to parliamentarians since, as has been explained (page 101), few have sufficient resources to corroborate the information on which they may rely to base support for amendments, Private Members' Bills and other lobbying matters.

Officials often take pains to check information supplied to them and will try to ensure that the real facts, and the case against the user's, are both exposed. The cost of deliberate misinformation is usually the denial of further credibility to those who may have felt they could get away with it. That does not mean that officials, particularly those who may occasionally over-zealously support the interests they sponsor, do not from time to time accept a particular version of the truth.

There are no undisclosed principals. Whether professional intermediaries or the user's own resources are employed, disclosure of identity and interest is vital in most work with Government. We say 'most' because an appreciable part of any user's Government relations strategy should be geared to impersonal information gathering, not personal liaison or negotiation.

It is not normally advisable to present a case to legislators, officials or Ministers without providing the honest and full reasons behind its presentation as well as strong arguments for its acceptance. As we have noted above, it is occasionally possible to deceive Government, but those who attempt to do so must expect to approach Government once only since attempts to mislead are usually discovered and either result in the opposite action being favoured by decision-makers or in the Whitehall telegraph creating an unofficial black list.

Example: International Services Ltd has bought a disused oil rig in the North Sea and has designated it an independent State, Maritimia. International Services Ltd's intention is to establish Maritimia as the largest 'University of the Air' in Europe, with programmes being transmitted to France, Denmark, Belgium, Holland and the UK. Since the rig is outside territorial waters, ISL also intends to turn it into a tax haven, but this strategy is known only to its directors.

The UK Government has created an Economic Resource Zone to extend its sovereignty rights to cover oil reserves beyond its normal territorial limits, but there is some doubt whether this still applies to exhausted fields and decommissioned rigs. ISL, in order to attract shareholders for its broadcasting project, needs to obtain the UK Government's recognition of the sovereign status of Maritimia as a safeguard of its inviolability for taxation, social security, defence and other purposes. It approaches the Foreign Office without raising its ulterior, tax haven motive. Not only would the Foreign Office's legal advisers be very cautious about creating precedent where doing so could open the door to a number of potential activities (even if they are not envisaged by ISL) that could be unfavourable to the UK's interests, but the deliberate concealment of ISL's true intentions would, even if other factors were promising, militate against the granting of recognition, since bad faith can never provide a basis for negotiations with Government.

In real life, there have been a number of examples of contractors to the Ministry of Defence and National Health Service being required to repay excessive profits gained on procurement projects through, for example, undisclosed transfer pricing. It is therefore advisable that the user's interest in dealing with Government is declared in full.

Another area where the rule applies is the employment of MPs as advisers to, or lobbyists for, organizations. Whether those organizations are trades unions or multinationals, those who employ MPs must insist that the link is declared on the Register of Members' Interests (see Members' Interests Committee, page 38) to prevent any mutual embarrassment arising through conflict of interests. Registration is not compulsory, so the onus lies on the employer of MPs to ensure that the requirements of the Select Committee are complied with.

The requirement under the ethical code to disclose interests in dealings with Government does not, however, mean that users need make public declarations of their commercial or policy intentions in this area. Disclosure of the object of any negotiation or lobbying strategy is still consistent with confidentiality. Thus the demands users make on Government and the sums they pay to MPs or other consultants are strictly their own business. The important requirement is only that dealings with Government are transparent.

Do not abuse the institutions of Government. This ethical principle does not concern the inadvisability of flooding MPs with letters or staging demonstrations – such tactics may or may not be suitable depending on the problem and the nature of the user – as much as the opportunities that our generally open system of access to the institutions of Government allow to the unscrupulous. For example, any MP can book the five private dining rooms in the Commons on behalf of outsiders if he is amenable, and that facility has been widely used by public relations firms seeking to impress their clients in a grand setting. A passing acquaintance with the same MP can gain an outsider access to the Commons and Lords Vote Offices, where free copies of legislation, Hansard and all other published official documents can be obtained in his name. Thousands of Parliamentary Questions are tabled each year by MPs on behalf of outsiders. They cost over £70 each to answer. Anyone may apply to an MP or Peer to become a researcher; if accepted, their new status will allow them (or most of them – there are two grades of research assistant) access to the resources of the Commons and Lords libraries, the Vote Offices and other facilities.

Only the second of the above four examples is illegal: it amounts to theft. But all of them indicate the fine line between necessity and unethical abuse in the strategies open to outsiders in dealing with Government. Users should not, therefore, be tempted by such opportunities to use the benefits afforded to a parliamentarian as may be offered to them.

If it is necessary to approach an MP to table a question because information is otherwise unforthcoming or because an official response on the record is required, the MP – no matter how willing he is to accede to outsiders' requests – should have the reasons for that approach fully explained to him since the question will have his name against it and, if he is on the Government side, he may be approached for an explanation by the Minister's PPS and, in the case of an Oral Question, the departmental Whip if the question is sensitive or calculated to criticize Government policy. He must therefore be aware of the potential consequences of his actions.

There are two further types of information that fall close to the borderline of ethics and involve more difficult decisions by users of Government:

- A relationship of trust between a user and Government may be so strong that he may be offered sight of confidental documents, such as drafts of Select Committee reports or Green Papers, by officials and MPs. However, it is unlikely that they are permitted to do so and any advantage obtained may be short lived if the breach of procedure is discovered. It is best to refuse such opportunities, no matter how tantalizing they may seem.
- Select Committee reports are always distributed to the media in advance of publication in Confidential Final Revise (CFR) form. It has been possible to obtain CFRs, as they are known, through Lobby correspondents and others, but most members of the Lobby now accept that the trade is an unwritten breach of privilege. If CFRs are offered other than by the Select Committee publishing them, users should ensure they take no action on the contents of the report until after the embargo deadline.

Many issues are considered immoral or unjustified by the majority of the population. They may still be advocated under the above code of ethics provided the truth is told and no attempt is made to suborn decision-makers.

Box 38 Giving MPs full information

> Study this letter as an example of the way to request the use of MPs' facilities in an ethical manner.
>
> G. Smith Esq. MP,
> House of Commons,
> London SW1A 0AA
>
> Dear Mr Smith,
>
> Consolidated Escalators is a UK-based firm with subsidiaries in 12 countries. One of our factories, which manufactures handrails, is situated in your constituency and employs 120.
>
> For some time we have been trying to obtain information about total expenditure by Government Departments on rubber escalator handrails. Unfortunately, it appears that the figures have not been coordinated in most Departments' procurement records. This data would be most helpful not only to us and our industry in general, but also to the many MPs interested in escalators and it would seem that the only way to secure it would be by PQ. SInce this is our final alternative, would it be possible for you to table the attached drafts to the 12 major departmental users of escalators?
>
> We apologise for burdening you in this way but hope you will understand our need to approach you. We completely appreciate that our request may be unacceptable, in which case please inform us.
>
> Etcetera
>
> If the principles on drafting of PQs, as set out on pages 155–6 are followed, it should be possible to attach 12 questions, each typed on a separate sheet, which could be tabled by the MP without retyping. The letter tells him what you want, why it is needed and why he is the most appropriate person to table the PQ. He need ask no further questions of you.

Parliament is lenient – perhaps too lenient – with those who try to interfere with the processes of representative decision-making. In recent years two examples stand out. Firstly, the successful attempt made by tobacco companies to use retained and sympathetic MPs to block a Private Member's Bill aimed at further controls on tobacco advertising. They did this by tabling dozens of amendments to the Bill due for debate before the Tabacco Products Bill, talking at length on each amendment in mock-interest until time for consideration of the next Bill had expired.

Secondly, it was reported that the Law Society, in opposing another Private Members' Bill, this time to remove solicitors' conveyancing monopoly, had allegedly considered advice that its members should invite MPs supporting the Bill to meetings away from Westminster on the day of the crucial Second Reading debate in order to keep them from voting against the Law Society's lobby. Thankfully, the alleged thought was not converted into action, but the opinion of many is that even conspiracy to pervert democracy should be the subject of at least a strong reprimand by the Speaker.

Government is still, notwithstanding the known (and unknown) cases of abuse, distortion or lack of disclosure, based on Voltaire's maxim: 'I disapprove of what you say, but I will defend to the death your right to say it.'

3.2 **Getting information**

Reliable and timely information – on policy planning, official or political attitudes to an organization or an issue, and on the many debates, questions, committee investigations, statements and reports that are part of our mechanism of government – is the foundation of any working strategy aimed at Westminster and Whitehall. Sound information can provide either reassurance or early warning of potential policy conflicts with personal, group or corporate interests.

Being well-informed does not simply involve a good knowledge of the sources of Government information. The user must first decide what he needs.

How much information do you need?

At its most comprehensive, a monitoring programme should seek to keep the user informed of everything that is going to happen and, where it is not possible to receive advance notification, of everything that has recently happened to touch upon his Government-related concerns. That means amassing the following data:

Who does what? Which officials and Ministers are responsible for your areas of interest; which Select, backbench and All-Party committees are involved; which other MPs and Peers are connected with or interested in your areas of interest? Since names and faces change, lists must be reguarly updated.

What are they doing? Information on the Government's commitments in your areas of interest; forthcoming legislation; likely future policy changes; project and contractual planning; notice of debates, Parliamentary

Questions and answers, legislative progress (including notification of amendments and the composition of Standing Committees); Select Committee investigations and reports; Green and White Papers and other relevant Government reports or documents; ministerial speeches and departmental statements; and manifestos.

Why are they doing it? The attitude of officials and politicians to you and your concerns; and pressures on officials and politicians to support or oppose you.

Any major commercial organization, trade association or pressure group should aim to be that well-informed, but experience will also allow for discrimination in the assessment of all that data. For example, advance notice of the tabling of a Parliamentary Question has marginal value if the MP or Peer is of little influence and has telegraphed his irrelevant motive. On the other hand, some innocuous parliamentary questions are in fact 'planted' – tabled by an MP on the Government side at the request of a Minister's PPS as a means of allowing the Minister to make a written or oral statement on policy (either clarification or change) to Parliament as a whole. It would be common, for example, for the result of the Navy Helicopter Replacement Contract (see page 83) to be answered in this way.

There are other advantages to the user of having a wide range of advance information at his disposal:

- notification of forthcoming Select Committee investigations gives affected outsiders the opportunity to make their case for submitting evidence;
- notice of parliamentary debates allows you to contact MPs and Peers to advocate your case;
- amendments can be tabled in Standing Committee if timetables for sittings are known;
- input to Green Paper and other departmental consultation processes can only be made if outsiders are aware of them – as mentioned earlier, Government is not always good at inviting comment on policy planning before those policies effectively crystallize and are presented to Parliament for endorsement.

You should draw up a checklist from the comprehensive data 'menu' above to cover the issues you wish to address.

138 Dealing with Government

Box 39 A typical information requirement

> The campaign to stop VAT on books in 1984/5 (qv.) drew up the following information needs:
>
> 1 The Ministers involved and their attitudes to the issue.
> 2 The officials involved.
> 3 The role of each Department concerned in influencing the VAT decision.
> 4 The time-scale of the Budget process.
> 5 The MPs directly involved: All-Party, Select and backbench committees and Opposition spokesmen.
> 6 MPs who could be interested: authors, publishers, educationalists, culture-based opponents of indirect taxation.
> 7 Potential opponents of the anti-VAT case – fiscally 'dry' MPs, Ministers, journalists.

How to get it – sources and method

Departmental information. There is a considerable amount of published material to enable outsiders to target official and ministerial decision-makers and be notified about policy. The most important guide is the *Civil Service Yearbook* (HMSO, annually) which lists all Departments with their divisional structure, and identifies all officials down to Assistant Secretary grade [and often to Principal]. It also includes a considerable number of contact telephone numbers. It does, however, have disadvantages: it is often difficult for outsiders to decide which part of a Department may cover their concerns from the information listed in the *Yearbook*; and, while enquiry numbers are given for each Division and Branch, there are few numbers given for the officials themselves. A good tip in obtaining information from Departments is always to add an official's direct line to the *Yearbook* whenever contact is made, since the vagaries of departmental switchboards mean that a call to Division or Branch enquiry points will usually involve a second call to the extension given.

The *Civil Service Yearbook* uses the so-called Unified Grading Structure, which gives grades numbers rather than names. For identification, the corresponding number and grades are:

1   Permanent Secretary
1a Second Permanent Secretary
2   Deputy Secretary
3   Under Secretary
4   An intermediate grade normally used for technical appointments

Box 40 The Unified Grading Structure

INNER CITIES DIVISION 5
Development and implementation of proposals for new urban development corporations. Co-ordination of UDC programme.
Head of Division (Grade 5)
Mrs D S Phillips
Enquiries: 01-212 0636
GTN 212 0636

PLANNING & DEVELOPMENT CONTROL
2 Marsham Street, London SW1P 3EB
Director (Grade 3)
N W Summerton

DEVELOPMENT PLANS; OTHER PLANNING TOPICS; LAND TRANSACTIONS
Development plan policies and procedures; land for housing; simplified planning zones; planning controls over hazardous development; environmental assessment; compulsory purchase and compensation; public acquisition and disposal of land.
Enquiries: 01-212 8561
GTN 212 8561
Grade 5
A H Corner

SPECIALIST PLANNING APPEALS
Tollgate House, Houlton Street, Bristol, Avon BS2 9DJ
Enforcement and established use; policy and appeals; purchase notices; planning control over outdoor advertising, and advertisement appeals; awards of appeals costs.
Enquiries: 0272 218600
GTN 2074 8639
Grade 5
D N Donaldson

DEVELOPMENT CONTROL
2 Marsham Street, London SW1P 3EB
Development control policies and procedures; the green belt; public inquiry procedures and liaison with the Council on tribunals.
Enquiries: 01-212 0798
GTN 212 0798
Grade 5
R S Horsman

LAND AND PROPERTY
2 Marsham Street, London SW1P 3EB
Director (Chief Estates Officer)
(Grade 4)
C K Howes
Professional and policy advice on all aspects of estates and commercial property work. Landlord and Tenant Act 1954 Part II (Business Tenancies) Secretariat to the Property Advisory Group.
Enquiries: 01-212 4992
GTN 212 4992
Professional advice on urban development grant applications; UDG appraisal team member.
Deputy Director (Grade 6)
J C White

PLANNING SERVICES
2 Marsham Street, London SW1P 3EB
Director Chief Planning Adviser
(Grade 4)
S P Byrne OBE

Cont.

Box 40 (*Cont.*)

PLANNING INFORMATION AND RESEARCH
2 Marsham Street, London SW1P 3EB
Planning practice, information systems and management of Planning Research Programme.
Enquiries: 01-212 3129
GTN 212 3219
Grade 5
R A Bird
International work in the urban policy and planning fields including UN(ECE), UNCHS, OECD and Council of Europe.
Enquiries: 01-212 4003
GTN 212 4003
Grade 6
D C Stroud

MINERALS
2 Marsham Street, London SW1P 3EB
Grade 5
R C Mabey
Policy, legislation and casework on planning control over mineral working, including guidelines for aggregates working, policy on coal and onshore oil and gas and advice to local authorities and mineral operators.
 Professional advice and research management on minerals planning, geology and land reclamation
Enquiries: 01-212 3521/3542
GTN 212 3521/3542

CARTOGRAPHIC SERVICES
2 Marsham Street, London SW1P 3EB
Map library; air photos unit; Drawing offices.
Enquiries: 01-212 4891
GTN 212 4891
Grade 7
P Morgan

REGIONAL POLICY
2 Marsham Street, London SW1P 3EB
Regional policy including European Regional Development Fund and Area Economic Development Studies.
Enquiries: 01-212 3541
GTN 212 3541
Grade 5
J A Zetter

Environment Protection
2 Marsham Street, London SW1P 3EB
Deputy Secretary (*Grade 2*)
Dr M W Holdgate CB

RURAL AFFAIRS
2 Marsham Street, London SW1P 3EB
Director (*Grade 3*)
T R Hornsby
Enquiries: 01-212 6930
GTN 212 6930

DIVISION 1 (COUNTRYSIDE DIVISION)
Tollgate House, Houlton Street, Bristol BS2 9DJ
Countryside Conservation policy; Countryside Commission; National Parks policy; public paths; access to open country; common land; village greens; allotments; caravaning and camping.
Enquiries: 0272 218178
GTN 2074 8178
Head of Division (*Grade 5*)
A Flexman

Source: *Civil Service Yearbook 1988.*

5   Assistant Secretary
6   Senior Principal

The Cabinet Office publishes lists of Ministers and their specific responsibilities, as well as Department Special Advisers. An annual publication from the same source, *Fringe Bodies*, lists all quasi-Departments, including advisory, regulatory and executive agencies, and all nationalized industries.

Each Department issues a number of statements, speeches and other documents each day through its Information Office. The Central Office of Information produces a booklet giving details of all departmental information officers with their direct numbers. It is possible to write to each Information Office and be added to the distribution list for departmental announcements. The Central Office of Information marshals all these on to a daily list which can be purchased. Some organizations arrange for delivery of all announcements to them each afternoon in order that they can examine the information as soon as possible after its publication.

In addition to the individual enquiry numbers listed in the *Civil Service Yearbook*, each Department has two general enquiry points. If outsiders do not know which Division or Branch would deal with their problem, they should ring the main Department number and ask for Enquiries. There is normally just one person who should, nonetheless, be able to place issues reasonably close to the relevant officials. The second enquiry point is only used if contact needs to be made with a Minister's Private Office, but the outsider may wish specifically to contact the Minister's Diary Secretary to see whether he would be free to receive an invitation. Asking for Ministerial Enquiries after dialling the Department's number will ensure that the outsider is transferred to the right person.

As mentioned earlier, even though for the user of Government the *Yearbook* is a bible, it has disadvantages. Since many officials at Principal Grade are not included, outsiders must complete the base of the pyramid of responsibility on their concerns by direct contact with the Divisions involved. It should be remembered that some subjects are considered sufficiently important to justify having several Principals working on them in detailed cells. The *Yearbook* also excludes those parts of each Department where access by outsiders is considered undesirable; namely those officials concerned with internal management. Contact with data-processing managers or travel units can often only be made by a circuitous route.

For the policy watcher, however, one part of each Department is hidden from the outside world but can be invaluable in dispensing advice if approached selectively – the Parliamentary Branch, which acts as the Department's link with Parliament. If a sufficient relationship of trust is established, the Branch will be able to tell the outsider whether particular parliamentary questions are 'planted', and to give prospective schedules for legislative stages and advice on the timing of other departmental business in either House where the week's Business Announcement (see below) has not included it.

Parliamentary information. As the public arm of government, Parliament produces a considerable amount of information about its proceedings and members. As with Whitehall, there is a standard reference work, called *Dod's Parliamentary Companion. Dod*, as it is usually abbreviated, contains the names of all Peers and MPs, with photographs, biographies, and other details such as constituency lists, a short guide to parliamentary procedure, and MPs interests by subject (although the list is by no means comprehensive and must be cross-checked with the other publications listed below). More detailed MPs' biographies are contained in the four-volume *Parliamentary Profiles* by Andrew Roth. *The Register of Members Interests*, which is published annually by the Select Committee on Members' Interests and is available from HMSO, lists the shareholdings, directorships and other commercial affairs of MPs, although it must be said that the list contains many omissions since disclosure is not mandatory.

The business of Parliament is well-documented. Each day, both Houses produce an Order Paper, listing the agenda for the coming day and other matters, and Hansard, an almost verbatim (bad grammar is improved) account of proceedings in either Chamber. The Commons Order Paper contains:

- a list of the Parliamentary Questions due to be answered orally on that day;
- details of Statutory Instruments tabled for positive or negative resolution;
- changes in the membership of Select Committees and details of Standing Committee membership on individual Bills.
- a summary of the items of business completed the previous day and details of the agenda for that day;
- lists of oral and written Parliamentary Questions still to be answered, with their likely date of answer (written Priority Questions (for quick answers) are marked by a capital W in the left-hand margin);
- lists of new signatories to Early Day Motions (EDMs); EDMs that have not attracted signatures the previous day are not reproduced;
- once a week, the Adjournment Debates for the coming week are printed.

The Lords Order Paper is a much slimmer document, largely because there are far fewer questions and no EDMs tabled in the Upper House. Compared to the 60 or so pages of its counterpart, it seldom exceeds 12 sheets. The

Lords Order Paper often lists business a week ahead, together with Unstarred Questions awaiting debate, written questions (there are no dates given for answer) and the timetable of committee sittings.

It is not necessary to spend hours sitting in the public galleries of the Commons and Lords in order to learn about comment on legislation and many other issues by MPs, Peers and Ministers. There are usually long queues, the taking of notes is prohibited, and parliamentary proceedings (except the two 15 minute sessions each week devoted to the Prime Minister) are rarely any more interesting in unedited form than the average court trial. Hansard allows users of Government to see those comments only a few hours after they are made.

Like the Order Papers, Hansard is also produced separately for either House, but is simpler in form. At most it is divided into four sections:

- Continuation report of the debates from the day before yesterday if they have lasted beyond 10.30 pm, when Hansard has to go to press. Thus, while Monday's proceedings are reported in Hansard on Tuesday, a late sitting may not be reported in full until Wednesday.
- Answers to Oral Questions given by Ministers the previous day.
- The day's debates and ministerial statements. (Such statements, on any subject from devaluation to changes in social security benefits, are normally made in both Houses at approximately the same time.) Hansard includes Division lists to show how MPs and Peers voted on a particular issue.
- Written answers to parliamentary questions.

There is also a Hansard for each Standing Committee, although there is often a delay of a few days before proceedings are published.

With practice, it should take only a few minutes to scan both Order Papers and Hansards, although reading a debate of six hours for important remarks may take longer.

Hansard and the Order Papers are available from HMSO but are expensive to buy. How should they be used? First, the Commons Order Paper, much of which should be irrelevant to the efficient user of Government, who will have taken the trouble to be informed about Statutory Instruments long before they are brought before Parliament and who will not be concerned by the bulk of parliament questions and EDMs. However, changes in Select and Standing Committee membership are important since they may increase or diminish your potential access or ability to secure the tabling of amendments.

Relevant Parliament Questions (PQs) should be studied in the light of all available information (from *Dod*, *Roth*, the *Register of Members' Interests* and newspaper comment) about the MP tabling it. The question may be less important than the motivation of the questioner. Remember that many PQs are drafted by outsiders and simply tabled by a willing Member. Written questions are normally given as bland an answer as possible, but Oral PQs may include unanticipated supplementary questions that could be directed at your interests. Making contact with Departments to assist with answering written or oral PQs is covered in the next section.

In pragmatic terms, EDM support is to be ignored unless a motion is tabled with over 50 Government-side signatories, an indication of considerable organization by its sponsors, or if it continues to attract support, which usually means that a pressure group or other lobby is working hard to interest MPs in the issue. It should be remembered that PPSs do not sign EDMs covering their Department and many of the more influential backbenchers prefer a more discreet and personal means of expressing their opinions to Ministers.

The Lords Order Paper is most useful for the details of Unstarred Questions tabled for possible debate in the coming weeks. As with Commons PQs, many will have been prompted by outsiders' requests to Peers; if they are debated, you may find that the only speakers could be antagonistic to your interests unless attention is paid to the Order Paper well in advance.

Turning to Hansard, watch ministerial replies to Oral Questions, since among officials' attempts to say as little as possible may be contained details of future publication dates of White or Green Papers or Government reports and other policy announcements. Supplementary questions, of which no one receives prior notice, indicate the real motivation of the MP. Through regular study of questioners and speakers in debates relevant to you, a list of MPs and Peers who support or oppose your interests can be compiled. Written answers occasionally contain valuable statistical information that could not have been obtained had the convention of answering questions from MPs not forced the Departments concerned to collate the data required. Occasionally, however, it is felt that information would be too difficult or expensive to obtain and the written answer will leave the MP, or those on whose behalf he has tabled the question, no wiser.

Standing Committee Hansard will only be of interest to you if you are following an item of legislation in detail, in which case you should also obtain from HMSO lists of amendments tabled for consideration (published every few days between appointment of the Committee and completion of a Committee Stage, and collated into what is called a Marshalled List perhaps twice during that period) and consult the relevant departmental policy Division or the Committee's clerk to find out when amendments of concern are due for debate (the Chairman may not select them at all) and, following that day's session, whether those amendments have been accepted. The Department will usually be able to indicate whether the Government will accept backbenchers' amendments or whether a close vote or upset is expected despite the efforts of the Government Whip.

Each week, the House of Commons publishes a *Weekly Information Bulletin*, a useful and clear record for those seeking to further their monitoring of the Commons. The first issue of each Session contains lists of all MPs; Ministers and Government Whips; officers of the House of Commons; Opposition spokesmen; delegations to international assemblies such as the Council of Europe; and MPs who are also members of the European Parliament. *Weekly Information* regularly lists the forthcoming week's business in the Chamber and Select Committees (although, because it is issued on Saturday, it is too late to cover Friday's motions, legislative and Adjournment debates – the coming week's Business announcement, which covers the Chamber only, is made by the Leader of the House on Thursday afternoons and runs from Monday to the following Friday) including the witnesses to be called by the latter. There are tables showing the progress of public and private Bills; and lists of the past week's official publications and Select Committee reports, Government responses, or individual transcripts of evidence. Overlapping with the Order Paper, it also reproduces the membership of Standing Committees when they are appointed.

Hansard, the Order Papers, Committee reports, Bills, Statutory Instruments, Acts and amendments are all available from the Sales Office of the Commons as well as HMSO. The *Weekly Information Bulletin* is only available from the Sales Office, which stocks all parliamentary papers for the past three years.

Another weekly publication (only produced when the House is sitting, however) is the *House Magazine*, which is available from Parliamentary Communications Ltd in London. It is the in-house newspaper of the Palace of Westminster, with an editorial board made up of MPs and Peers. Each issue lists the All-Party and other meetings notified to the Whips for the following week (many All-Party Group meetings are not, however, publicized by being included on the Whips' list that is sent to all MPs at 6 pm on Thursdays) and tables giving full details of the parties' spokesmen in both Houses and of PPS are regularly reproduced. The magazine now tends to concentrate each issue on a subject, such as the national heritage or information technology, with articles by the relevant Ministers, information about those Ministers and Opposition spokesmen, and views from backbenchers. Every MP and Peer receives a copy, making the *House Magazine* a favourite target for corporate or pressure-group advertising, and the public can also subscribe.

Lastly – at least as far as parliamentary hard copy is concerned – each Select Committee issues press releases covering its future programme and

146   Dealing with Government

announcing the publication of its reports, often accompanied by a press conference. Anyone may call the office of each committee (through the main Commons number, 01-219 3000 or by using the direct lines listed in *Dod*) and ask to be included in the distribution list for these releases.

There are two further sources of printed information about legislation, public policy and the components of power. The first is the Press, whose lobby correspondents – journalists allowed to work in the Palace of Westminster, with close, confidential and non-attributable access to MPs, Peers and Ministers – and specialist reporters are recipients of leaks, interviews and policy announcements that would not be available to any except a few full-time government affairs consultants. While the analysis by political editors of current affairs and, to an even greater extent, their predictions about electoral behaviour, ministerial reshuffles and Budget proposals, are invariably both conflicting and inaccurate, the media's revelations about Government policy, ministerial intentions and back-bench attitudes should be studied closely. To some extent, the media's insight on political issues may be more valuable than information direct from MPs and Peers: the Conservative holding a marginal seat may understandably feel that the SLD is a serious electoral threat; a political editor can both distance himself and take the national view, pointing out traditional mid-term dissatisfaction with the Government of the day and the use of public relations techniques by third Parties to persuade the dissatisfied electorate that they are a more viable alternative than may be the case in practice.

For those without Hansard, which reports the new week's parliamentary business announcement on Friday, the main newspapers list the work of both Houses on the same day and Select Committee agendas each Monday.

The second source is often ignored by users of Government. Legislation is the law; before making a case for changes in the law or policy, that legislation and the basis it gives to policy must be understood. Any law library will keep a set of current statutes and Statutory Instruments with annotations that clarify the drafting and give details of judicial decisions covering the Act in question.

We turn now to more personal ways of satisfying the Need to Know about what is happening in Parliament, Departments and the Executive. So far, the user of Government has needed only the gift of discrimination to select relevant information from the mass of facts available in hard copy form. From now on, he will also require an understanding of, and sensitivity to, the considerations of legislators, Ministers and officials that can only be acquired through experience.

Both the Commons and Lords have established public information offices to answer enquiries from outsiders about MPs and Peers, constituencies (if the user is in doubt, the Commons Public Information Office (PIO) will tell them in which constituency a particular street or other location falls), parliamentary procedure, forthcoming business in the Chambers and committees, the membership of those committees, the officers of backbench committees and of those All-Party groups that have kept the PIO up to date, and other queries. The Commons PIO has produced a series of free factsheets on procedure, All-Party groups, and the history and institutions of Parliament. Their numbers are 01-219 4272 (Commons) and 01-219 3107 (Lords).

We have mentioned that contact with the Clerks to Standing Committees can provide details about proceedings at Committee Stage of a Bill that are not available in printed form. Similarly, the offices of Select Committees can be helpful in providing information about future investigations, witnesses to be called, publication dates of reports and the chances of reports being debated.

Less institutionalized forms of information gathering inevitably centre on the strength of relationships outsiders can develop with the components of the power structure. If, as an example, information is wanted about matters discussed at the weekly PLP meetings or the agenda of backbench committees; if a PQ is needed to obtain otherwise unobtainable information; if details of the following week's schedule of debates is to be obtained in advance of the Thursday afternoon announcement, there is no alternative but to know and be trusted by MPs (Opposition spokesmen in the last of these two cases). While there are no short cuts – it may take months or even years to develop sufficient understanding of, and confidence from, MPs – the technique of developing that relationship is covered in chapter 3.3.

Policy officials, information officers and parliamentary clerks in Departments will, except on non-sensitive issues such as publication dates or guidance on officials' responsibilities, need to satisfy themselves of the bona fides of those seeking information on anything from future policy planning to a Minister's diary commitments.

Officials have no duty to provide outsiders with the information they seek, but they usually do so if asked courteously and concisely. It is in their interests to avoid concerned parties learning of policy developments too late to present them only having recourse to the tabling of last-minute amendments or mobilizing the media and mass public pressure to make their case, all of these techniques causing more work for Departments.

Early warning by officials, provided a timely approach is made to them, therefore encourages negotiation, rather than the adversarial tactics that keep civil servants drafting answers to PQs or writing speeches for Ministers and then sitting late at night through Unstarred or Adjournment debates in the officials' box in the Commons or Lords. Box 41 takes a hypothetical

148 Dealing with Government

Box 41 Developing information links with officials – the example of the Machine Tools Federation

> The Machine Tools Federation was formed a year ago to promote the image of the industry and negotiate with and monitor Government on its behalf. In carrying out the last of these responsibilities, it concentrates on three departments:
>
> - *Department of Trade and Industry* – for information on the department's attitude to the industry; progress on current policy planning; possible future policy developments; policy on some of the main industries using machine tools; the motor, shipbuilding, aerospace and textile industries; future lines of credit and the Department's attitude to including machine tools in aid and trade packages; and, since most of the Federation's members are based in the Midlands, official consideration of changes in regional policy.
> - *Department of Employment* – for information on changes in employment policy and training schemes that could affect the Federation's members.
> - *Treasury* – monitoring Budget planning, since the Federation is seeking reliefs on capital expenditure.
>
> The Federation initially contacted each Department at Principal level, telling the officials who it was and stating that it wanted to ensure it was kept informed about any policy that could affect it. On first liaison, which was by telephone, it asked officials whether they were able to disclose if anything was in discussion on a range of subjects and about progress on current policy developments. It ensured, in asking officials for this information, that it conveyed its understanding of the discretion civil servants have to exercise in disclosing information as yet unannounced publicly.
>
> In a meeting shortly afterwards with its sponsoring officials (requested by the Federation) it was revealed that a Green Paper would shortly be published on a subject affecting the industry. The Federation asked about its publication date and for guidance on the considerations of the Department in examining submissions. It later contacted the relevant Division to find out how many submissions had been made in response to the Green Paper.
>
> The Federation is careful never to ask officials, even those in the Divisions with which it now enjoys regular and close relations, for information that could compromise that relationship. It does not ask for sight of documents while still in confidential draft form although it does ask if officials can tell it anything about their content on the basis that the worst answer it can receive is no. It has asked for, and received, information on a number of matters: on the decision-making structure, particularly where that structure is unrecognized – its members often need to know about the composition of teams working on individual departmental procurement contracts; how the interdepartmental process will work on some of the issues affecting the Federation; and on timing of statements; the White Paper following the Green Paper's consultation period, and the introduction of legislation.
>
> *Cont.*

Box 41 (*Cont.*)

> The Federation has found that it often has to make contact at Assistant Secretary level for information about ministerial attitudes to the issues in which it is interested. Once again, it never pressures officials but makes them aware of the consequences to it of not being properly informed and of its awareness that officials may not be able to release the information it needs. Its approach is invariably deliberately naïve when contacting civil servants with whom it does not have a close working relationship: having identified itself, it asks for help with a problem, states that problem, and then asks if the official can tell them anything about – legislative timetables, departmental attitudes or concerns, consultation processes or whatever. It further demonstrates its understanding of Whitehall by mentioning that officials may request its inquiry in writing (if they do, it always calls them no more than ten days after receipt of the letter) or that they may wish to meet it to discuss the enquiry or to save them drafting a lengthy response.
>
> The Federation learnt early that some officials are more cautious than others about providing information and that this problem is more evident below Principal grade because of the frequent need to check upwards before responding.
>
> Like many industry groupings, the Machine Tools Federation has little money and therefore makes maximum use of free sources of information. It learns about the parliamentary timetable from the Friday and Monday papers; it studies those papers' Lobby gossip; it is on the mailing list for all Department of Trade and Industry, Department of Employment and Treasury press releases; and it consults the reference books in the public library next door for lists of MPs. It takes the view that resources are not a great problem if the system of acquiring information is understood and the user knows how to target officials. It has seen that many large and well-funded organizations thinking that Hansard reading is enough can be beaten at the monitoring game by more humble users who realize that the formulation of policy is similar to the conception of life: it grows, takes form, and by the time it emerges into public view – parliamentary consideration – it may be too late to do anything except try to lose some rough edges. Advance warning can best be gained through seeking information from Departments.

interest group as an example of developing and then using information links with Whitehall.

The Machine Tools Federation's approach is a standard and reliable technique for liaising with Departments to acquire information. There may, however, be instances where an organization needs anonymously to acquire details on policy or assess official attitudes to them or their concerns. It would be wrong for this book publicly to advise on techniques of approaching Departments without an organization disclosing its identity, although it acknowledges the need to do so under such circumstances.

Officials recognize that this happens and are understandably careful in responding to those with whom they are not familiar.

Information about Departments, the policies formulated by them and Parliament's opinions on those policies is not just available from Whitehall and Westminster. The research departments of the Party headquarters maintain close links with their political leaders and with backbenchers who may prefer to rely on sources other than the Commons Library or outside groups and companies for issue information. Briefs on important legislation may be prepared and circulated to backbenchers in advance of Second Reading debates; and the role of Party research departments in preparing the basis of election manifestos means they can often advise outsiders on current, and likely developments in, Party policies. The Conservatives, for example, produce before each election a bulky guide for candidates which covers every aspect of public policy and campaigning. They also keep detailed biographies of each of their MPs, which are available at a small charge to members of the public.

Away from London, the annual round of Party conferences provide a valuable source of political information, since most MPs and all Lobby correspondents attend and can usually be found in and around the conference hall. Attending Party conferences is, however, increasingly difficult since the need for security involves observers in applying for passes well in advance and the Labour Party has sharply restricted access to its conference by those who are not members of constituency delegations. Accommodation is also scarce, since Party organizations, MPs, the Press and constituency associations fully book all the best hotels, in particular those close to the conference hall, up to 18 months before the due date. Nonetheless, a large number of pressure groups and commercial organizations not only attend and meet many MPs individually, but also hold receptions for MPs to gather views and convey theirs. We will return in chapter 3.3 to the advisability of organizing such receptions, whether in Westminster or at Party conferences, for legislators.

Lastly, there is a plethora of research, representative and campaigning organizations that closely follow policy planning and development within tightly defined sectors. Bodies ranging from the Disabled Living Foundation to the Publishers Association can be helpful guides to Government-related information about their concerns, since a fair amount of their time may be spent monitoring their Departments and Parliament, negotiating with officials and Ministers, and keeping lists of supportive or antagonistic MPs and Peers. However, no list large enough to detail all these organizations has yet been published, so some lateral thinking may be required to find a specialist body in your area of interest.

Dealing with Government   151

What you cannot get – information that is difficult or impossible to obtain

Even when armed with every word published by Whitehall and Parliament, even when a full understanding is developed of the technique of identifying and then obtaining information from departmental and parliamentary sources, there is still a great amount of material, comment and planning, the details of which are either denied to those outside Government or are difficult to uncover.

Like Parliament's place in the power structure, the substantial volume of releases, statements, reports of debates, Green and White Papers and other publications issued by Departments and Westminster are only the visible tip of a more significant iceberg. As already explained, the assiduous user of Government needs to know about policy planning before it reaches published form; and the motivation behind the actions of Whitehall and of legislators is as important as the actions themselves.

Any question about underlying motivation or advance disclosure of forthcoming policy change is inevitably sensitive. Unless a strong relationship of trust is established with officials, they will simply tell you that all decisions are made by the Minister; revealing the true identity of the power behind the throne, whether at Permanent Secretary or lower levels,

Box 42 The importance of understanding the motives of Government

---

An MP delivers a strong and well-publicized parliamentary attack on an organization or its concerns. The real interest of that organization should not be with the speech itself but in the MP's motivation, which could indicate greater repercussions than short-term adverse publicity – is an organized campaign directed at the organization, with the MP as a willing parliamentary mouthpiece? Has a Minister asked MPs to apply pressure to him as a means of providing the excuse to overturn the advice of his officials and substitute his own policies? Is the MP simply trying to appease a constituency interest, without any intention of developing the matter further?

A Green Paper is published proposing stricter controls over the activities of companies in one industry. Has the issuing Department bowed to pressure from a sector that feels threatened by those companies? Do officials have views about those companies or their activities that have been allowed to prevail over the industry's attempts to defend itself before the Department? Is the attitude expressed in the Green Paper part of a wider, as yet unexpressed, change in departmental policy that may have further adverse implications for that industry? To what extent are Ministers in control: has the initiative come from them or, at the other extreme, have they simply endorsed the case put to them by their advisers without having the time to corroborate it?

cannot be expected of officials unless they are satisfied that the information they give will be treated with discretion. The reality may anyway lie between their formal and unguarded statements, since most Whitehall decisions are a product of ministerial setting of form and official provision of substance. It may well be that Principal and Assistant Secretary grade officials, with whom primary contact on information requirements should be made, have not been privy to decisions made at a higher level and it may be impossible for you to gain a full picture of the background to those decisions unless long-standing contact has been maintained with Under Secretaries and above, or officials at lower grades are prepared to find out more for you from their superiors. If, however, officials are reluctant to provide sensitive information for whatever reason, it would be unethical to do other than accept their judgement since they have no duty to tell outsiders anything.

A Minister's thinking is conditioned by a wide range of factors: Prime Ministerial pressure; the decision of a Cabinet Committee; the advice of the Whips if the issue is likely to be politically sensitive; media pressure; officials' advice; the counsel of his Special Adviser; and his personal prejudices or ambitions are but a few. Officials with whom firm contact has been established may provide some insight into his views; his Special Adviser and PPS can also help; and the relevant backbench committee on the Government side may have discussed the issue in question with him. The last three sources can be more frank than officials on initial acquaintance if approached properly:

- write to them (do not telephone) having identified them by contacting Enquiries in the Department in the first two cases and the PIO or Labour and Conservative head offices for the names of backbench committee officers in the latter;
- explain who you are, what the issue is and the nature of your interest or concern, with its relation to the Minister;
- relate the letter to your target's role *vis-à-vis* the Minister;
- request ten minutes of their time (in the Department in the first case; in the House of Commons in the last two) to seek their advice.

Thus, for example, a letter to a Minister's PPS from Consolidated Escalators:

> We have followed with great interest your Minister's recent statements about the need to cut maintenance costs in his Department. As one party that would be affected by this move (our work for the Department had a value of £19,000 in 1984), we have been keen to discover the frank reason for his decision, which does not seem to have been followed in other Departments.
>
> We are of course aware of your Party's commitment to value for money and a Department's constant need to monitor its establishment costs, but it would

Dealing with Government 153

be most helpful to us if we could fully understand his thinking. In view of the closeness to the Minister that is part of your role, we would be very grateful if we could talk to you for ten minutes to take your advice.

The above principles are directed at those making initial contact with the machinery of government. For those who have developed established relationships with any of the sources of information about decision-makers or the decision-makers themselves (having first identified the real power centre in the case of officials) liaison may be more informal, ranging from being able to see Special Advisers, Deputy Secretaries and PPSs at shorter notice and through a telephoned appointment, to a close personal friendship with the Secretary of State. Even under these circumstances it pays to remember the administrative and political pressures on them and the fact that the Prime Minister, Secretaries of State and all other Ministers only infrequently divorce their personal decision-making power from the need to seek corroboration of facts and logistics by referring downwards.

Only if the outsider's relationship with Ministers and Cabinet Office officials is extremely close, and probably not even then, will the proceedings of Cabinet Committees be divulged. Since they are mot officially supposed to exist, members of the Government are expected to exercise the highest level of discretion over whether a Cabinet Committee has discussed an issue and its outcome. There is no ethical reason why outsiders should not ask the officials they contact in a Department whether they have been involved in interdepartmental discussions on an issue through the Cabinet Committee sytem and, if not, who has; but it is unlikely that anything other than a non-committed answer would be given and officials may feel that the outsider is prying excessively. It is better to ask how interdepartmental liaison works on the issue in question without mentioning the Cabinet office and its machinery.

Similarly, it is highly unlikely that a Department's internal memoranda expressing views or advice on an organization, an issue or on legislative formulation would be shown to outsiders unless officials felt there was good reason. It is pointless for you to ask for sight of such documents, which may be used, for example, to brief Ministers or more senior officials and collate views of other Divisions or Departments in advance of legislative or other drafting and on commercial matters.

A decision to allow companies to tender for an allocation of frequencies to operate a new national radio telephone network would involve the Department of Trade and Industry's Radio Regulatory Division, because of the allocation of radio lines; Telecommunications Division; and, following the principle outlined in section 2 (page 94), OFTEL might be called upon to assess tenders and advise the Minister of its decision, subject to policy considerations on which he will be briefed by the two Divisions. OFTEL may appoint a technical consultancy to assist it. The factors behind the form of the call for tenders, the basis of assessment and official opinions on the technical and managerial competence of the tenderers, and the policy reasons that may weigh against the tenderer offering the lowest bidding price and most efficient network scheme are all contained in memoranda that flow between the four components of judgement before the final submission is prepared for the Minister. Sensitive liaison with OFTEL and the Department of Trade and Industry (appreciating that the decision itself is in effect *sub judice*) may discover all or most of those points and increase a tenderer's understanding of the background in which he must present his bid; but he will not be able to obtain the memoranda themselves other than by unethical means.

Parliament is generally open with information, but four sources may present difficulties:

- The Library prepares excellent briefs on a large number of topical subjects for MPs, but they are not available to the public and it is not permitted to contact Library research staff for documents or advice. Outsiders should not write to MPs to ask them to obtain Library briefs on their behalf. Even if an MP is retained as an adviser by an organization (see page 210) this applies; and it is doubly unethical to ask an MP to commission the hard-worked Library staff to produce individual papers ostensibly for that MP but to be passed to an outside body.
- Evidence given before a Select Committee cannot be reproduced verbatim in advance of publication of the Committee's report without its permission (*Weekly Information* details transcripts of evidence released in advance by each Select Committee). Unless outsiders attend the session in which the evidence they seek is given (*Weekly Information* lists witnesses a few days in advance but the Committee's clerks may be able to give more notice), they must contact the witness to ask for permission to see the transcript that will be sent to them by the Committee for correction. Government Departments are unlikely to give that permission. Copies of witnesses' written submissions are often available to the Press in the Committee Room and the Clerk may agree to give outside observers a copy, but he will not release written evidence submitted by those not called as witnesses or supplementary memoranda requested by the Committee to provide information on a point. The Clerk may, however, disclose which bodies have submitted evidence.
- Most All-Party groups may provide lists of their membership to the public, but a substantial number are established and run by outside bodies, some of whom may request that the Group's officers do not

release any details of members or activities. Since this policy may also extend to restricting access by the public to a Group, it is quite wrong that this practice should be allowed. However, while it continues the public must come to terms with it. The practice has led to some strange results: a seminar held for members of the All-Party Pensioners and Retirement groups experienced difficulties because one of the groups, run by a vocational organization for the elderly, was under instructions not to release details of its members. This policy prevailed despite the fact that organization was the leading speaker at the seminar and would have benefited from a larger audience.

- The agenda and proceedings of backbench committees are notified only to MPs of the same Party. Outsiders can learn of backbench committee affairs only by developing a good relationship with the officers (or members, if the committee is Labour, since Labour MPs have to join the groupings that interest them). All Conservative MPs are assumed to be members of all their committees and it is impossible to know, other than through a committee's secretaries, who has attended a meeting.

We have referred to the technique of tabling PQs to obtain otherwise unobtainable information from Departments. When information only is needed, Oral Questions are unnecessary since their purpose is to force a statement from a Minister to the House or publicly to put forward a supplementary that may cause the Minister some embarrassment. The art of drafting their less dramatic partner, Written Questions, may seem simple until it is realized that many are disallowed by the Table Office, the Department of the House that deals with the processing of PQs. Its rules include:

- questions covering more than one Department must be individually tabled to each Department;
- questions must always be addressed to the Secretary of State of the target Department;
- questions on interdepartmental coordination must be addressed to the Minister for the Civil Service (at present, the Prime Minister);
- questions cannot ask a Minister whether he agrees with a particular statement or to state an opinion. They must not be rhetorical;
- separate points should be made in separate PQs. A PQ may, however, ask for information on a number of connected points (for example, details of (a) capital and (b) maintenance expenditure on micro-computers by a Department);
- questions must not refer to a debate in the current Session or criticise a decision of the House. They must not be based on rumour or

unauthenticated reports, and cannot cover State security matters, Government research contracts or commercially sensitive matters.

Since Departments will answer nothing but the question, it must be drafted to ensure officials have no option but to provide the information needed, unless it would cost too much to gather it.

Example a road safety organization is keen to encourage the compulsory fitting of rear seat-belts in cars. The Department of Transport has the task of monitoring compliance with a new Construction and Use Regulation endorsing the organization's lobby. The Organization has been unable to obtain fitting figures or details of compliance from the Department. An MP agrees to table a PQ. It considers two drafts:

1 *To ask the Secretary of State for Transport whether he will make a statement on the number of cars sold in the Uk that were fitted with rear seat-belts in (a) 1987 and (b) 1988; and on compliance with the Construction and Use (Seat-Belts) Order 1988.*

  The request to make a statement could be interpreted by officials as a request for an opinion only. The answer could therefore take the form of 'There has been an appreciable increase in the number of cars fitted with rear seat-belts in 1988 compared with 1987. Police reports indicate that few prosecutions have taken place for non-compliance with the Order.'

  While this answer may slightly exaggerate the starkness with which poorly prepared PQs can be treated, it is not untypical.

2 *To ask the Secretary of State for Transport to state the number of cars sold in the UK that were fitted with rear seat-belts in (a) 1987 and (b) 1988; to list the percentage level of compliance with the Contruction and Use (Seat-Belts) Order 1988 within the past six months; and to make a statement on the operation of the Order.*

  This question is much more specific. Officials have no alternative but to provide the answers needed. The statement may disclose further information as a bonus.

If the matter is genuinely urgent, you may ask an MP to table a priority question for answer within twelve sitting days. The answer will be correspondingly shorter, however. Type your drafts on blank paper, double spaced in all cases.

3.3 Techniques of advocacy

Acquiring information about the activities of Government is the first and most important step towards ensuring that harmony can be established between corporate, group or individual strategies and public policy.

Information should flow both ways, however. Government has a need for information if its policies are not to be formulated in a vacuum or be based on misconceptions. Officials do not wish to jeopardize their position by producing unrepresentative advice to Ministers. MPs do not wish to risk their seats by endorsing the product of that advice. Those who need to deal with Government must provide it with information, and provide it in a proper and timely way if they are to achieve the results they seek.

The need to advocate a case to Government is the second part of the two-way communication that should exist between Government and the governed. Advocacy in this context takes three forms:

- Informing Government about you and shaping the opinions of decision-makers as a means of pre-empting problems or encouraging actions that could benefit you. It means making contact with Government without the immediate aim of policy change – simply initiation of wide-ranging liaison, ensuring that sponsoring officials and legislators are well informed, or just getting a Minister to open a factory.

Information, in this context, must therefore be interpreted broadly, for this area of dealing with officials, Ministers and legislators is aimed at ensuring they understand the operations, interests and concerns of those:

- to whom they are accountable;
- for whom they are responsible;
- in, or against, whose interests they formulate and enact policy or with whom the Government is involved in its commercial strategies.

Work with Government in this area differs here from its pure legal counterpart: unlike the law, advocacy to Government is not just about how to make your case but to whom and when. There is no need for a plaintiff to be known by the judge when he goes to court (although it helps if he understands the mentality of the judge); but it is a great advantage if Government knows and trusts you before you make a case to it. There may be no pressing need to stop Government or to make it do something, but the establishment of rapport between an outside body and those who could affect its interests pays considerable dividends, including the possible elimination of the need to lobby or negotiate with Government at short notice, both involving cost and mutual disruption to your operations and the processes of government.
- Negotiating with Government on contractual matters, concessions of a financial or commercial nature, and legislative or policy change. It is a situation where you are advocate for your own case and Government is the court. You may have counsel facing you – another lobby. It is the opportunity for Government to consider your case and be persuaded to accept or reject it.

It may seem that a fine line exists between making contact with and informing Government, and negotiating with it. The difference is that the latter is concerned with specific objectives; the former may either avoid the need to negotiate or facilitate it by establishing liaison in advance with decision-makers.

- Lobbying Government where it is appropriate to add external pressure to the making of representations to Government. Lobbying is most appropriate where an issue involves strong political or public interest considerations or where negotiation has failed. It can be regarded as the equivalent of the right of appeal or as the final resort on essentially administrative issues.

All three of the above areas of advocacy are different levels of the same skill: the ability to persuade, which, once again, is dependent on:

- *Who you make your case to*: too low a level and your targets will carry little influence; too high and access is difficult or your representations will be passed down to those with sponsoring responsibility for your concerns.
- *When*: too late and the process of policy gestation will have been completed. The power of Parliament may, however, be a determinant in the case of late representations, particularly involving legislation. A small majority may mean that the Government is vulnerable to amendments.
- *How*: meaning the presentation of issues in a form that can be understood and assimilated by the policy-making process; the technique of marshalling support from those who can influence decision-makers; making sure the message gets through; defending a favourable position, or attacking it; the skill of taking legislation through Parliament; and initiating it.

Who to deal with

If the techniques of monitoring and research are intelligently applied, you should be able to identify decision-makers and those who are in a position to influence them. However, in making a case to Government, four further considerations also apply:

- Only experience will tell you how much responsibility and influence officials at particular grades in one Department may have in comparison with their counterparts in another. In certain areas, HEOs and Principals may have the respective power, scope and access of Principals, and Assistant Secretaries in others.
- Contact with a Department by MPs, for example through letters to a Minister, is usually dealt with at a higher grade than similar representations from the public.

- Where the need is to inform Government without specific negotiation on an issue, Parliamentary candidates are an important target, either in your constituency(ies) or nationally, except in seats with a safe majority for the incumbent. Remember, however, that a seemingly safe seat, with a majority of 5000 or more, could still be threatened if there were a general swing against the MP's Party at the next election. Do not ignore candidates.
- Lobbying – the adding of pressure to the making of representations – involves considering further influences on decision-makers than just those components of the structure of central government: the power of the media and public opinion, properly mobilized, are the two most important factors.

Broadly, there are seven categories of target that should be considered:

1 *Ministers* in the Department(s) of greatest interest to you.
2 *Ministerial assistants* – PPSs, who are close to their Minister's thinking and can ensure that information is conveyed to him if there is any risk of emasculation by over-zealous officials; and Special Advisers who, in this context, can perform not only a similar function to PPSs but also act as a ministerial opinion former. In writing many of the more political speeches delivered by Ministers, they also indirectly speak for them.
3 *Officials* – divided between those with sponsoring responsibilities for your main area of operation and those whose work could affect your interests. A group representing small country landowners would possibly liaise first with the Department of the Environment if their greatest concern is over protection of the countryside; but they might also need to establish contact with the Treasury if a long-term aim is to seek changes in the tax treatment of woodland. Having decided on the Departments that need to be contacted, the same procedures in identifying appropriate decision-making Divisions and Branches to obtain information apply here. The level of contact may be at Principal/Assistant Secretary grades, if information about your operations and interests is to be given, or in the Assistant Secretary–Deputy Secretary band if your aim is the forming of opinion that may eventually influence the decision to amend or maintain policy.
4 *MPs* – at constituency level; as Party spokesmen; as members of backbench, Select or All-Party committees; or as identified potential supporters or opponents of your interests (identified by background or by 'on-the-record' opinions expressed in Hansard, the Press, or in letters to you).
5 *Peers* – as members of groups such as Committee on Overseas Trade or the North Atlantic Assembly; or with interests linked to yours – either

declared in debate or from known business connections and career training.
6 *Influential external organizations* – whose advice or representations may shape policy through their exercise of opinion forming and briefing skills; through being involved in departmental advisory committees or through their central role (Party research departments as an example) in the political machinery.
7 *Other ad hoc targets* – such as the Commons Library, which may welcome objective information on a major or topical issue.

Why does Government want to be contacted?

Ministers want to be associated with success. A visit to or other public contact with successful organizations that they sponsor gives them that opportunity. Contact with outsiders that does not involve specific negotiation allows Ministers to explain Government policy to a small group of people, in the case of a private meeting, or nationally, if a major representative function (such as the annual Lord Mayor's Banquet) attracts widespread publicity. And, as mentioned above, they need to receive feedback on their plans and ensure that they obtain information about the concerns of large or representative bodies personally as well as through officials. There must, however, be a definite reason for contacting Ministers; they do not have the time to meet outsiders simply to maintain a relationship.

Ministerial assistants need to be aware of future campaigns that could be directed at turning MPs against their Minister's policies, of views that could influence ministerial speeches or which may not be fully represented to a Minister by his officials in advance of a decision being required of him.

Officials need information. They cannot be confident of the genesis of policy or of its efficient administration without knowing who will benefit or be affected. They are obliged to take a representative range of views into account in formulating policy: inevitably, they turn to the bodies they know but are more confident that they have discharged their duties if other organizations contact them. Sponsoring officials have the task of helping their charges with the solution of problems and the realization, where possible, of Government-related objectives. They must also answer PQs and letters about the industries, pressure groups and issues within their responsibility.

Officials are also cautious by training or nature. It takes time in many cases for them to satisfy themselves of the credentials of outsiders with facts or opinions to offer. The onset of consultation periods may not give them enough time to do that. For them, as well as outsiders, opinion-forming must start before action is needed. The top three grades also benefit from the many informal contacts with outsiders that arise in their representative role, enabling them to take soundings to assist with their advice to Ministers.

At constituency level, MPs need to keep their electorate happy by maintaining contact with organizations in their area and learning about local industry and issues. Most MPs are outgoing by nature and want to know their constituents and understand their problems. They also need to be seen to be meeting constituents; they need publicity, and visits or publicized meetings are usually regarded as useful by them.

In groups or committees, MPs need contact with outsiders if they are to act as informed representatives of backbench opinion on departmental subject matters or if they are to take on a Department or major interest group without being out-argued on points of fact.

Individual MPs need to ensure that the views they express are accurately based. They also take a genuine interest, possibly because of their background, in certain subjects and welcome the opportunity to learn more.

Why should you bother?

- Because advance contact helps to keep policy on track.
- Because it gives decision-makers guidance towards the strategic objectives of outsiders.
- Because it allows Government to secure an understanding of you and your objectives.
- Because it allows you to defuse potential opposition from, or forge friendly relationships with, decision-makers.
- Because it allows you to shape opinions in advance of negotiation.

Contacting your targets

Contact with Government may be impersonal or personal. In the former case, it may be made through letters, submissions, brochures, videos, company publications or the briefing of influential organizations; in the latter through individual or mass meetings, visits, and entertainment. Briefing and opinion-forming must start with personal contact – cold information is treated by most of Government as it would be by you. *Most*, because Westminster, if information is presented properly, will pay attention to relevant facts and opinions – in many cases (for example in response to Green Papers) impersonal contact is the only way for a Department to approach the gathering of information and comment from a wide range of

Box 43 The Independent Retailers Group – informing and opinion forming

The Independent Retailers Group (IRG) represents the collective interests of small shopkeepers to Government, the public and the media. Each year it draws up a strategy of liaison with Government, setting out potential threats to be covered and the policy changes it seeks to benefit its membership. This strategy is constantly reviewed to ensure that IRG's monitoring of potential legislative and policy planning is not ignored and that it can maximize its input to the planning process before policy crystallizes.

This year, IRG's strategy document includes an assessment that action is needed on the following issues:

- Sunday Trading and extended shop hours;
- employment subsidies for small firms;
- rating policy;
- small firm audit requirements;
- conditions of storage and sale of fresh food;
- restrictions on advertising;
- assistance to preserve village shops.

On some of these points, IRG has already built on its intelligent exercise of research and monitoring techniques by contacting its sponsoring Branch in the Department of Trade and Industry and ensuring that the Principal is kept well informed about its concerns, objectives and statistics; and that its annual strategy is discussed with the Assistant Secretary to see where the Department could help to achieve IRG's aims or advise on their chances of success. It meets the Under Secretary in charge of the Division including the retail industry at least twice a year for an exchange of views and will also have developed regular contact with the Department of Employment on small firms policy and training matters. It meets DTI and Department of Employment Ministers around once a quarter and liaises with Special Advisers in both Departments every two months; its size allows it easier access than some to Ministers, who are invariably keen to be informed about developments in an area important to the economy and the comments of groups representing a large number of electors or which has substantial lobby muscle. These meetings give them a warning of sensitivities that should be considered, or of factors that must be taken into account if future policy planning is not to be unrepresentative. These meetings also sow some of the political seeds (the others being with the various Party research departments and with MPs) to add to those planted at policy adviser level that IRG intends to cultivate to ensure either that the policy status quo is maintained or that the case for change can be made, if needed, to a receptive audience.

In requesting ministerial meetings, IRG is conscious of the need only to talk to the Secretary of State on broad issues or those he has brought into his own portfolio of specific responsibilities. Otherwise, their copy of the Cabinet Office's *Ministerial*

Cont.

Box 43 (*Cont.*)

> *Responsibilities* gives them all the guidance they need on which Minister to approach on particular matters.
>
> The IRG meets each backbench committee that covers its interests on both sides of the Commons (Trade and Industry, Home Affairs, Employment, Finance and others); and maintains contact with members of the same Select Committees, with Opposition spokesmen and with the All-Party Retail Group. It seeks to ensure that all MPs know they can contact it for information about small shops and that it can gauge parliamentary reaction to its strategy and to current Government policy planning as well as keep abreast of investigations, rising stars and changes in the composition of committees and groups.
>
> The IRG prefaces specific action on its annual strategy by adding to its list of developed targets the officials and MPs who would either be responsible for handling policy or who might actively support or block its progress. In the former case, the *Civil Service Yearbook* and a few enquiries of their sponsoring officials gives them the information they need; in the latter, scanning debates and PQs, as well as reports from members' liaison with MPs at constituency level, gives them some idea; discussions with the officers of relevant backbench and All-Party groups tells them more. Officials occasionally give them help in identifying PQs going back over a year, since it would otherwise take many hours to read through Hansard.
>
> With members in every constituency, IRG has no trouble in contacting legislators; and the officials it contacts rarely reject the opportunity of a meeting if it may contribute to their understanding of the issues that could be developed into a campaign, backed by other components of the decision-making process, that would be aimed at their Division.
>
> The time spent by IRG on all this activity is worthwhile for three reasons:
> - It develops trust among decision-makers and influencers. It is important that they are familiar with an organization before it has to make demands of them.
> - It allows IRG to establish its existence, aims and concerns without having to press a specific case.
> - It means that when IRG tackles the issues above, it can do so from an informed base: not just about the Government's own policy plans – their use of standard research and monitoring techniques has taken care of that – but also a knowledge of the extent of receptiveness to its own aims that has been built up in the key decision-making areas of the system as a result of IRG's opinion-forming programme.

sources. MPs also pay regard to a volume of letters from their constituents on an issue, even if they suspect that the letters have been deliberately orchestrated, if they feel that ignoring the impersonal representations of constituents could make them unpopular.

We will assume that all contact that may so far have been made for information-gathering purposes has been impersonal. The need now is to secure access, convey your message properly and ensure that the relationships you develop are maintained.

Personal contact. Having decided whom you need to inform – through research, monitoring, and an understanding of those whose responsibilities and interests could impinge on your own; having also decided on your objectives in dealing with Government, your need is then to approach your targets in the right way and at the right time.

Ministers must always be contacted direct, but that contact can be reinforced by their departmental advisers and by supportive MPs.

Whether you want to meet a Minister in his Department, invite him to address a conference or lunch or visit your organization, the first step is to ring Ministerial Enquiries in his Department and ask for his Diary Secretary. Explain who you are and who you represent. State that you will be writing to the Minister for an appointment/to invite him to your function/to invite him to visit you, etc. To avoid a clash of dates, you are trying to find out whether the Minister would in principle be free before you send a formal request. If a visit outside London (or, if the Welsh, Scottish or Northern Ireland Offices are being contacted, Cardiff/Edinburgh/Belfast) is part of your plan, it also helps to ask whether the Minister is planning a tour of your area.

The Diary Secretary will usually ask you to put your request in writing before any judgement can be made on the available space in the Minister's diary. This puts the advantage on his side because it is much easier for the Minister to claim a full list of engagements if he is advised against accepting your request or because he personally does not want to meet you. However, if the Diary Secretary agrees that a particular date might be free, you should then write as follows:

The Rt Hon Jack Smith MP[1]
Department of Environment
2 Marsham Street
London SW1P 3EB

Dear Mr Smith[2]

We are writing following our conversation with your private office to confirm[3] our request for a short meeting[4] to present and discuss the research our organization,[5] which is involved in commercial construction, has carried out on urban renewal. Having liaised in detail with Inner Cities Branch[6] (1/2/3 etc) we feel that the conclusions of the research have significant implications for current policy development and for any decisions that may be required on infrastructure development.[7]

We would be grateful for any time that you could give us in order that we may add to your understanding of this issue.

Yours sincerely

Notes
1. Pay careful attention to form of address. *Dod* lists titles – all Cabinet Ministers become Privy Councillors and are allowed to add the Right Honourable prefix. Papers should be consulted for changes in Queen's Birthday and New Years Honours lists, which include knighthoods and peerages for MPs. Ministers in the Welsh, Scottish or Northern Ireland Office can be addressed in London or in Cardiff, Edinburgh or Belfast.
2. A Minister can either be addressed by name or as 'Dear Secretary of State/Minister'. There are five exceptions: Dear Prime Minister/Chancellor/Home Secretary/Foreign Secretary/and the Minister of Agriculture (who is addressed as Minister).
3. Shows that contact has already been made. If you wish to meet the Minister on a specific date and have been able tentatively to clear that date with the Diary Secretary, mention it at this point.
4. All meetings should be short – in intention at least. Ministers rarely have more than 45 minutes unless the matter is very important; however, two hours for a visit outside the Department is considered quite acceptable. In the latter case, remember that he may have four factories in a wide geographical area to visit in one day.
5. Tell the Private Office – which handles all mail addressed to the Minister – who you are.
6. Helps to assess relevance. It shows the Private Office that there is no point in telling you to start at square one because you have already liaised properly with the officials responsible for inner cities. A meeting with a Minister should be the culmination, not the starting point, of contact with Government on an issue. Do not say you have met the relevant officials if you have not done so – they will see your correspondence as a matter of course.
7. Relate the purpose of the meeting to the Department's considerations – helping them to obtain a better understanding of a key issue.

The letter also shows an important point – contact with Ministers cannot just be a familiarization exercise. It must be specific and therefore must bridge the gap between the imparting of general views and the realization of definite aims. Some bodies (the TUC and CBI, for example) meet Ministers within an institutionalized framework for wide-ranging talks, but the rest of the electorate must follow the normal rules.

If no reply is received within ten days (remember that Private Offices get many letters each day) telephone any of the Private Secretaries to the Minister and find out what has happened to your letter. Influence on the Minister to accept or not can also come from the officials sponsoring the issue or organization; the Minister's PPS and Special Adviser; or your constituency MP. Since you should have liaised with the relevant officials first, they should be told of your wish to see the Minister and asked to support your request. They will have to produce a brief for the meeting – more work – or may therefore be disinclined to agree that a meeting is necessary. If so, you can write to your constituency MP explaining your need to meet the Minister and asking him whether he could be approached on your behalf. This method of applying pressure is particularly relevant where your need is for the Minister to visit you. Keep the letter to your MP to one page – a universal rule in writing to MPs. Ministers are more likely to accept a request for a meeting from an MP, particularly if he agrees to accompany you.

If your request is for a visit to your constituency, it is in the MP's interests to support you, if he is on the Government side, because the visit will generate publicity for him if he is there; if he is not a member of the Government Party, he would be more inclined to stress the Minister's responsibility to the area or to the subject of your interests. Remember that antagonism between the parties is more apparent than real. Ministers may have a very good relationship with the Opposition.

As an alternative, the same process could be followed with the Minister's PPS or Special Adviser, who may be more receptive to your needs than Private Office or Branch officials. A direct approach to the Minister's political advisers may help to ensure that the Minister, rather than his assistants, makes the decision to see you or not.

These techniques cannot, of course, guarantee success, but they will improve your chances.

Special Advisers and PPSs should both be approached in the same way: on the basis that you are involved in a number of sponsored areas falling within their Minister's responsibilities and would be grateful for the opportunity to brief them as part of a programme of ensuring that all levels of the Department are informed. With PPSs, it helps to mention that the issues of concern to you will or may form the basis of forthcoming legislation – your contact with officials should give you an indication – or that you will be, or have been dealing with a number of MPs on those subjects.

Officials – it is not usual for senior officials to accept a request for a meeting until outsiders have first discussed the issue with their specialist staff at Principal and Assistant Secretary level. An exception to this is an invitation to address a meeting or attend a particular event. Contact can be made by telephone or letter, although many officials prefer to receive details about organizations and their problems or statistics by letter before responding with an appointment. Any first contact letter or call should follow the standard procedure of stating:

- who you are;
- their relevance to you, either as sponsoring official or because their branch handles issues affecting your interests;
- why you want to see them. If your organization is small and little known, you will have to give a reason. Expect parts of the Department of Trade and Industry, Department of the Environment or Department of

Transport to refer you to their regional offices, which are run by Under Secretaries, in your area.

It is better not to invite senior officials to visit you without having met them first, unless you are contacting regional offices of Departments, where there may be a less formal atmosphere.

MPs and Peers cannot be contacted initially direct by telephone. You should write to them at the House of Commons/Lords, stating the reason for writing at the start (for example, 'As an organization in your constituency employing $X00$ people concerned with Y', or 'Our company produces economic forecasting software. We would like to meet you in your role as Secretary of the backbench Finance Committee to discuss developments in the Treasury model which we feel would be of future value to your Committee'. A variation on the second example would be 'since you have shown an interest in high technology/Treasury affairs (etc.) to show how the Treasury model may now be inaccurate/how MPs, the City and business can now access forecasts for the UK Economy (etc.)'). If you are writing to your constituency MP, you should ask for a meeting either in London or in his constituency: if others are your targets, then meet them only in London unless it is important and relevant that a committee or grouping should visit you or attend an event outside the Palace of Westminster. If a meeting is required with a Select or Labour backbench committee, write to the Chairman. If you wish to contact a Conservative or All-Party committee, either the Secretary or Chairman can be approached.

If you are writing to a number of MPs and Peers to arrange a meeting or visit, make the letters as personal as possible – MPs, as mentioned on page 102, are wary of mass-produced letters and may share secretaries who may give identical circulars a lower priority in presenting them to their boss. Constituency mail is the most important item for any MP and it is preferable that an invitation for a visit should be sent to a constituency MP by companies or organizations in that constituency, not by a parent or umbrella organization. You should also include items of information about them gained from your research material to show that you have taken the trouble to write to them, not to MPs or Peers as a whole. If their position on committees or past training, for example, is of relevance to your concerns, say so. Before requesting a meeting with a group of MPs or Peers, despite your feeling that their interests are close to the issues you want to discuss, it helps to meet one of them (for instance, the Secretary of a backbench committee) to ensure that the request would evoke a positive response. While you may be deeply concerned about particular matters or may be in no doubt of the importance of your organization to Parliamentary affairs, those who work there may be less convinced. Your desire to make contact with decision-makers or influencers is competing with many others for the attention of MPs and, to a lesser extent, Peers.

Impersonal contact. It may only be possible to make contact with Government impersonally to deliver your message. You may be based too far from Westminster or Whitehall to do any more than meet your constituency MP. You may be too busy to allocate the time needed to meet your targets – although that may be a false economy. Or you may prefer not to commit yourself too far beyond ensuring that you are well informed.

Whatever form of communication with your targets that is chosen – letters, brochures, company or organization news sheets, recorded material or advertising and publicity – the following should be considered.

If you seek to make identified targets aware of your existence and views by letter, it must be written – or appear to be written – for them and them alone. Clearly, there is no point – and it is also discourteous – to send a circular to Ministers, whose Private Office will pay little attention to an issue that is not part of their Minister's responsibilities. If you are seeking to put forward views to all Cabinet Ministers on a major public spending issue in the hope that they will support your position, only personal contact can help since there is a tendency for all letters not directed at the Treasury or the Department in question to be diverted to them and, as has been suggested in section 2 of this book, the influence of third-party Ministers on the Cabinet or Cabinet Committees is limited. If letters to those third parties are to have any effect, they must highlight the strong and direct relevance of your views to their Department and to them. Thus, the VAT on books case discussed earlier (page 25) would have involved its campaigners in contacting Cabinet Ministers other than those in the Treasury, Department of Education and Department of Trade and Industry. In doing so, they will have referred to the specific effect that VAT on books would have had on employment in bookselling and publishing; on education in Northern Ireland, Wales and Scotland; and to the need for the implications the campaign had identified for those Ministers to be represented by them to their Treasury colleagues.

There is no point, on the same principle, in contacting officials as a group since any circular would either be too imprecise to be of any interest or would be sent by other officials to the relevant Branch. It is possible to copy to the Under Secretary at the head of a Division a letter sent to one of his Branches, but it is wise to ensure that the Branch is aware of your action. There is no point either in trying to make contact with senior officials over the heads of their subordinates, if for example you are not making satisfactory progress with negotiations at Branch level, and hoping that you can do so without the Branch knowing since it is normal for them to see any letter or minute of a conversation that concerns them.

It is even more important to satisfy officials and MPs of your bona fides if impersonal contact is made. They must therefore know who you are, your relevance to their area of policy responsibility, why you are contacting them, and what you want from them (if your contact is not simply to give them information).

Consider the volume of material that can be assimilated by your targets. With MPs or Peers, observe the same rule that Churchill laid down in the War: the information should be set out in one page unless the reader has a strong or specialist interest in the issue or the material has strong visual impact. Given that an MP may easily receive 70 letters, internal circulars and telephone messages each day, and in most cases has only his secretary to assist him, information that does not make its mark within a few lines is more than likely to be thrown away. Information must also be presented objectively: the annual report, company newsletter or detailed research statistics that fascinate you will be unlikely to interest any legislator or Minister for whom you and your cause is one of many. Even with civil servants, it helps to highlight relevant pages or passages in lengthy documents (Departments, because they are divided into specific sections, can handle more detailed information) since they may be required to summarize them for more senior officials or Ministers or because they are likely to think better of you and your case if they are given the feeling that you understand the pressures on them and the way in which they have to work.

MPs commonly send letters from outsiders to Departments for reply. This gets them off the hook, giving them a response on minsterial letterhead that impresses some but is unlikely to help. It is better to state clearly that your letter is designed as a brief for the MP only, not for the Department, and that if he accepts your case you will happily draft a letter or brief for him to be sent to the Minister in his own name. Remember that there is a big difference between an MP agreeing to send your letter as a brief to Ministers and committing himself to argue your case. MPs as mere postboxes are usually ignored by Whitehall.

Refresher

To take stock at this stage:

- You have decided on your objectives in working with Government.
- You have established a monitoring system and/or have researched into current and likely future policy in the areas of interest to you.

- You have identified those who either make or influence decisions in Government that could affect you.
- You have precisely and concisely contacted your targets with the aim of making your existence known and of building familiarity between you and them.
- You have developed an understanding of the working practices and considerations – administrative and political – of the power structure and have thought carefully, in contacting elements of it, about the most effective way of selling your organization and ideas to them.

Now ask yourself again, and keep asking yourself:

- Do our targets really have the power to help or damage us?
- What do we want from them?
- Can they give it to us?
- How would we react to our approaches if we were a disinterested MP or an official who had not met us and who may have strong policy reasons for opposing our views?

The last of these refresher questions is of greatest importance in considering the next step to be covered, that of meeting your targets. The MPs and officials who assisted with the preparation of this book were unanimous in their advice that too many organizations wishing to deal with Government fail to ask themselves why, in objective terms, they or their case is important not to *them* but to *their* targets. As pointed out earlier, working the system of Government is no different from trying to win a case in court – *their* procedures, rules of advocacy and susceptibilities must be followed, not *yours*.

Meeting your targets

Form and timing. Before considering the next step, should the Minister, official, adviser, Peer or MP you have contacted agree to meet you, the form of contact must be considered. You may seek a meeting pure and simple; a discussion over lunch or dinner; an invitation to your reception or to address your formal dinner; or agreement to visit a factory or project. Bear in mind the following:

- Do not invite ministers to a private lunch or dinner unless you are very well acquainted with them. If they are invited to a reception, a representative lunch/dinner or visit, they must be the guest of honour unless senior Royalty is to be present. Even then, they may not agree to share top billing.

- Consider carefully the level of Minister with whom you wish to make contact. Study their responsibilities and tailor their position to the need you have. If you are organizing a major representative function for an industry or important policy area, the Secretary of State can be invited. Otherwise, approach the Minister whose designated responsibilities fit specifically with the subject of function. Your size is important – Rover is more likely to get the Secretary of State for Trade and Industry to open a new plant than is a small machine tools factory far from London or the Minister's constituency unless the latter has an outstanding growth/ export record as a result of the favourable effects of Government policy, or is in receipt of public funds, or because it produces something of key importance to a policy area. The Secretary of State and, in some cases, Ministers of State will often pass down the line invitations if they are wrongly targeted or if they simply do not wish to accept. Junior Ministers, unless advised to attend by their superiors, may not react favourably to being considered a fall-back. It is therefore important to consult with the Private Office of the Secretary of State if in doubt on who should be approached.
- Principals or Assistant Secretaries should not be entertained until a relationship of trust has been developed. They may be invited to larger receptions and visits through cold contact. More senior officials can be invited to lunches provided they are not the only guest and if it is for a purpose related to their responsibilities.
- Members of Parliament receive many invitations to lunch or dinner. Most Conservatives in particular could be fed for free throughout the day for the rest of their Parliamentary career. They prefer information to be imparted in ten minutes rather than two hours. However, they can be invited for entertainment on first contact and there is no doubt that two hours of conversation can forge a stronger link than even the clearest and most concise imparting of information. Peers are less lobbied than their counterparts and may have fewer demands on their time. Both sets of legislators are more likely to respond if the entertainment you plan is for a linked group of legislators such as a backbench committee.
- For events outside the House such as visits to your company, organization or project, or for organized presentations of information to your targets, bear in mind the daily, weekly and annual timetables of legislators. Members of Parliament should be seen in their constituency only on Fridays and Saturdays. (Some stay in London on Fridays, restricting their time in their constituency to one available day a week. Even then, their Constituency Agent may hear constituents' grievances if the MP wishes to be elsewhere. This is particularly the case in large constituencies.) The rest of the time, he must be met in London unless your liaison with him

would involve a fact-finding foreign visit or an organized excursion. Peers may spend less time in London and only come up for debated matters affecting them. Do not try to see MPs during Prime Minister's Question Time or on a day when other questions are being answered in which they are known to have a specific interest. The Order Paper and Weekly information will give you advance notice, and a chart listing the subjects to be handled at each Question Time for several weeks ahead is available from the Sales Office in the House of Commons. The Order Paper for the Lords gives similar notice of the four Oral Questions to be answered each day in any week. The 1922 Committee and PLP meetings are attended by many MPs and should be avoided as a meeting time. Remember also, in the case of legislators, that their working hours stretch into the late evening; be prepared to meet them after 6 pm since their day is only half finished when most people leave work. There are fewer restrictions for Ministers and officials, except that it is not easy to meet the Minister you may have targeted in the period immediately following the end of the parliamentary year because most Ministers take a long holiday in August, leaving only one or two of their colleagues on duty in their Departments.

- It is very difficult to see Ministers, MPs and Peers at short notice. You should plan at least three weeks to one month ahead for Ministers and two weeks at least for MPs. Special Advisers, the Policy Unit and officials may be more flexible but you should expect all of them to have a heavy workload and realize that others are competing for their available time.
- Meetings with Ministers should almost always be regarded as the culmination of representations and discussions at official level unless you are being blocked as the issue is a political or party matter. In 90 per cent of cases do not contact Ministers first.
- Unless your invitation is dedicated or it is objectively attractive, the response is likely to fail in direct proportion to the distance your targets will have to travel from Westminster, Whitehall or their regional office and the length of time it would take to get to your venue.
- Consider the value of entertainment, whether it is a briefing lunch, reception, function at the Party conferences or sponsored visit. Does the expenditure justify the possible benefit? How important will those targets be to your objectives? Forget about the fact that some of the names are well-known – how much power do they have? As a rule, entertain sparingly – not with legislators after your first contact unless the cost–benefit is objectively good or unless it would take more time to convey the same message to a series of MPs or Peers than it would to entertain them collectively. Officials are generally more cautious about such invitations because they are bound to resist any attempt to influence them other than with factoral argument. Project teams working on procurement contracts

may also refuse the opportunity of a sponsored visit to acquire facts unless the Government pays their fare.

Strategy. Ministers may keep you waiting for a few minutes before your meeting with them as their oficials will usually take them through the two page brief that has been prepared as an *aide-mémoire.* Your 45 minute allocation may therefore be cut to 35. The production of these briefs shows the importance of contact with officials before any ministerial meeting takes place. There is no point in trying to take them or the Minister by surprise since it will only involve more explanation. When meeting officials in advance, therefore, tell them what you intend to say and give them all the information on you and your organization that they have not already got and which they could find pertinent in briefing the Minister.

The meeting will be held in the Minister's office. He will be accompanied by his Private Secretary to take the minutes – for corroboration of statements made as much as anything else: another reason for them listening to and noting all ministerial telephone conversations with outsiders – and by at least the relevant Principal, probably an Assistant Secretary as well and, if it is a large or important delegation that is meeting the Minister, an Under Secretary or higher. You should also be accompanied if possible in order that your notes can be corroborated if necessary.

When meeting a Minister, he may be addressed as 'Secretary of State', 'Minister', or by his name. Ministers are good listeners, like most MPs. The onus will be on you to lead the meeting, but give the Minister the option: either that you should make a few brief remarks which he can question or respond to; or that he can interrupt as he desires. In either case state your identity and interests unless it is self-evident since you cannot assume that the Minister has read his brief. Reiterate the reason for seeing him and say what you have to. Do not recite reams of statistics; keep the message simple and relate to his concerns and political sensitivities – this again is why it is so important to establish contact with those close to the Minister who can advise on his likely reactions to your interests in advance of your meeting, which should be the culmination of all those contacts.

Your aim should be to leave the Minister with two or three points that give him a clear impression of you and your interests. You should question him by asking him to comment on your views: can action be taken (or not, depending on your objectives)? Would he like more detail if he is interested in your proposition? (If he agrees, do not delay in submitting additional views or research to him and his officials – with the amount of paper in his Red Boxes and on their desks, matters that are of interest today can be almost forgotten next month and they are very unlikely to press you for the material you promised to provide.) Your meeting must not, therefore, be left hanging. The Minister must receive definite information about your concerns and interests; you must expect comment from him.

Immediately following the meeting, write to thank the Minister and remind him of comments made by him that help you or of a commitment on your part. If you believe that it would be worthwhile to meet him regularly and you are of sufficient representative size or your work is of sufficient importance, then say in your letter that 'it would be most helpful if we could meet again once you have considered this new information/in six months' time (etc.) to review progress' or suchlike.

If the Minister is to address a function, it is most important that his Private Office receives full information on the guests who will be present and on the precise timing of everything he is expected to do. They need to know who will meet him at the door and to whom he will be introduced. Will other speeches be made, and by whom? Officials in the relevant Branch should be briefed on the subject matter of the function for two reasons: they make input to his speech and produce a brief for the occasion, on you and the policy areas involved in the event; and, if it is a visit, because the Minister may bring one of the Branch Principals – even if no invitation has been extended – it is therefore courteous and sensible to invite the officials yourself.

If a representative body is being visited and the occasion will be publicized, the Minister may make an important speech (see A visit to Associated British Airports – page 81), and it would be helpful to consult his Special Adviser, who may help with the speech and who can add to the judgement of officials on whether the Minister intends to say something important to your, or a wider audience.

Officials should again be met in their Department (not necessarily in London, because of the number of Department of Trade and Industry/Environment/Transport regional offices and the dispersion of technical advisers in Departments such as the Ministry of Agriculture to rural offices) with a time limit of one hour. A first meeting is essentially a familiarization exercise, combining a description of your organization, its activities and objectives – policy or commercial – with a request for information from officials about how your objectives fit into their policy plans. Always ask how you can help them by providing information and suggest that they may wish to visit you or receive a demonstration of your technology or other work. The more understanding you show of what officials can and cannot do or say, the easier it will be. For example, do not ask them to make decisions on policy: they will only say that they cannot assess what the Minister will do. But they will often add their supposition – usually a very educated guess – as a rider.

If your aim is primary or secondary legislation, Circulars or other concrete action, ensure that it is feasible before mentioning it. Ensure that officials understand that you are aware of the case against yours so that they may feel you have thought through your strategy carefully. However detailed your discussion of objectives may be in subsequent meetings, your first contact will aim to establish your credentials and assess the calibre and outline views of the officials affecting your interests.

Visits by officials need not be as structured as those of their political masters, but they must be worthwhile for them. Your visitors must therefore be given briefings and have the opportunity to have all their questions answered. At the same time, such visits should be organized to make a point, for example, the need for change in the funding of research. If your first contact with your official targets will be at an event such as a factory opening or reception, ensure that someone is deputed to look after them and fulfil the same objective as an initial meeting in their Department.

The rule of thumb in liaising with officials on the first and subsequent occasions is to treat them exactly as you would treat stockbrokers' analysts – as people whose actions can affect your concerns, who corroborate the information you give them, whose judgement determines their future as well as yours and who therefore will do you no favours, and who should be treated with respect. They deserve the same amount of trouble and expense that organizations would take over liaison with those analysts.

Officials must be approached sensitively. Start from the assumption that civil servants can themselves do nothing. A typical professional request is therefore couched gently: 'Is there anything that can be done to take these views into account; and is there any more information we can give you to clarify those views?' Do not press your views on them or seek action too quickly – build the relationship as a company would with a prospective client: the soft sell.

Again, a first meeting should be concluded with an arrangement on how both sides may wish to progress: it may be that giving your targets information at that initial encounter is enough and the principles of getting information could apply thereafter with informal telephone contact; or there could be regular meetings.

Constituency MPs can be met either at your organization, at his constituency surgery – but only if there is an immediate problem to be solved – or in the House of Commons. If the latter is most mutually convenient, arrive in good time since it may take some time to pass through the security check, particularly in Summer (tourists) and on Tuesday and Thursday afternoons (Prime Minister's Question Time). Expect your MP to be late, since he may have had a number of appointments before yours, and do not take up more than half an hour of his time. Even if his majority is safe, he is likely to make a special effort to see you unless your organization has political objectives strongly at variance with his own views. Most MPs, however, are apolitical on constituency matters – the welfare of their constituents is their only concern and a Conservative will make as strong a series of representations to a Minister on local unemployment as a Labour MP. Do not, however, turn up unannounced: always confirm your arrangement with your MP's secretary in advance.

Your first meeting with your constituency MP is to tell him about you: your size; who and what you represent; what you do; your investment plans; the state of your market; whether you have been affected by policy in any area, for example retraining, and your views. And the ubiquitous offer of help with any information he may need. If he is a Labour MP, meet him with representatives of your workforce if you are a company. Again, keep emotion out of your message: his job is hard enough without having to rely on exaggerated facts. These first meetings are particularly useful to constituency MPs if legislation that could have local implications is imminent, for example a Bill to control the supply of animal feedstuffs if he represents a rural area. He needs to know that he has a reliable source of contact on subjects of mutual interest. There is no need to arrange subsequent meetings, but try to see your MP twice a year. Ignore recesses – with the exception of a holiday at the end of the Session, MPs are available all year round and are more accessible in their constituency when Parliament is not sitting.

With constituency MPs, as with all other legislators, no attempt should be made to pressure them except by reasoned argument and appeal to their sense of political expediency. It would be quite wrong to threaten to vote against them if they do not accept your objectives. As counselled earlier, treat Government as a court and MPs as you would judges.

If your first meeting with an MP takes place in his constituency, you may wish to publicize the event. He will usually be delighted since coverage in the local press registers his presence in the area.

With issue-based individuals or groups of MPs and Peers, your approach to an initial meeting will be dictated by the reasons given in your introductory letter. Those reasons must be related to the interests and powers and duties of your targets, not to your more general concerns. You must be able to answer 'What's in it for them' satisfactorily before the meeting takes place. Is the information you wish to convey likely to tell them anything they do not already know? What is so important or different about your organization? If you can positively answer those questions then proceed on the basis of concise information communicated on the assumption that even specialists have less knowledge about your activities or problems than yourselves and should not be blinded with jargon or detail – you should see your presentation from their point of view and remember that, as mentioned above, they may have had six other meetings that day, do not know you and may not be immediately sympathetic to your views. Your information can only be registered if the message is simple and delivered with an understanding of why they should be hearing it.

Do not be scared to ask MPs for advice on others whom they know have similar or opposing interests to your own, or for guidance on the action you might take to progress your Government-related strategies. Bear in mind, however, that legislators are inclined to gear their advice to a parliamentary-based course of representations, given their affiliation to their own component of Government. Only Whips, PPSs, former Ministers and a small handful of other MPs have first-hand experience of the internal decision-making machinery of Government Departments.

So your first meeting should be based on the impression of offering help to MPs and Peers while conveying or seeking information or advice and canvassing their support or help. Subsequently, once your targets are aware of your objectives and how you see their role, you may be more direct. However, remember that they are busy and if your case can be made in ten minutes, do not take up more time by considering entertainment that may be more attractive to you than to them. No meeting with an MP or Peer need take more than 45 minutes unless a visit or a detailed seminar for them is planned.

With candidates, access and approach can be both easier and more direct. They need your vote and therefore welcome the opportunity to explain their views and hear your demands. Meet them in your constituency and contact them every three of four months since promises are easily forgotten. As with sitting MPs, however, they are likely simply to follow their Party line in responding to representations on matters, even from constituents, that do not relate directly to the constituency and in which they have little direct personal interest.

Having met your targets, do not abuse the access that exercise of these initial contact techniques may give you. Liaison with officials can be maintained on the Getting Information basis (chapter 3.2) between meetings to inform them. Legislators should be contacted again well in advance of the implementation of a strategy of specific representations to Government that will involve Parliament. The aim is to form opinions: to ensure that Government supports your organization or industry and the aims of either, or that it does not adversely affect, through misinformed comment or policy discussion, the activities of your organization. You must seek to avoid the risk of, for example, widely reported speeches or Oral Parliamentary Questions that criticize the safety of your products or your practices and which could cause loss of revenue, membership or confidence in you.

Producing briefs and submissions

Well-presented written information coupled with oral submissions are the two keys to successful advocacy to Government. Legislators need written briefs as *aides-mémoires* for speeches in the Lords or Commons Chambers; in committee, either as a background to Select Committee questioning sessions or to propose or attack amendments to legislation; and to enable them to grasp an issue before deciding whether to support or oppose any case put to them. Officials need them in order to provide balanced information to Ministers, to compile statistics and to provide a concrete manifestation of the views of outsiders on policy. Ministerial political advisers need to ensure they are kept informed on matters on which they could be consulted.

Briefs to all components of Government must be totally clear, as short as possible, and as dispassionate as possible. They must include some or all of the following points:

- who you are;
- why you are submitting it: for example, in response to a Green Paper's call for comments. Always state both your connection with the issue and/or your motive;
- an analysis of current legislation/policy, with its defects;
- your case – what you want,
  - why you want it,
  - a rebuttal of the case against yours;
- cost/benefit and time-scale required to implement your proposal;
- the action required to progress your case.

They must not, even on emotive issues, be couched in emotive prose: let the facts speak for themselves. They must not contain unsupported statements: source all facts and bear in mind that expressions such as 'X will lead to catastrophic unemployment' will be impeached or ignored unless you produce the information to corroborate them.

Box 44 Writing to MPs

> When you write to MPs, your letter or brief will almost always be filed. If you write in the future, the MP's secretary will have to retrieve your earlier correspondence for him. In order to make her life easier, attach copies of previous papers or letters to which you may refer and, where appropriate, remind him of his response to your past representations unless he is known to be very familiar with you and your cause.

They must be capable of being assimilated quickly by legislators and Ministers and, in briefs to officials, they must show an understanding of the realistic limits of policy planning.

In addition to the above principles, pay attention to the separate considerations of legislators, officials and Ministers. MPs and Peers, on receiving a brief, will ask:

- Does it affect my constituency?
- If not, does it relate to my training/interests/party sensitivities?
- How *representative* and *accurate* is the advocate and brief?
- What is being required of me?

even if you have met them and have already explained your case. Unless briefs are handed to the MP or Peer personally, they should be delivered with a covering letter. Unless the brief is sent from a body in an MP's constituency, it helps to head both letter and brief with the subject being raised in order to present the issue immediately. If that subject is legislation being considered by Parliament, include the stage and sections concerned in the heading. For example:

The Viscount Walmer
House of Lords
London SW1A 0AA

Dear Lord Walmer,

Civil Aviation Bill – Committee Stage, 11th February, Airport landing charges

The Airline Passengers' Group, which represents the interests of air travellers, is concerned over the landing charges provisions of clauses 18–19 of the Civil Aviation Bill.

In view of your speech at Second Reading[1], we hope that you will be present at Committee Stage and that the views of the attached short brief may be persuasive to you. If so, we would be grateful for the opportunity to present an amendment (also attached) for tabling.

Should you require more information, please contact us. We look forward to your response to our case and will be present at committee stage should it be helpful.[2]

Notes
1 Your study of Hansard will have indicated who spoke at Second Reading.
2 Telling an MP or Peer that you will be in the chamber or, better, in the committee room to hear them move or support your amendment is a good idea: they cannot duck the issue in front of you if they have promised to help you.

Box 45 Briefing legislators

The Country Landowners Association sent this brief to a selected list of MPs, arriving three days before Second Reading of the Agriculture Bill in 1985. It is clear, concise, and correctly tailored to the rules of Second Reading (see page 65)

―――――― COUNTRY LANDOWNERS ASSOCIATION ――――――
AGRICULTURE BILL

SECOND READING: HOUSE OF COMMONS: MONDAY 25 NOVEMBER 1985

The Power to Charge for Advisory Services (Clause 1): The CLA objects to the provision enabling a charge to be imposed for advice on conservation. This is contrary to the spirit of the Wildlife and Countryside Act 1981 and contrary to the Minister's Written Answer (Hansard, 7 November 1985 Col 7) when he stated that the Government "do not however have any plans to introduce charges for the kind of advice now provided to farmers free of charge on conservation". There is a vital need to encourage conservation and the CLA feels strongly that MAFF should be seen to be playing its part by providing this most necessary advice free of charge. However, we welcome the Government's commitment to give advice on the diversification of rural enterprises as, while the ADAS socio-economic advisers are already there to proffer such advice, a greater emphasis should be given to this work.

Capital Grants: We would like to see a new Clause in this Bill empowering MAFF to provide capital grants for diversification of farm businesses. In our view, the Government should be encouraging such diversification. We feel that this Bill presents a good opportunity to broaden the definition of agriculture so that it encompasses all those activities set out in Clause 1(1)(a).

Home-Grown Cereals Authority Research (Clauses 4(5) and 5): The CLA is concerned that the levy which the HGCA is empowered to impose (Clause 5) might be expected to

Cont.

Box 45 (*Cont.*)

cover the full research costs of fulfilling the Authority's non-trading functions described in Clause 4(5)(b). We see it as vitally necessary that considerable research resources are devoted to funding new uses and processes for cereals and straw. Government funding must be both continued and increased, to avoid the risk of the HGCA having to fund the total research costs out of levies envisaged by Clause 5.

Environmentally Sensitive Areas (Clause 9): CLA finds this Clause worrying. It seems likely from its wording and from what it leaves to subsidiary legislation that an ESA might end up as prohibitive as an SSSI, or even more so, but without the benefit of the procedures and safeguards laid down in the Wildlife and Countryside legislation. The vagueness of Clause 9(1) contrasts with the detailed and restrictive provisions of 9(5).

We are particularly concerned at the apparent one-sidedness of 9(4), in that the Minister "may make an agreement with any person having an interest in" the land. We would much prefer to see power to offer to enter into an agreement and make provisions as to its terms. Above all, if the terms of the agreement are to be binding on successors in title (9(7)), there must be much more detailed provision to cover the position of the owner of the land.

If such detail as there is in Clause 9 is justified in the primary legislation, let there be more detail as to the voluntary nature of agreement procedures and as to the safeguards for the landowner.

For further information, please contact Susan Bell or William de Salis.

SUSAN BELL
JONATHAN CHEAL
Country Landowners Association
16 Belgrave Square
London SW1X 8PQ

Tel: 01-235-0511

21 November 1985

This letter is short, but says all that is needed. The attached brief should be arranged in a series of numbered points and should not exceed two pages (for MPs, one page). It can be written in an abbreviated form as long as it is clear. In this case, the brief must cover the basis of the clauses in question (you must liaise with the relevant Department for this information) and *either* the reason why they will not achieve their objective *or* the objections to that objective or the means of achieving it.

In aggreeing to table a Parliamentary Question, particularly one for oral answer, some MPs and Peers may request a brief. In the case of written PQs, this should include a justification for seeking the information required and the case it is meant to support. This can normally be summarized in a few lines. Oral Questions require the questioner to play the same game of Battleships as the Minister facing him and the MP or Peer acting on your behalf must be briefed on the possible answers that could be given to your question (unless it is addressed to the Prime Minister, in which case the question itself is by tradition too vague to allow him to anticipate the Supplementary with any degree of certainty).

Example: briefing an MP on an Oral Question. In 1985 the Government published Green and White Papers covering home taping of copyright material. In them, a levy on recording tape was considered in view of the extent of copyright infringement taking place in the home. Opponents of levies strongly believed that the Government's assessment of the extent of home taping was based only on the record industry's statistics and had ignored radically lower figures produced by them at the suggestion of officials.

Action. Opponents of levies might therefore have decided to try to expose what they believed to be the one-sided thinking of the Government by asking an MP sympathetic to their case to table an Oral PQ. It could have been phrased as follows:

> To ask the Secretary of State for Trade and Industry, to provide details of the current extent of home taping of copyright material in millions of hours per year.

They should have produced a short brief, reproducing the PQ at the top to save the MP from having to refer to other papers, and continuing as follows:

The Minister may give two responses:

1 *He may give a figure of X million hours/years of audio taping*. This is the record industry's estimate. One rebuttal could be 'Will he acknowledge that the research from which that figure was drawn was conducted by the record industry, which has an interest in proving that a considerable amount of home taping is going on, and that his assessment of the extent of home taping fails to take into account the research conducted by other sources, which indicates that Y hours/year is a more realistic estimate. Does this not therefore call into question the basis of his statement in the White Paper that the extent of taping of copyright audio material justifies a levy?'

Box 46 Impersonal briefs for MPs and Peers

> If you have no alternative but to send mass-produced letters to legislators, try at least to insert a few phrases that make the MP or Peer feel you know why *he* should be receiving your information or request for help. If you cannot do this, it mollifies legislators somewhat to explain that the letter he has received is also being sent to a defined group, such as all qualified teachers in the Commons or other members of the same Select Committee.
>
> Never send circular letters without personally addressing them, even though it may take a great deal of time.

2 *He may give both figures (X & Y)* He should be asked why Y does not seem to have been taken into account in the statement in the White Paper that the extent of music taping justifies the imposition of a levy since it shows that home taping is far less of a problem than it was alleged to the Minister by supporters of tape levies and since the Green Paper seems to be based only on the record industry's very high estimate.

Question time can be nerve-racking for MPs and Ministers. Therefore do not refer your MP to other areas of the brief; reproduce information where he needs it since he must not stumble while he searches for supporting facts or statements.

Submissions to Select Committees are far closer to briefs to Departments on policy matters: they should contain more detail and are therefore invariably longer and more complex. The Clerk to the Committee – either if it wants evidence from you or if you have approached it to make a case for your wish to submit evidence on a future planned enquiry that is directly relevant to your interests – will be able to guide you on the particular issues the Committee will wish to address.

You will also have your own views to convey. An effective technique for doing this is to ask questions that you then answer. The use of this technique is best exemplified by the submission of the Association of International Air Courier Services to the Industry of Trade Committee's 1982 investigation into the Post Office and the impact of legislation liberalizing certain areas of postal monopoly. We reproduce an extract in box 47.

Indeed, there may be on occasion no difference at all between the structure of submissions to Select Committees and Departments, since the former are occasionally established to conduct consultations on contentious issues in place of a Department. Responses to Green and White Papers, or other calls for comment or papers submitted to a Department on an organization's own initiative to support a case, should bear in mind the

Dealing with Government

Box 47 Briefs to Select Committees

Extract from the submission of AIACS to the Select Committee on Industry and Trade in 1982:

Memorandum by the Association of International Air Courier Services (PO6)

Competition between international couriers and postal services

The Association of International Air Courier Services is the official representation body for UK-based international couriers.

In this brief submission AIACS intends to address four points:

1 What is the business of international couriers?

2 Which markets are served by them?

3 Do they compete with postal services and, if so, to what extent?

4 Is competition detrimental to the Post Office or the consumer?

1 What is the business of international couriers?

International air couriers carry urgent business documents and parcels from desk to desk between countries in every continent.

Collection, international transportation and delivery are all either undertaken or controlled by each individual operator. This ensures maximum security, reliability and speed.

Most companies operate on a network basis whereby they maintain offices in major international cities (the largest operator has 300 offices in 68 countries) and connect them by the use of 'on board' couriers who travel with their consignments which are then checked in as passenger baggage for secure and fast handling. The speed of air couriers, whose operations are specifically based around the international transmission of time-sensitive material, enables banks in London, for example, to convey an average of millions of dollars in cancelled cheques and other financial instruments across the Atlantic each evening in time to reach their offices and the New York Clearing House.

The main commodity carried by air couriers is business documents of no intrinsic value — contracts, tenders, accounting information, plans, shipping papers and suchlike. A smaller part of their operation involves the carriage of small parcels typically containing computer tapes, spare parts, advertising copy, medical samples and other items that require special handling.

2 Which markets are served by them?

Air couriers do not carry correspondence unless specifically associated with business material. Demand for their service arose from world business as a result of rising interest rates, and a general commercial awareness that time saved was money saved, coupled to an increase in the pace of international trade that certain postal services were not able to accommodate. A system was needed to ensure that urgent material could be rapidly and reliably conveyed to any part of the world and this has now been provided, to the extent that many international companies would not now be established in the UK or British companies competitive in all the markets they serve, if it were not for their ability to use air couriers.

The main users of international courier services are banks, construction and computer companies, shipping lines, lawyers, advertising agents and accountants. In total, they provided the UK-based air couriers with revenue of £47,900,000 in the year to 31st December, 1981. Almost 40 per cent of this is attributable to routes to third world countries not currently served by Datapost. In many cases they provide the only reliable physical communication link between firms involved in development projects across the world and their head offices.

way a Department itself would marshall facts. Consider the Inland Revenue's paper on the National Heritage to the *ad hoc* Select Committee that was established to consider the Government's 1975 Wealth Tax proposal (box 48).

The most common failing of written representation to Government is that they fail to appreciate that the reader of that brief or submission may be antagonistic or neutral to the case being put forward. That is why no one should have the opportunity of pencilling 'Why?' or 'Source?' against any statement made. As counselled earlier, the best submissions consider the case against theirs and rebut it.

Officials, in considering a case, will ask themselves different questions of those of legislators. They will want to know:

- Will this proposal work?
- What are the political implications?
- How much work would the proposal involve?
- Does the submission show an understanding of the way in which this proposal would be progressed?

It is therefore important to show an understanding of current policy and the reasons for it – research will be needed here. If, however, you are simply briefing officials to keep them informed, you must in your brief indicate what the information is required to do – to maintain or ultimately change

Box 48 One component of Government briefing another

Extract from the Inland Revenue memorandum on the national heritage submitted to the Select Committee on a Wealth Tax in 1975.

Outright Exemption of all Works of Art
16. It may be said that outright exemption of all works of art would be the surest way of preserving the national heritage and would avoid the practical problems which are inevitable with any charge, whatever its basis. These problems turn on the provision of public access, the valuation of assets and the decision whether objects satisfy the criteria for inclusion in the heritage.

Practical difficulties if works of art are not exempted:
(i) *Public access*
17. First it would be difficult to lay down rules for public access to some works of art which would be fair and could reasonably be interpreted. There may on the one hand be little difficulty in respect of objects on more or less permanent loan to public collections or with regard to the contents of historic houses – the Historic

Cont.

Box 48 (*Cont.*)

Buildings Councils already have considerable experience in linking grants to such a test – although the extra cost to the owner of providing the necessary facilities, security, insurance and advertising can be quite heavy. Equally it may be possible to lay down rules for works of a scientific or research nature, or for objects which are particularly delicate and require the most careful treatment, for which the demand for access either would or should be limited to a few scholars and specialists. For such objects the test might simply be that the owner should be prepared to make arrangements for them to be viewed by appointments in some cases no special steps might be required to publicize them since those interested might in any case be aware of their existence and whereabouts.

18. However, there is a middle group of objects for which it is less easy to see how public access could be provided. Where, for example, the owner of valuable pictures or furniture lives in a flat in London or in quite an ordinary house in the suburbs, it would not be reasonable to expect him to be able to open it to the public. Moreover since museums and galleries have not the facilities to acquire, borrow or display many more works than they already do, a test along the lines of exhibition for, say, three months every five years might also be unreasonable. In such circumstances the test might simply have to be that the owner would have to express his willingness to lend his works for any reasonable exhibition which might be mounted by a museum or gallery and/or to give an assurance of first refusal to a public collection. Clearly however the conditions for such a test would need careful consideration by the Department of Education and Science. The lower the standard set for inclusion in the national heritage the more difficult the condition of public access: the revised interpretation of the test (see paragraph 5 above) might suggest the possibility of its being lowered.

(ii) *Valuation*

19. There are two aspects to the practical problems of valuation – the difficulty of the valuation of any one object and the magnitude of the task overall. As to the first it is not easy to establish values in an area where the market is notoriously volatile. Professional opinion varies widely, fair market comparisons are difficult to find for certain items and may not be easy to specify rules to determine whether items should be valued separately or what the unit of valuation should be. On the other hand works of art have had to be valued for estate duty and capital gains tax purposes for many years and, despite the criticisms which are levied from time to time, there are no grounds for suggesting that the task cannot be reasonably done. However, it has also been argued that the provision for controlling valuations suggested in paragraph 63 of the Green Paper – that following a sale in the open market either party may backtrack a number of years – may be particularly difficult to operate in the sphere of the arts.

20. There remains a problem of the size of the task, both because of the area which would have to be covered and the recurring nature of the tax. There would be a considerable increase in the demand from taxpayers for professional valuations and, even though the Inland Revenue might well be able to expand its own staff working in this area, provision might have to be made for specialist advisers for appeals. It is doubtful whether museum or gallery staff would be able to do much to help.

Cont.

Box 48 (*Cont.*)

(iii) *The test of quality*

21. If objects falling within the national heritage are to receive more favourable treatment than works of art generally, there would be an increased load on those staff in the museums and galleries who are responsible for advising the Treasury whether objects should be regarded as coming up to the required standard for inclusion in the national heritage. Although as we have pointed out exemption has already been granted for very many such objects, there might be a substantial number which would fall within the charge to tax for the first time or where an owner would seek exemption in respect of an item where it had been refused some years previously. This is a task which would of course be quite outside the province of the Inland Revenue. It would also be for consideration whether the impact of the wealth tax would require the introduction of appeal machinery even though no appeal currently lies against the Treasury decision for estate duty (or capital transfer tax) or capital gains tax purposes.

22. Apart from these practical difficulties another reason which has been advanced* in favour of exempting all works of art (whether or not of sufficient quality to form part of the national heritage) is that the fine arts market will move to overseas countries which are not affected by anything like a wealth tax. The reason for this argument has not been fully explained (and it might appear to conflict with the suggestion that the tax could cause forced sales, so bringing business) but it seems to us that if any tax were to have the effect suggested, it would be more likely to be one on the transmission rather than the holding of assets. However, capital gains tax has applied to gains on the disposal of works exceeding £1000 in value for all but ten years, while estate duty has run for eighty years: there is no evidence that the auction rooms and dealers have been affected adversely.

23. The Government are fully aware of the practical problems mentioned above and are concerned that the difficulties should not be belittled. At the same time they do not consider that the problems are such that any attempt to charge works of art should be ruled out. As was made clear in the Green Paper there are strong arguments against exemption. First it would do nothing to widen public enjoyment of the national heritage; there seems no good reason why special treatment should be afforded to works of art which could be, but are not, made available to the public. Second exemption of all works of art would do nothing to further one of the aims of the tax which is to reduce concentrations of privately held wealth. Third it would provide wealthy tax payers with an incentive to invest in non-productive rather than productive assets. Finally it would depart from the general principle suggested in paragraph 23 of the Green Paper that all assets with a realisable value should be chargeable to the tax: any departure from this principle will lead to distortion and inequity between taxpayers.

24. In the view of the Government these arguments against exempting all works of art whether or not they are within the national heritage are very strong. The possibilities discussed in the remainder of this paper consider ways in which the various aims of the Government, both in relation to its tax policy and to its policy towards the arts, could be met within the practical considerations set out above.

* By, for example, Mr St John-Stevas (*Hansard*, 13 December, 1974, col. 1069).

their Department's policy concerning you (grants; procurement blacklists; and subsidies, for example) or your areas of interest.

A brief produced for a Minister is, in effect, a brief to his officials unless it is channelled to him through his Special Adviser or PPS, or is given to him by an MP, or by you in a meeting with him. In each of these cases, the tactic should be used sparingly since it is only needed where briefing through more normal channels has failed owing to the opposition or intransigence of officials; or where the Minister believes that the full facts might be moderated by his Department and, for his own purposes, requests a personal account of your case. If, in visiting or meeting you, a Minister asks for details about points you have made that are of interest to him, he invariably means that you should produce a brief for his officials to analyse, summarize and present to him in essence only (usually with their observations attached, whether he has asked for them or not). Any other request could only be made at a private meeting (with officials present), through his parliamentary office – as Jack Smith MP, who happens to be the Minister of State for X, not the other way round – or via his Special Adviser or an MP or Peer who may have made representations to him on your behalf.

Officials will take a view on the production of information purely for a Minister if they find out about it. In the case of material innocently and mistakenly targeted at him, they will not be unduly concerned except perhaps in feeling that some major organizations should know better. They are more certain to view you unfavourably if it is clear that an attempt has been made deliberately to circumvent them. Since you should only use this ploy, as suggested above, when there is no further possibility of persuading officials with your case, your decision to attempt to produce briefs for Ministers alone must be carefully considered.

Should, however, you feel that it is necessary to make a case to a Minister direct, it is essential that your points drive home immediately since he may have only a few minutes to read your brief and assimilate your arguments.

Box 49 Delivering briefs to MPs and Peers

If letters and briefs are delivered personally to the Palace of Westminster, there are a number of procedural requirements:

- All letters must be stamped (not franked). You are allowed to deliver one free of charge.
- Only Peers who give their address as the House of Lords can have mail delivered there unless they have requested that letters should be left for them, for example on the day of a debate for which they are travelling up to London. Home addresses are listed in *Dod*.

Box 50 Presenting a case to officials

In 1985, a company manufacturing emergency alarms for the disabled and elderly sought to obtain a ruling from Customs and Excise that its new alarm could be zero-rated for VAT purposes, thus lowering the price and increasing demand from a market with a high proportion of low- or fixed-income consumers. It faced two problems: the earlier version of its product had been turned down by Customs and Excise; and the very strict interpretation then applied by officials to the relevant section of the VAT Acts, which provided that products specifically designed or adapted for the disabled could be zero-rated. Products designed for the disabled *and* the elderly would not qualify.

The company initially contacted the Assistant Secretary responsible for the Branch covering this area for advice on the information he would need in order to reach a decision on their application and for guidance on the considerations he and his colleagues would apply in judging whether the new alarm complied with the statutory requirement.

Having gained an understanding of their court, the company decided to base its case on the difference between the current model and that which had previously been examined by the Department; and on proof that the new model had been so designed and priced that only a person with recognised disabilities, as opposed simply to those 'at risk', would be prepared to pay the extra price for the special features of the equipment compared to other, inapplicable systems. Its brief to the Assistant Secretary therefore included the following:

- A description of the applicant and its market (type and size)
- The history of its previous application to the Department and the reasons given for its rejection.
- An explanation of the history of product development following that rejection to show, irrespective of the applicability of the new model, that the company had sought to adapt the rejected product to meet the needs of the disabled. A statement was included from the Chief Engineer on the problems of use by the disabled that the new model was intended to overcome.
- A detailed comparison of the facilities of the new model compared with its predecessor, together with a photograph, to show that by design as well as by intention the product had been adapted for use primarily by the disabled.
- An analysis of the important clause and of all other statutory definitions of disablement to show not only that the company fully understood the conditions with which its product would have to comply but also that its facilities were consistent with needs dictated by the accepted understanding of disablement.
- An offer of a demonstration.

The brief gave officials all the information they needed, but the company nonetheless took no chances and contacted the Assistant Secretary ten days after receipt to assess his reaction and see whether any more detail would be required.

In proving its case beyond all reasonable doubt, the company secured the zero-rated status it required and was able to increase the availability of its product to many who could now afford the new price and, as a result, itself benefit commercially.

The obvious example of the need for simplicity and clarity in a short, easily understood brief is the instance of representations being made to a Minister by an MP sympathetic to your case during a Division in the House. Divisions are usually held late at night, when the Minister may have had to rush from a dinner engagement or, if not, is likely to be tired after a 13 or 14 hour working day. A number of MPs (or Peers, if the Minister is a member of the Lords) may be competing for his attention. Your points must therefore, as with MPs, be set out in one page. The note must tell the Minister who is making the representations; it must summarize the issue in question, avoiding technical terms or abbreviations unless you are certain he will understand them, and it must state why the Minister himself should take the action you desire. That action must be politically, pragmatically and administratively feasible.

Think also of the questions most of interest to a Minister in judging your case:

- What is the Government trying to do?
- Can I earn credit by supporting this?
- Is it feasible – what about all the representations I have received (directly, through or from my officials) against this view?
- What will it cost; what are the administrative problems involved?
- Could I experience problems with Parliament or the media over this? (i.e. how well organized are these people; are they telling the truth when they suggest there is considerable parliamentary support for their views?)
- I may have committed myself to taking *some* action. Even though their case is good, will they cause trouble (as above) if I go against them anyway.
- They may have put forward a good case against us doing anything, but can they now give us alternative proposals that we could use in place of our own?

Advocates often overlook the last of these questions in particular. The offices of officials and Ministers ring with choruses of disapproval by organizations for any measure Government considers. Few, however, appreciate that governments often commit themselves to taking some action, whatever it may be. Unless objectors can come up with something better, some idea with which officials and Ministers can run, even the best-argued case may be negated by the latter's need to be seen to act.

In most circumstances it is very helpful not just to meet with officials in advance of a ministerial meeting or visit but also to provide them with a short brief, the main facts of which they can then incorporate into their own document for a Minister. Similarly, if you have requested, or know that the Minister will make a speech at your function, liaison with his Special

Adviser, even if only in the form of a note on your organization, its aims and achievements, will be regarded as helpful by him and will maximize your chances of the Minister presenting your version of the truth to your audience.

Constructing your case

The advice given so far has involved the technique of presentation of your case: the channels through which contact with Government should be made and the form in which information should be presented to those channels. Before continuing to expand on the techniques of persuading Government of your views, we must pause to consider those views themselves. How objectively reasonable are they? Are they capable of acceptance by your targets, given the financial, administrative and political constraints of their position? (Not to mention the realities of time: new principles cannot be introduced into legislation after Second Reading, for example.) Have you taken into account their personal views, as far as you have been able to ascertain them? Is the tone of your case calculated to appeal to the sensitivities of your targets, whether in Government or peripherally, such as the general public?

In order to secure the greatest possible acceptance of your case, you may have to be prepared to compromise between views you may hold strongly and those to which Government will be most susceptible.

Example: *VAT on books*. The initial aim of the wide range of interests that coalesced in 1984 to prevent the imposition of VAT on books in the 1985 Budget was to show the Chancellor of the Exchequer that taxing publications would damage the publishing industry and the British cultural tradition. It was quickly realized that the first argument would be seen as no more than a defence of the interests of publishers and the second would make only limited inroads on the hard-nosed Treasury. Neither would be likely to attract the widespread public support necessary to generate pressure on MPs and Ministers to oppose the proposal.

The campaign's research indicated that publishers were regarded as well able to afford the tax and that literature and culture were notions considered largely unimportant in political terms. It was therefore decided that, instead of being presented as a 'tax on knowledge', VAT on books would be represented as a tax on education, which would enable more interests to be brought into the campaign and have greater public and political appeal. Opposition to the VAT plan would henceforth centre on the effects of book price increases on schools, universities, and the ability of parents to provide educational material for their children. The concentration on the educational aspects of the anti-VAT case also enabled representations to be made to the Department of Education and Science and the Welsh, Scottish and Northern Ireland Ministers as well as

Customs and Excise and the Treasury. More legislators could also be targeted since education is of general interest.

From a position where the campaign's members were seeking support for their interests, their case was changed to emphasize a strength that also directed attention away from damage to publishers and towards more politically sensitive consequences.

As a reinforcement to the factual and emotive educational arguments targeted at politicians and the public, the campaign felt it also had to tailor its case to the needs of those officials whose job it was to advise the Chancellor on the implications of possible Budget items. It concentrated on the need to maintain books as a special exception to the principle of positive rating of all retail items on the basis of tax efficiency – that an economic value could be applied to education and that the elasticity of demand for books is such that tax-induced price increases would raise less VAT revenue than they would lose in educational value.

It is therefore necessary to think carefully about the tone of your case. The reasons for the views you advocate are less important than the reasons your targets want to hear. When you deliver them also conditions the feasibility of your case. Once legislation has been introduced into Parliament by the Government, it is pointless to attempt to delay its passage beyond that Session or to expect that the Bill will be withdrawn owing to the pressure you may be able to mobilize (with the exception of Private Members' Bills, where the balance of support is always more uncertain than that for Government legislation). Opposition to legislation once it is in Parliament must concentrate on amendment, with the arguments supporting your case being changed depending on the stage in the legislative process at which they are deployed. Your case will probably also have to be adapted to the targets you are addressing, possibly emphasising constituency aspects to MPs, logistical implications to officials and electoral or political implications to Ministers.

The 1981 campaign to confirm the legality of private sector international couriers succeeded not because of the benefit that would result to a growth sector, which was all that interested the industry, but because it represented the opportunity to Trade and Industry Ministers to apply the Conservative Government's competition policies and thereby encourage the air courier industry to thrive. The success of that *policy* was more important to the Government than the success of the *industry*. If, therefore, you wish to succeed in your dealings with Government, objective facts presented unimpeachably must be advocated with an understanding of the pragmatic position of decision-makers and your other targets. The air courier example shows that Government is itself driven by self-interest. Your interests can only be progressed if they appeal to the principles that motivate decision-makers in Whitehall and Parliament.

Reminder

- Lobbying government is the art of the possible; swim with the tide of Government's intentions as far as you can. Antagonism should not be your starting point: 'Yes, but' is better than 'No'.

3.4 Promoting and amending legislation

At least 40 per cent of any large organization's time in dealing with Government should be concerned with legislation that has an impact on its interests. Legislation, in this context, is taken to mean the complete public legislative process, covering the pressures that leads to the formulation of Bills and Regulations through to their enactment and subsequent extra-legal interpretation or clarification by officials. It is impossible for most outsiders who seek to work with Government to their benefit to ignore the law – whether in monitoring it, analysing it for benefits, weaknesses or harmful provisions, or taking action to promote or amend legislation or block amendments that are against your interests.

Methods of changing the law

Apart from judicial interpretation and the direct applicability of EEC law, there are only three direct causes of legislation or amendment of existing statutory provision:

- *Party and ministerial pressure* – political commitments either specifically decided on before a Party assumes office or, subsequently, as one of a number of measures to satisfy a broad policy aim such as nationalization or encouraging worker participation.
- *Pressure from officials* – whose advice to Ministers, particularly on technical or administrative matters, is often persuasive. Their role is especially strong where secondary legislation is involved. Departments often propose measures to Ministers, either to remedy inadequacies in existing legislation that could not be solved by reinterpretation through departmental Circular or because new circumstances require new statutes – for example, the information-technology boom led to the need for data protection legislation on an international basis.
- *Pressure from MPs and Peers* – through Private Member's Bills; through mobilized parliamentary pressure to persuade the Executive of the need for change (for example, a large group of Government MPs persuading the Chancellor that the application of VAT on books would be

unacceptable to his Party); or through defeating Government legislative proposals in part by amending them. A further alternative, that of defeating legislation by forcing a No Confidence vote against the Government on a Bill and securing its resignation, occurs too rarely for the user of Government to consider it as a feasible tactic.

Which course to follow?

New legislation essentially seeks to remedy deficiencies in existing policy, whether that is governed by current statutes or not. The approach you take to find the appropriate solution to the deficiencies you have identified will be conditioned by a number of factors:

What is wrong with the existing policy or legislation? You must have a complete understanding of the extent of existing statutory provision or policy and must be able to show that they either embody drafting inaccuracies; or should be amended to bring them up to date; or that social changes/economic factors/new technology/new evidence, or whatever, indicate that a different approach must be taken. At the most obvious level, a demand for a Circular must be backed by evidence that statutory provision and secondary legislation covering a policy area is too unclear or complex to be implemented effectively. That evidence can only be obtained by analysing the legislation and collecting opinions from those affected by the alleged inaccuracy.

In presenting your case to the court of Government, you must be clear about your facts and have good witnesses. Remember, however, that even the most obvious of deficiencies may not be capable of equitable remedy – and policy in a democratic system must be equitable. Thus it was clear to all that the provisions of the 1956 Copyright Act covering the unauthorized taping of copyright material were unenforceable; but attempts to secure a tax on recording tape to compensate copyright owners were defeated since the tax could not be applied fairly: existing policy may not be ideal, but there may not be a better alternative.

What are the alternatives for change? Having assessed the need for change, you will need to think objectively about the advantages and pitfalls of your proposal. How much will it cost? How much administration will it involve? What is the extent of central or local Government's involvement in that administration? What are the political implications (does your proposal fit with the general policy of the Party through which you may seek to develop it? Will it earn that Party bonus points with its members and the electorate? Can the policy be implemented within the normal span of a Government's life?) What are the projected results of your proposal; and could they be achieved in a more cost-effective way? In proposing new legislative policy, you are likely to be met by one of the following responses:

- No, because of (X, Y or Z).
- We agree with your objective, but the means of achieving it would be politically impossible for us to adopt.
- We agree with your objective, but your proposal would be too costly/administratively unworkable.

You must therefore be able to demonstrate to decision-makers the Civil Service skill of having assessed all possible alternative remedies to an identified problem, evaluated their merits and tested them according to the above criteria to produce an answer that is as close to being incontrovertible as possible.

Would more than one Department be involved? Usually. Most measures, for example, have financial implications – either requiring greater public resources, reducing the drain on the Exchequer or changing the way money is raised to fund departmental programmes – which would usually involve the Treasury, which is more than just a sophisticated accounts office. As the key functionary of Executive policy, its deliberations are geared to the Government's welfare. Your campaign for legislation to remove planning controls in designated areas of the country, with associated financial assistance for infrastructure development, would be aimed at the Department of the Environment and might be opposed by a Treasury committed to a counter-inflationary policy involving cuts in public expenditure. Close to an election, however, Government may feel the need to reflate somewhat in order to revive employment, in which case Treasury Ministers would be more willing to agree to those proposals. (Whichever policy the Government decides to pursue, the Departments of Employment and Trade and Industry would also be involved.)

Even aside from financial aspects, the VAT on books case study (page 24) shows how many Departments are involved on apparently simple issues since every possible effect of new legislative policy must be considered. If your proposal is for removal of planning controls in England only, the other Departments covering the UK would normally be consulted unless it were clear that the need for such a policy is proven to be highly localized.

Is this a political or an administrative issue? Most issues have more complex implications than appear at first sight. Clearly, if your objective is to seek greater acceptance by the UK Government of the South African Government's policies, your case will almost exclusively be decided by legislators and Ministers, with a fair element of public pressure. At the other extreme, a Regulation to enforce minimum spray density per acre in order to prevent *Phylloxera* returning to vines would be of concern only to officials, the junior Minister who would authorize it, possibly the one MP who is a Master of Wine and the handful of others connected with the wine trade. Those two examples are respectively obvious political and administrative issues, but most other causes cannot be as distinctly categorized. In advance of launching your campaign for change, you should evaluate the extent to which the components of power could become involved. Among the variables are:

- The extent to which an essentially administrative matter could be turned into a political one by involving public opinion expressed to Parliament, to strengthen your representations or as a tactic of those opposed to your case.
- Would the issue, no matter how worthy, divert parliamentary time from the Government's more election-winning measures?
- How will opponents of your case react?. The higher profile (i.e. media and public pressure) the issue becomes, the more likely it is that you will have to devote considerable effort to calming the sensitivities of Parliament and Ministers.
- Whether it is likely that the Prime Minister would become involved. Does your case involve a major Cabinet decision, and could ministerial acceptance of it be overridden by the feeling of the Prime Minister that the measure would not be in the best interests of his Party's image?
- The impact of EEC law. If your measure seeks to amend or replace legislation which has been implemented throughout the EEC, it may only be possible to progress at European Commission level. EEC legislation is Directly Applicable, meaning that Member States must translate Regulations and Directives into their own domestic law either literally or with some changes allowed to account for differing national circumstances. If in doubt, check with an expert on Community law or with the officials responsible for the issue that concerns you.
- The timing of your action. The later you seek to amend proposed legislation, the more likelihood there is that you will have to rely on securing a parliamentary majority, with or without the help of the Whips, for your amendments. Without the Whips' support, it can be almost impossible to obtain the endorsement you seek throughout a Bill's passage unless the Government has seriously miscalculated the feelings of MPs on the issue. The chances of incorporating your amendments into a Bill once it is tabled in Parliament are roughly 1 in 20.
- Whether Ministers see your proposal as an administrative or political

issue. To return to the case of tape levies, the legislation in which it was envisaged they would be included was apparently non-controversial and legalistic: copyright amendment and consolidation. The levy issue could have been considered as just another part of the Patent Office's work on seeking copyright remedies to the impact of new technology, but Ministers became concerned, following representations to the anti-levy lobby, over the political implications of new taxation and the effect of a levy on the youth vote.

New law need not, therefore, be based on existing principles. One of the main reasons for proposing legislative change is that the basis of existing law is no longer valid. Departments, instead of basing their drafting on an interpretation of current statutes, should be considering the law as it ought to be. Ministers, who are able to impose innovation and equity on the policy-making process (as well as political pragmatism) must be targeted to harness that asset.

Will the Government be interested in, or find the time for, your measure? You should not adopt the Private Member's route until you have either achieved no progress over a sustained period in pursuing your case with the Government or have received an undertaking from it to support a Private Member's Bill on the subject since it welcomes the idea but would have no space for it in its own programme.

A Private Member's Bill would also be appropriate as a means of attracting publicity to, and identifiying parliamentary support for, an issue, with both then being used as levers to extract concessions from the Government. The Bill introduced in 1983 by Labour MP Austin Mitchell, aiming to break the solicitors' monopoly over conveyancing, followed ten years of campaigning by the Consumers' Association and National Consumer Council in which successive Governments had failed to accept their arguments. The unexpected support and public attention gained by the Mitchell Bill resulted in a promise by the Government that it would implement the tone of his measure even though it ran out of time before completing its parliamentary passage.

Lastly, the Government may prefer that Private Member's legislation be introduced in preference to its own measure where the matter is one that crosses Party boundaries, is of general concern, and would therefore probably not be whipped. Two examples have been the abolition of the death penalty and various attempts to amend the Sunday Trading laws.

Similarly, amendments to Bills should, wherever possible, be negotiated with the officials and Ministers responsible before they are tabled in Parliament. High-profile pressure may be created and directed at the

Department concerned without also targeting Parliament. Since, realistically, amendments will only succeed if the Government accepts them, it is sensible to make your representations while draft legislation may still contain some room for flexibility. Amendments to Private Member's Bills should again initiate via the Department concerned before attempts are made to mobilize the support of MPs and Peers. While that support can also sway Ministers to accept your case, the difficulty of obtaining sufficient interest from MPs and Peers on other than the most public issues should not be underestimated. The case must either appeal to their personal principles or interests or be pressed upon them by constituency representations.

What is the extent of support or opposition for your case? By this, we mean not just support or opposition within the components of power but among all outside groups that may be affected by your interests. In some cases, the main forces can be easily identified and should either be contacted (if they are groups outside Government) in order that supporting representations may be coordinated or, if they are opponents, they can be taken into account in your arguments in the suggested way by rebutting their likely objections to your case. In moving beyond defined interest groups, supporters among the population as a whole can be identified and mobilized in a number of ways.

If your case is sufficiently topical, hold a press conference. Depending on the support you wish to attract, your invitations could be sent to the national, local or trade press and, if the matter is of national or important local significance, television and radio stations. It may be necessary to structure the campaign supporting your case around the use of publicity in order to inform potential supporters of the policy threat or opportunity on which your case is based, but PR should never overwhelm the need to produce a sound and dispassionate case to decision-makers and to understand the system. Ministers are deeply resentful of modern-day 'hype' techniques and may ignore the good points of your case if it is felt that you have deliberately attempted to exaggerate the extent of your support. Nor should it be thought that pressure can succeed unless it is precisely targeted; and that requires good research in advance.

Example: In November 1985 the British Medical Association launched a series of booklets containing the results of research on UK smoking-related deaths. The booklets, each covering a geographical area, listed deaths by constituency and were sent to each MP. At the same time, the BMA sought and obtained national publicity for its campaign to restrict tobacco advertising because the issue was of general interest; the BMA is a representative and respected body; and its case was powerfully made in a way that would also reach the strongest sensitivities of MPs – to what happens in their own constituency. That should not obscure the detailed discussions that proceeded in parallel with the DHSS. Few letters to MPs were generated, but the publicity itself was sufficient to strengthen the BMA's case.

There is no doubt that the success of the VAT on books campaign was to a great extent due to the campaigning body's ability to galvanize support from a large number of interested organizations and, by making the population aware of the threat it perceived through coverage in national, trade and local publications and on TV and radio, to generate a considerable volume of individual representations to MPs, many of whom passed them on to the Chancellor.

The advantages of media coverage, if your case is sufficiently persuasive, is that the arguments are seen by a great number of potential supporters and are advocated by an influential medium rather than by an obviously interested party – you.

You may have to produce a leaflet which very simply (if your target is the population as a whole) sets out the problem, your arguments, and the action people can take to support you. That action is likely to be writing, in one page, to their MP, with a copy and covering letter to their local paper, making sure that the letter is written in their own words. The problem must be perceived through the eyes of those whose support you seek. All that will sway them is a current or threatened state of affairs that affects them and your advice on how they can defend their interests. You are not important to them – note the way the anti-VAT case was changed to take into account this point (page 191).

Other action you can suggest could involve the production of petitions which could be returned, together with responses from MPs, to you or organizations with whom you have coalesced. Arrange to have the petition presented to the signatories' MPs and have all the forms sent to the relevant Departments or committee chairmen. A petition is no different from an opinion poll. Both can be used to demonstrate to Government the extent of support for your views. If you can afford it, the opinion-poll course is more effective, particularly if you use a well-known firm, since Government can be certain that no undue influence has been used to obtain the results with which they are presented. In keeping with our advice to think legal, remember to provide full information on methodology, sample base and questions asked in any research that you intend to present to Government. Once again, use the media, which seems to have an inexhaustible hunger for surveys and reports on topical issues.

Try to secure the support of personalities who are either well-known or well-respected by Government and the public. Even if your concern is not of general public interest – for example, your firm seeking endorsement of its proposal for restructuring of State-backed credit insurance – the support of a former Permanent Secretary to the Department of Trade and Industry or the Treasury, who will not only have access to Government but whose experience also carries credibility, will greatly benefit your cause.

It pays to think carefully about how your case could be adapted or moderated in some areas in order to obtain support from officials or Ministers for the core of your proposal. Those who opposed a levy on tape initially did just that; with time, they accepted the need to distinguish between those copyright owners who lost revenue through home taping of borrowed material, on which no royalty would have been paid, and the taping of material owned by the taper, on which a royalty would have been paid in the purchase price and for which further compensation might be considered inequitable. Although still opposing tape levies, their arguments appeared more reasonable and attracted considerably more support from MPs and Peers at a time when the Government was beginning to reconsider the viability of its own legislative proposals.

Time scale

It is much easier, and it usually takes less time, to block or amend legislation than to promote it.

Securing the acceptance of major ideological commitments by a Party and then by a Government may take years of planning and persuasion. Such a process can best be started while that Party is in opposition, when it has more time to consider its policies and is less accountable to the public if it changes its mind. Your targets will be the Party leadership and its research department and you will usually need the support of influential organizations to add weight and credibility to your case.

Pressure to accept new ideas often comes from the media: the Conservative Party's commitment to privatization of State-run services and competitive tendering for such services had its genesis in a pamphlet published by a Conservative councillor (now a Minister) in the late 1970s and adopted by a right-wing research/pressure group whose ideas were themselves gaining favour with the Party's leadership. Although a number of senior Party figures adopted the pamphlet's proposals and progressed them within the Party's policy-making machinery, their author had to lobby MPs, speak at Party conferences and elsewhere and promote industry pressure before privatization of services became accepted both by the leadership and local associations. In this campaign he was assisted by thee publicity he was able to obtain, but he was also fortunate in that the susceptibilities of the Party leadership at that time were particularly attuned to the sort of ideas he was promoting.

So establishing the policies that lead to legislation is a long-term process requiring sustained energy. Ideas must be published and publicized, supporters and influential patrons within and outside the Party must be mobilized and the support of the Party's grass roots must be obtained. In addition to speaking around the country, the author of the privatization plan may have circulated his pamphlet to constituency association chairmen or may have especially lobbied a Party-controlled local council to adopt his ideas as an experiment, providing an invaluable case history for him.

On a more defensive level, pre-emptive contact with Parties before they take office is invaluable since the fear of 'U turns' can commit them to policies set out in their manifestos despite the realities of power they will face. There is therefore good cause to establish contact one Parliament ahead with Party organizations, spokesmen and leaders if you need to suggest that there should be no legislation (for example, on regulatory matters) in a particular area.

Highly political issues, which may embody elements of the governing Party's ideology but are more specific – repeal of the Sunday trading laws or controls on vivisection – also require a long-term strategy. The pressures of the legislative timetable and the difficulty of giving new ideas momentum within Whitehall means that at least two years' preparatory work should be allowed. Once again, the media, both as a force acting on Government and as a means of informing public opinion, is important. Local newspapers should not be underestimated since most MPs need their support. MPs are important in these cases since direct representations to Ministers (which should not only argue persuasively on the need for your proposal but should show an understanding of the implications for the Government: how would it sell your proposal in order to gain maximum advantage for itself?) need also to show that your proposal would be acceptable to their Party. You must persuade backbench and All-Party committees to put your case to Ministers. Evidence given to a Select Committee investigating the general area in which your concern may fall, or representations to the Committee's Chairman and members (by organized presentation or individual meetings) to consider a specific enquiry should also be part of your campaign.

All relevant MPs and peers must be targeted during your campaign, and it should be anticipated that major political legislation would involve the establishment of a committee of enquiry to which you must seek to give evidence. The period of persuasion before a commitment to the policy or legislation you seek will inevitably be prolonged on political issues because of the opposition you must tackle outside Government: any political measure evokes strong feelings and one of your tasks will be to reassure Ministers, and the sources on which they may rely for corroboration, that contrary views to your own can be overridden in the public interest. Advocates of a fixed link across the Channel had to devote time to facing opposition from ferry operators, environmental groups in Kent and some Northern interests who feared a further concentration of trade in the South-East. Legislation to progress the proposal could not proceed until the Government was satisfied that all parties had been given their say and that it had been given a fair impression of representative opinion on the issue.

Administrative legislation, by contrast, can be proposed, accepted and formulated quite rapidly since it is invariably less public in nature and may simply require that existing measures be brought up to date by the exercise of secondary legislation powers. Your focus will turn to officials rather than legislators or the media, although the political nature of some highly detailed matters – milk quotas as an example – may mean that officials could support your case but Ministers would not. A great many cases straddle the political/administrative boundary and are prolonged accordingly.

Where officials are the predominant influence on acceptance of your views, your work should be geared to making as little work for them as possible. Your case for a new Circular to clarify the powers of local authorities to make grants to help the elderly and disabled buy emergency communications equipment would therefore have:

- researched all current statutory provisions;
- commented on the difficulties of interpretation or questionable applicability after considering unsatisfied problems of definition (for example, the definition of 'telephone' was unchanged in English law from before the First World War until BT's Operating Licence was drafted in 1984) and any clarification that judicial or tribunal opinions may have given to the law subsequent to its enactment;
- interviewed various local authorities at metropolitan, county and district level to obtain their views on problems of interpretation;
- proved thereby that real problems exist;
- suggested a viable structure for the Circular you desire

in advance of approaching the Departments of Health and the Environment. You would seek the support of organizations representing the elderly and disabled and the major local government bodies such as the Association of County Councils; and, as a fail-safe, you may add the opinion of a respected lawyer that the clarification you seek is consistent with principles of interpretation and with the exercise of discretionary powers.

It is unlikely that the exercise of compiling your case and influencing officials in both Departments, even though they may only have to read your dossier and agree, could be completed in less than six months, with a further four for preparation of the Circular. It is occasionally possible to expedite procedures by appeal to the relevant Minister if there are good reasons for urgency, but officials' objections will usually override yours.

From time-scale, we must also consider timing of representations to amend policy or legislative formulation. The earlier in the process that you access decision-makers and put your case to them, the greater your chances of success and the wider the range of techniques and conduits to those decision-makers that you can use.

Intelligent liaison with officials as part of an ongoing programme may alert you to future consultation periods, allowing you to make representations to Departments either to consider revising the terms of consultation or to ensure that your views are taken into account in the drafting of Green papers.

You should make the fullest use of consultation periods that follow those Green Papers by producing a clear submission within the period specified. Submission dates are occasionally extended owing to unexpectedly great public interest in the issue or new facts arising, but otherwise only exceptional factors will allow you to present your evidence after the final date. Officials will normally be happy to discuss the Green Paper while you are preparing your evidence if there are points on which you seek clarification. Following that, they sift the representations of the most important bodies and others that make specific points within the ambit of the Green Paper. Unless you are a major firm or representative body, your evidence has far more chance of being considered if it sticks to comment on particular matters rather than the Green Paper in general. Your next step is to maintain contact with the officials responsible for summarizing submissions (usually a Principal and an Assistant Secretary) for ministerial consideration. To what extent can they comment on your views?. Do they want you to provide supplementary evidence?. Have new facts come to light

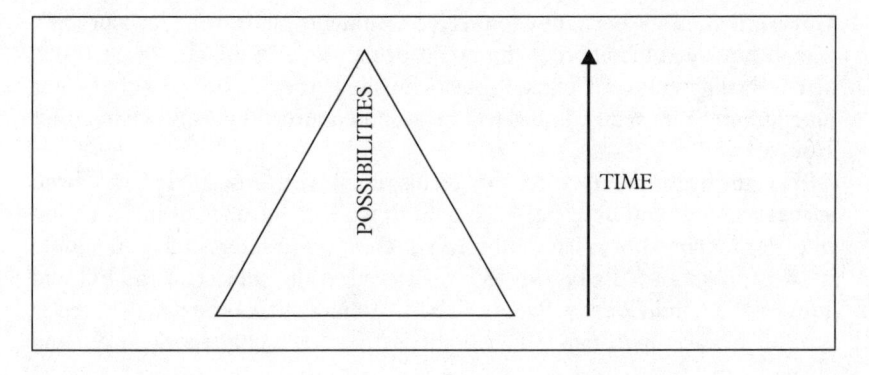

Box 51 The later you start, the fewer choices that are open to you

since you submitted your evidence? A good example of this last point occurred in the tape levy consultation period. Following the submission deadline, new technology – very small 8 mm video cameras, equipment that could print still photographs from video film, and tape that combined audio and video functions – was marketed which both created new non-infringing uses of tape and blurred the distinction made by the Green Paper between audio and video levies. That information had to be considered by the Department of Trade and Industry even though it was produced after the closing date for submissions. With the aim of mobilizing parliamentary opposition to any levy proposal prior to drafting of legislation, a demonstration of this new technology could have been arranged in the House of Commons with the sponsorship of a sympathetic MP and the agreement of the Sergeant at Arms' office to bring in equipment. Such a demonstration would have immediately shown those who were invited that non-infringing uses of tape are growing and would be attractive to them since, like the rest of us, MPs and Peers love new toys; and on this issue, a visual presentation would be worth more than even the best written brief.

There may be only six to eight months from publication of a Green Paper, which may give a two-month submission deadline, and completion of the final draft of the White Paper that usually follows it. You must therefore react quickly and take every opportunity that is offered to liaise with the sponsoring Department. The Minister responsible for examining representations (usually a Parliamentary Under Secretary) will only have time for a limited number of meetings with concerned parties. You must request one of those slots and try to persuade officials that your use of the Minister's time will be justified.

At the next stage, you should take the opportunity to comment on legislative drafting before a Bill is presented to Parliament (although sight of draft clauses is often restricted to key bodies crucially affected by them); and negotiate amendments with officials and Ministers rather than be forced to table them in the House against the wishes of the Government. While the Government is always happy to receive comments on drafting inaccuracies, it is in practice unlikely that the broad principles of a Bill can be amended after Parliamentary Counsel have finished their work or that new amendments on specific issues will be accepted after Report Stage in either House.

If your negotiations with the Department concerned have not been successful or if you have not been able to work in advance of introduction into Parliament of the legislation in which you are interested, you should draw up a list of MPs known to be involved in the subject of the Bill and contact them individually. Some will agree to meet you; others may accept a written brief impersonally. The point is that MPs only speak at Second

Dealing with Government 205

Reading if they are motivated to do so and the membership of Standing Committees is partly taken from those who have shown an interest during the Second Reading debate. The more MPs on the Government side that you can persuade to support your views about the principles of the Bill, the greater are your chances of having friends in the Committee who may be prepared to table your amendments, and speak to, and possibly negotiate privately with the Minister, or his PPS and Whip, on your behalf. Unless such negotiation can take place and the Minister be persuaded that the amendment would correct an inaccuracy or benefit the Party without either undesirable administrative implications or affecting the tone of the Bill, your realistic chances of success are slim. Negotiation between Committee and Report stages may result in the Government relenting provided an acceptable reworking is produced. Once again, public and media pressure timed to coincide with consideration of your amendments can make the difference between Government rejection and at least a sympathetic hearing.

The need to work in advance of legislation being tabled is most evident in the case of Budget representations, where your campaign should commence perhaps a year in advance if you seek concessions, or before the beginning of December if you wish to avoid penalties in the March statement.

Those two time-scales illustrate the difference between guiding and amending fiscal policy. All representations should have been made by the end of January, although mobilized public pressure can continue up to Budget Day. The Chancellor not only meets his backbench Finance or Treasury Committee and has to face the views of the PLP or 1922 Committee, depending on his Party, in advance of the Budget but is also aware of Early Day Motions with substantial support from MPs on his side, so constituents' views expressed to MPs are important. Parliamentary activity also attracts press coverage, so you may wish to approach potentially sympathetic Peers to sponsor an Unstarred Question debate on your lobby, whether it is to keep VAT off books or to promote the extension of mortgage tax relief. The Government is traditionally non-committal in advance of the Budget since it must not disclose its plans (given the volume of lobbying that was inspired by the 1985 Budget, such openness is unlikely to be repeated for some time) but debates and letters from MPs and Peers to the Treasury, Customs and Excise and Inland Revenue at least give it an indication of the support for your cause. You may of course be arguing against something that is not even under consideration by the Government, but that is a risk you must take.

If the tone of fiscal policy, or rumours, are such that your interests could be affected, it is futile to lobby post-Budget. The Government packs the Finance Bill Standing Committee with its supporters and it is even more loath to amend major legislation since it does not wish to lose face. You must carefully assess your chances of gaining support from both Government and Opposition before investing time and money in post-Budget lobbying.

Technical legislation involves different considerations. Firstly, you will not be able to generate widespread parliamentary and public interest unless the Bill or Regulations could impinge on an emotive area: electrical standards being changed as a result of deaths through faulty plugs, for example. There is therefore an even greater necessity to work within the sponsoring Department and influence drafting.

Secondly, contact with standing advisory committees or *ad hoc* panels of experts is important. The Department will consult them during drafting of primary legislation and, on Regulations, often while the Bill that allows for them is still in Parliament.

Thirdly, your response to the consultative document that precedes publication of Regulations should be produced in great detail since each Regulation will usually only cover highly specific areas. You must ensure that officials are happy to include you on the circulation list for the consultative document. You may be unable to obtain a copy from the Department, but the representative bodies covering your interests may be luckier if you ask them.

3.5 **Using help**

As we explained in the introduction to this book, it is not possible to produce a manual on working with Government on the same basis as an accountancy or law textbook. There are few established procedures and precedents to guide practitioners and no certainty, even if recognized techniques are used, that Government will wish to be bound by them. An established empathy with decision-makers and judgement in the selection of techniques to suit your demands cannot be gained other than by experience. If you lack that experience, do not have friends at court, do not have the time to satisfy your needs or are too geographically remote from those with whom you need to liaise, you may need to employ outside assistance to augment your resources, advise you or act as your advocate. Although it is *de rigueur* to use Parliamentary Agents for drafting of amendments and the promotion of, or opposition to, Private Bills, your choice of counsel for other works is both wider and more discretionary.

Representative bodies

Most commercial organizations can call on the services of one or more representative bodies to assist them – and, unlike the use of professional consultants, the services of those bodies are free to members.

There are four advantages of making use of a trade association, professional body or other representative organization (such as the National Consumer Council):

- Government prefers to deal with representative bodies because it feels they carry a constituency opinion with them when they deal with Whitehall or Parliament.
- Consequently, representative bodies find it easier to secure access to Government and many have very close and long-standing relationships with their Departments and with Ministers, All-Party Groups and backbench committees.
- Representative bodies are able to benefit from the collective experience of their members. In advising on the solution of individual problems, they are often aware of the results of another member's dealings with Government on a similar or identical issue.
- Their staff can be a valuable source of information, either by monitoring Parliamentary and Departmental decision-making on behalf of their members and then regularly circulating the results, or by being available to answer members' questions.

However, they also have their shortcomings:

- Since they have to represent all their members, the views they submit to Government may understandably have a tone of lowest common denominator about them. They may be reluctant to take up individual or special interest cases since to do so may put them at odds with what they may feel is a different, but consensus view.
- Not all representative bodies are as efficient as, for example, the Consumer's Association. Some are poorly funded and others use their access to Government poorly. Partly, this latter may be due to the tendency in many bodies to form decisions by committee; partly because staff of the right calibre may not be available. This is not unduly to criticize representative bodies – there are precious few people outside Government who really understand how it works.
- Members will often acquire information faster (but at a cost) if they monitor Government themselves.

Taking both sets of arguments together, the best advice is probably to take a close and dispassionate look at the abilities of the body representing your interests. Ask MPs for their views on the quality of that body's dealings with them. However good the organization – and some are very good at working on behalf of their members – you will probably have to fight your own battles and will therefore also need to consider other sources of information and advice.

Government affairs consultants

Government affairs consultants are specialists in dealing with Government. Their work involves one or more of the following:

1 Legislative and policy analysis.
2 Monitoring of and research into legislative and Government public and commercial policy planning.
3 Advice on advocacy to influence public policy.
4 Direct advocacy to influence public or commercial policy and legislation on behalf of their clients.
5 Auditing in-house capability.

Some firms purely provide monitoring services, but most satisfy points 3 and 4 above, each with a distinctive character. Most specialize in parliamentary work, although a few cover Whitehall and still fewer have sharply defined subject expertise such as oil, information technology or commercial negotiations with Government. While some of these firms are divisions of public relations companies, the rest work only in this area and have no connection with public relations except in using techniques of mobilizing public or media opinion where necessary. The firm you employ will, as with other professional consultants, therefore depend on your requirement: organization of meetings and visits; access to decision-makers; advice on case-making and negotiation; opinion-forming; commercial advocacy; work with Parliament, Whitehall or both; monitoring and research. Essentially though, consultants can be divided into two types: those who facilitate access to Government and those who understand how Government works. While the two streams are not mutually exclusive, the first approach tends to be based on contact techniques aimed largely at Parliament; the second on a working knowledge of the way decisions at Westminster and Whitehall are made and on structuring a client's case after detailed research. This is the difference, in broad terms, between using a PR adviser and a barrister. In dealing with Government, it is advisable to use professional help and the latter type of consultant is invariably more effective than the former.

Regrettably, there is as yet no professional qualification or official vetting of practitioners to provide you with a guarantee of a minimum level of competence. In considering whether to appoint Government affairs consultants, you must therefore be certain that the quality of advice you receive is not more apparent than real, since the best firms are invariably those who are least visually impressive.

Why should you use government affairs consultants?
- To provide you with information;
- to augment your own expertise and resources where there are weaknesses;
- to replace in-house resources if it would be more cost-effective to do so, even if your own skills are equal to those of the consultants you appoint.

Considerations in appointing them:
- What is their background? Have they any experience of working inside the components of power?
- What is their consultancy record? Have they handled any other work in the same area as yours or with the same targets?
- Are you satisfied that their assessment of your targets is based on a real understanding of the way Government works? Do they appear to be steering you towards Parliament to the exclusion of the rest of the system; if so, what do they intend to do with the Departments that may be important centres of power for you?
- Do they have a mastery of the techniques of working with Government, or are they simply trying to apply PR skills to your needs? PR is useful if you need to influence media and public opinion only, for example on environmental issues, but for all other work involving direct contact with Government, consultants must demonstrate the lawyer's skills of objectivity, advocacy techniques and a full grasp of the system of decision-making in Government.
- Can they justify their advice: why are the targets they recommend important to you? Can those targets give you what you seek?
- How fast and extensive is their monitoring?
- Are they sufficiently independent to advise on restructuring your case or to disagree if your methods or objectives are inappropriate or unattainable, no matter how attractive you may find them?
- Reject statements suggesting that a firm has 'tame' MPs at its disposal, or that it can stage events for you in the House, unless you are happy that such activities are worthwhile and the use of Parliament and parliamentarians in this way would be ethically justified.

Treat government affairs consultants as you would a lawyer or accountant – as professional advisers who should be a regular part of any corporate armoury or pressure group campaign team. The use of government affairs consultants should not be considered as part of your PR activities, even if a PR firm is used for this work. The US practice of treating the legal and regulatory affairs manager as the reporting officer on matters relating to Government (also followed by many British organizations, such as the Consumers' Association, who have regular dealings with Government but may not be able to establish a full-time government affairs department) is more appropriate in view of the close relationship between the law, legislation and public policy.

Other professional advisers

The work done with Government by advisers who are more established in other areas should not be overlooked. The privatization and consultancy work undertaken in recent years by solicitors, accountants and merchant banks has given some of them considerable experience in dealing with specific Departments and particularly, in the case of banks, with the Treasury, Department of Trade and Industry and Monopolies and Mergers Commission. The leading City accountants may be consulted on fiscal negotiations and occasionally on public procurement and the implications of complex corporate and financial legislation. Solicitors are also, of course, legislative analysts but are most valuable in advising on the clear presentation of your case.

In many ways, government affairs consultants combine the skills of other professional advisers in dealing with Whitehall and Westminster, but the proven expertise of some of the major City firms now working in this field may be helpful.

Retained MPs and Peers

At least 100 MPs and an indeterminate number of Peers (since the latter do not have to register their interests) are retained by organizations to provide them with advice; to act as spokesmen for their interests or to assist them with obtaining access to other MPs, Peers and Ministers. They have several advantages:

- No one understands Parliament better than an insider. Even the best government affairs consultants, if acting ethically, cannot see the volume of information that reaches MPs and Peers – details of backbench and All-Party committee agendas; the plans of the Whips; the private discussions that take place in the PLP and 1922 meetings, and much more besides.

Dealing with Government

- They have better access to Ministers and other MPs than do most consultants, making it easier for them to produce their colleagues for meetings and receptions (however, be careful in the latter case: knowing that many clients are impressed by weight of numbers, the temptation is to invite those whom the MP can most easily persuade to attend if it is not possible for the most relevant targets to be there – another example of the apparent versus real problem of which you must be wary).
- They are less expensive to retain than are other professional consultants.

However:

- Their value depends on their position and popularity. An Opposition MP or Peer will not enjoy the same degree of access to Ministers as a colleague on the Government side. Many MPs have less mobilizing ability than may be expected because they are not liked by other parliamentarians or are too junior. A former Minister is ideal because he will also understand the workings of Whitehall.
- They may not have enough time to help you, in which case you will have to augment their advice with that of other consultants or devote more of your own time to addressing your objectives.
- They cannot deal with Whitehall. While some officials are happy to answer enquiries from parliamentarians, most still refer MPs and Peers to the appropriate Minister's Private Office. Negotiation with, or even access to officials on your behalf, should be discounted.
- They may be seen by their colleagues as the hireling of your organization and therefore disregarded as an objective advocate. That is why their standing in Parliament is so important and also why, as a general rule, they should not speak on behalf of their clients.
- You must insist that any MP you retain should declare his interest to the House.
- They may have little individual power.
- It is advisable, if you wish to retain parliamentarians, to employ members of both Government and Opposition sides since you may require All-Party action.

Public relations firms

Generally, PR firms are retained by government affairs consultants, who would advise on their choice depending on your needs: it may be advisable to mobilize grass roots pressure; to produce visual presentations or video information (for example, outside organizations can stage exhibitions in the Upper Waiting Hall, or just outside the Committee Corridor in the House, by arrangement with the Sergeant at Arms); or to obtain press coverage nationally and locally. For pressure groups, the use of PR may be a more effective tactic on public issues than negotiation with Government. It should be remembered, however, that a battering ram is not needed if you can walk through the door. Pressure should in most instances be a subsidiary weapon in your plans. Guidance on selection of a reputable firm can be obtained from the Public Relations Consultants Association, Premier House, 10 Greycoat Place, London SW1. It is advisable, however, to treat with some scepticism those firms claiming to provide professional PR and government affairs services: the difference between the two disciplines makes it sensible to use separate specialists rather than be tempted by the facility of having your requirements serviced, probably less professionally, under one roof.

Appendix 1

The courts and the Ombudsman: action against executive and administrative decisions

Where negotiations with, or pressure on Government makes no impression, it may be possible to secure results through recourse to administrative law or the Parliamentary Commissioner for Administration.

If significant error can be found with the way a decision by a Minister, or in his name, has been reached, it can be quashed by the High Court and the Government told to think again. The courts cannot substitute a more reasonable or accurate decision for the Minister's: they can only rule that a mistake has been made.

Examples: In 1985 the DHSS issued a decision to alter the lodgings rule for young people living on supplementary benefit. The court ruled that it was invalid since Parliament had not been given the opportunity formally to approve the new Regulation. The Minister was acting without jurisdiction.

In 1985 the Secretary of State for Transport directed the Greater London Council to hold a public inquiry before imposing a night and weekend ban on heavy lorries. The court ruled that he had no legal power to issue such decisions. Even if he had, it would have been unreasonable to direct that an inquiry took place in view of the lengths to which the GLC had gone to examine the issue before deciding to impose a ban.

This power of the courts is known as judicial review. The principle allows them to review and condemn the actions of Government as:

Irrational, meaning that a decision is so unreasonable that the decision-maker must have been influenced by an improper motive, have taken into account irrelevant matters or omitted relevant ones. The test is that no reasonable person or authority looking at all the facts and circumstances could have taken the decision in question. In practice, it is very difficult to prove.

Illegal, meaning that the decision has been based on an incorrect interpretation of applicable law.

Procedurally improper, meaning that there has been some unfairness in the way a decision was reached, for example, by ignoring the principles of natural justice. Considerations of national security are usually accepted by the courts as overriding natural justice.

Other earlier examples, successful and unsuccessful, of judicial review illustrate its scope:

Appendix 1

The Secretary of State for Environment successfully defended the Conservative Government's legislation to control local authorities' rating powers against legal action. The same Minister's 1985 refusal to reopen a public enquiry into a plan for an airport in London's dockland was upheld as being neither illegal, unreasonable or unfair. In 1980, as Secretary of State for Health and Social Security he was told that his decision to replace an area health authority with commissioners, in a clash over cash limits, was illegal. A Labour Secretary of State for Education was overruled in his attempts to compel a Conservative-run education authority to implement a plan for comprehensive schools. The Attorney-General's refusal to intervene when Post Office workers blacked mail to South Africa was ruled illegal. The Secretary of State for Trade was adjudged to have exceeded his powers in refusing to grant Laker Airways a licence for its Skytrain service.

On occasions, judicial review may be the only remedy available to you, but actions are rarely brought against governments and the decision to consider recourse to administrative law can only be reached after consultations with an experienced practitioner.

The Ombudsman investigates cases of maladministration by Government bodies – delays, wrong advice, bias or discrimination, refusal to act where there is a clear duty to do so, or failure to follow prescribed procedures. Most of his work concerns DHSS and the Inland Revenue but any Department can be investigated and a number of public bodies also fall within his remit:

ACAS
Agricultural Wages Committees
Arts Council
British Library Board
British Council
Building Societies Commission
Certification Officer
Charity Commission
Civil Service Commission
Commission for the New Towns
Cosira
Countryside Commission
Crown Estate Office
Data Protection Registrar
Department for National Savings
Department of the Registers of Scotland
Development Boards Agencies
ECGD
Equal Opportunities Commission CRE
Forestry Commission
General Registry Office, Scotland
Health and Safety Executive/Commission
HMSO

Housing Corporation
Industrial Training Boards
Intervention Board for Agricultural Produce
Land Registry
Legal Aid Boards
Medical practices committees
MSC
National Debt Office
National Tourist Boards
Nature Conservancy Council
Northern Ireland Court Service
Office of Fair Trading
OFTEL/OFGAS/OFFER
Ordnance Survey
Public record offices
Public Trustee
Registry of Friendly Societies
Research Councils
Residuary bodies
Royal Mint
Scottish Courts Administration
Scottish Homes
Sports Councils
Treasury Solicitors
Urban Development Corporations

He cannot investigate nationalized industries and similar bodies such as British Rail, the Post Office, and electricity and gas boards. Nor can he consider complaints about Government policy or legislation in general or contractual and other commercial dealings with Government, except compulsory purchase of land. He looks at the way Government deals with governed, and does not act as a court of appeal from its decisions. He is not an alternative to statutory appeal procedures and will only act in lieu of the courts if it is considered unreasonable for you to take legal action: cost is not a consideration. He will not take up your case if you have already gone to court.

Complaints to the Ombudsman must be referred, within one year of the alleged maladministration becoming apparent, through an MP, although not necessarily your constituency Member, and all correspondence you have had with the Department must be attached with your complaint. You must be personally affected and have suffered an injustice such as financial loss or gross inconvenience, and you must be prepared to wait – the Ombudsman's investigations can take up to a year.

The Parliamentary Commissioner for Administration is based at Church House, Great Smith Street, London SW1P 3BW.

Appendix 2

Components and mechanics – finding out more

Despite the large number of books written on the British system of government, there are few that do more than analyse the public face of decision-making or provide a classical, and now outdated view of the British Constitution in terms of effective checks and balances. There are three reference books, however, that are essential for any serious student of the practical workings of the system:

- *The Civil Service Year Book* (HMSO);
- *Dod's Parliamentary Companion* (Dod's Parliamentary Companion Ltd); and
- *Roth's Parliamentary Profiles* (Parliamentary Profile Services Ltd).

As a general and well-informed guide to components and mechanics, we recommend two books by MPs: Nigel Forman's *Mastering British Politics* (Macmillan, 1985) is excellent, as is *Honorable Member* by Richard Needham (Patrick Stephens, 1983), a guide to the Commons and the lives of MPs. The Industry and Parliament Trusts *Commons Select Committees – Catalysts for Progress?* (1984) covers one specific area of the House's work.

Very little has been written about the Civil Service. The most comprehensive study is *Whitehall*, by Peter Hennessy (Secker and Warburg, 1989). *The Crossman Diaries* (Methuen, 1979) and Joe Haines' *Politics of Power* (Jonathan Cape) provide personal descriptions of the work of a Cabinet Minister and 10 Downing Street. Joel Barnet's *Inside the Treasury* (Andre Deutsch) is self-explanatory. Richard Crossman's *Inside View* (Jonathan Cape, 1982) gives a broader insight into policy-making from a Minister's angle. Gerald Kaufman's *How to be a Minister* (Sidgwick and Jackson, 1980) and Kellner and Crowther-Hunt's *The Civil Servants* (Macdonald, 1980) throw further light on the work of officials and their masters. The most revealing book on the Cabinet system is Peter Hennessy's *Cabinet* (Basil Blackwell, 1986).

Two publications commend themselves to the EEC-watcher: Vacher's *European Companion* (A. S. Kerswill Ltd, quarterly), which acts as a combination of *The Civil Service Year Book* and *Dod* for the institutions of the EEC; and John Drew's *Doing Business in the European Community* (Touche Ross), which provides a clear guide to the work of those institutions and the techniques of working with them.

Appendix 3

Movement of officials to the private sector – rules and concerns

Extracts from the Treasury & Civil Service Select Committee's report on acceptance of outside appointments by Crown servants (1983–4, HC 302)

Rules on the Acceptance of Outside Business Appointments by Crown Servants

It is in the public interest that people with experience of public administration should be able to move into business and industry, and that the possibility of such movement should not be frustrated by public concern over a particular appointment. It is also no less important whenever a Crown servant accepts a particular business appointment that he should not be open to any suspicion of impropriety. Therefore the rules set out below have been designed to safeguard against such criticisms both the public service and individual officers who wish to leave to take up these appointments. The rules aim at avoiding any suspicion—however unjustified—that serving officers might be ready to bestow favours on firms in the hope of future benefits to come. They also seek to guard against the risk that a particular firm might be thought to be gaining an unfair advantage over its competitors by employing an officer who, during his service, had access to technical or other information which those competitors could legitimately regard as their own trade secrets.

2. All officers of the rank of Under Secretary (or, in the Diplomatic Service, Counsellors) and above, and of the equivalent ranks in HM Forces, are required to obtain the assent of the Government before accepting within two years of resignation or retirement offers of employment in business and other bodies:[1]

(a) which are in contractual relationships with the Government;
(b) which are in receipt of subsidies or their equivalent from the Government;
(c) in which the Government is a shareholder;
(d) which are in receipt from the Government of loans, guarantees or other forms of capital assistance; or
(e) with which Services, or Departments or branches of Government are, as a matter of course, in a special relationship;

---

[1] The words "particularly those" have since been inserted at this point: see Appendix 5 of the Fourth Report from the Treasury and Civil Service Committee, Session 1980–1981. HC 216.

and in semi-public organisations brought into being by the Government or Parliament. In addition there are posts of a special or technical nature (below the rank of Under Secretary) to which Departments must apply a similar requirement. The Government's assent must similarly be obtained if an officer wishes to accept an appointment in the service of a foreign government.

PROCEDURE

3. Assent to an application will take the form of approval by the Prime Minister in cases referred to an Advisory Committee, or by the Minister in charge of the Department in all other cases. It would however be open to a Minister to approve arrangement under which defined categories of case would be dealt with at a specified level without reference to the Minister.

4. *Permanent Secretaries and Second Permanent Secretaries*

All cases concerning Permanent Secretaries and Second Permanent Secretaries (and those of equivalent rank in HM Forces) must be referred to the Head of the Civil Service and to the Minister responsible for the Department. Where the Head of the Civil Service and the departmental Minister are agreed that the proposed appointment is to a non-commercial body of such a nature that this procedure would be inappropriate (eg a University), the appointment may be approved without reference to the Committee. All other cases will then be referred by the Head of the Civil Service to the Prime Minister to be laid before the Advisory Committee (see paragraph 10).

5. *All Other Heads of Departments*

All cases concerning Heads of Departments other than Permanent Secretaries will follow the procedure for cases concerning Permanent Secretaries, with one variation; where the Minister responsible for the Department and the Head of the Civil Service are in agreement about whether consent should be given or withheld and, if the former, about any conditions to be imposed, the case may be decided, without reference to the Advisory Committee, by the departmental Minister.

6. *Deputy Secretaries etc.*

All cases concerning Deputy Secretaries, officers of higher rank below Second Permanent Secretary and HM Forces personnel of equivalent rank (other than those covered by paragraph 5 above) will similarly follow the procedure for Permanent Secretaries, subject to the exception that where the Head of the Department concerned and the Head of the Civil Service are in agreement about whether assent may be given or withheld and, if the former, about any conditions to be imposed, the case may be decided, without reference to the Advisory Committee, by the Departmental Minister.

7. *All other cases*

Save for the exception referred to in paragraph 8, the CSD must be consulted in all cases not covered by paragraphs 4–8 where there has been "contact with the prospective employer" as defined in paragraph 16.

8. Departments need not consult the CSD in cases covered by paragraph 7 up to and including Senior Executive Officer level (or the equivalent rank in HM Forces) where the contact with the prospective employer in the previous two years had been only casual, and there appears to be no risk of criticism from the trade secrets angle.

9. In putting cases forward to the CSD, Departments should explain why they recommend that permission should be granted. They should say whether they consider that a satisfactory answer could be given in the event of the Government being criticised for allowing the appointment to be taken up.

ADVISORY COMMITTEE

10. The Advisory Committee will consist of three members having experience of relations between Civil Service and the public or private sectors of industry. The members will on each occasion be drawn from a panel. Cases will be referred to the Committee by the Prime Minister and it will report to him. The Committee will consider the cases defined in paragraphs 4–6. It many also consider, exceptionally, cases falling outside those grades which are referred to it. The Committee will not act as a court of appeal against decisions reached in cases not referred to it.

11. In considering cases the Committee will have regard to the purpose of the rules as described in paragraph 1. The Committee will take into account the views of the Department concerned and of the CSD.

12. In all cases referred to the Committee, the final decision will rest with the Prime Minister who will be answerable in the House for the decision; the responsibility for all cases which do not go to the Committee will however remain with the departmental Minister concerned. The Prime Minister will be free to accept or reject the Committee's report together with any recommendations which it may make.

13. Except as noted in paragraph 14, in all cases referred to the Committee which concern Permanent Secretaries (and their equivalents in HM Forces), a minimum period of three months must elapse between leaving the Service and taking up an outside appointment within the scope of the rules.

14. Exceptions to the waiting period described in paragraph 13 may be made only in cases where the Prime Minister agrees that the national interest is overriding, eg where the appointment is to another post in the public sector (see also paragraph 18(*c*))

CONDITIONS WHICH MAY BE IMPOSED

15. It will be open to those considering applications in accordance with paragraphs 4–7 to recommend outright refusal or unqualified approval; or to recommend approval subject to conditions. Such conditions may include:

(*a*) a waiting period lasting for up to two years, the duration to be determined according to the individual circumstances of the case. (In the case of

Permanent Secretaries, the automatic three months' period will form part of any longer period which may be imposed);

(b) a ban on involvement in dealings between the prospective employer and the Government, either absolute or with reference to a stated issue or issues, lasting for up to two years, the duration to be determined according to the circumstances of the case;

(c) a ban on involvement in dealings between the prospective employer and a named competitor (or competitors), subject to the same conditions of scope and duration as those at (b) above;

(d) a requirement to seek the approval of the prospective employer's competitors for the proposed appointment, should this not already have been done.

CONSIDERATIONS TO BE TAKEN INTO ACCOUNT

16. One of the main factors which will be relevant to the consideration of cases will be the degree of contact there has been between the applicant and the prospective employer. Sometimes the prospective employer's relations with the Government may be relevant irrespective of any involvement on the part of the individual concerned. But normally some measure of personal involvement on the part of the applicant will be necessary for this factor to be relevant. Such involvement should be assumed when the individual concerned, either directly or personally or indirectly through those for whom he is responsible (whether or not they normally work to him) at any time in the course of his official duties during the two years before his resignation or retirement or earlier if the association has been of a continued or repeated nature, has:

(a) dealt with the receipt of tenders for and/or the awarding of contracts between the firm involved and the Government; or

(b) dealt with the administration and/or monitoring of such contracts after they have been awarded; or

(c) advised in a professional or technical capacity about such contracts either before they are awarded, as in (a), or in the exercise of a monitoring brief, as in (b); or

(d) been involved in contact of an official but non-contractual nature with the firm involved—where, for instance, the firm operates in a field in which the Government as a whole or the individual's Department has a special interest of a financial, policy or other nature.

17. Previous contact as outlined in paragraph 16 should weigh heavily in the consideration of any application. But the decision of what conditions (if any) should be imposed or whether the application should be rejected will depend on the full circumstances of the case, including the extent and nature of the previous contact.

18. Other considerations which should be kept in view include:

(a) The possibility that the applicant may have had access to information about one or more of his prospective employer's competitors which could legitimately be regarded as their "trade secrets". This may arise independently of any contact with the prospective employer—when, for instance, the prospective employer is a newly-created company or consultancy in the relevant field. It would be normal to consult these competitors to see if they had any objection to the appointment;

(*b*) An appointment may be on a part-time or consultancy basis. If so, this may be a factor tending to reduce the likelihood of public criticism, especially if the consultancy service is to be offered without favour to a number of firms competing in the same field;

(*c*) There may be occasions when a Minister considers it in the national interest that, although the normal weighing of the factors to be considered might dictate the granting only of qualified approval or even the rejection of the application, the appointment may nevertheless be allowed. In all such cases, the procedures set out in paragraphs 4–7 should be followed, including reference to the Advisory Committee where that is appropriate.

(*d*) Many senior Crown servants are engaged in dealing with private interests on behalf of the Government. Moreover, such senior officials would have a special knowledge of how the Government would be likely to react to particular sets of circumstances, and how the Government would be likely to legislate to give effect to its policies. An official in this position could well be, or be thought to be, of considerable assistance to an outside body which had an interest in matters on which policy was developing or legislation was being prepared. It is important to take into account the advisability or otherwise of permitting Crown servants to join outside interests with whom the Department had been, or was, in a negotiating relationship. It may also be relevant that a senior official was involved in policy discussion which led to a decision the effect of which was considerably to the benefit of the firm offering him an apppointment.

19. In cases involving Permanent Secretary Heads of Department subject to the automatic waiting period (see paragraph 13), formal applications to take up an outside appointment should not normally be made until after the successor to the individual concerned has been named. Cases where the individual intended to resign before retirement in order to take up an outside appointment would have to be considered earlier.

WARNING TO STAFF

20. When an officer to whom the rules apply is nearing retirement his Department should remind him of the rules and should take the opportunity to suggest that, if he is in any doubt as to whether he needs to seek permission to take up a particular appointment, he should in the first instance approach his Establishment Officer for advice. It is important that the officer should be aware that permission must be sought not only for the initial appointment taken up on retirement, but for any subsequent appointment during the two year period which comes within the scope of the rules, including appointments to subsidiary or associated companies.

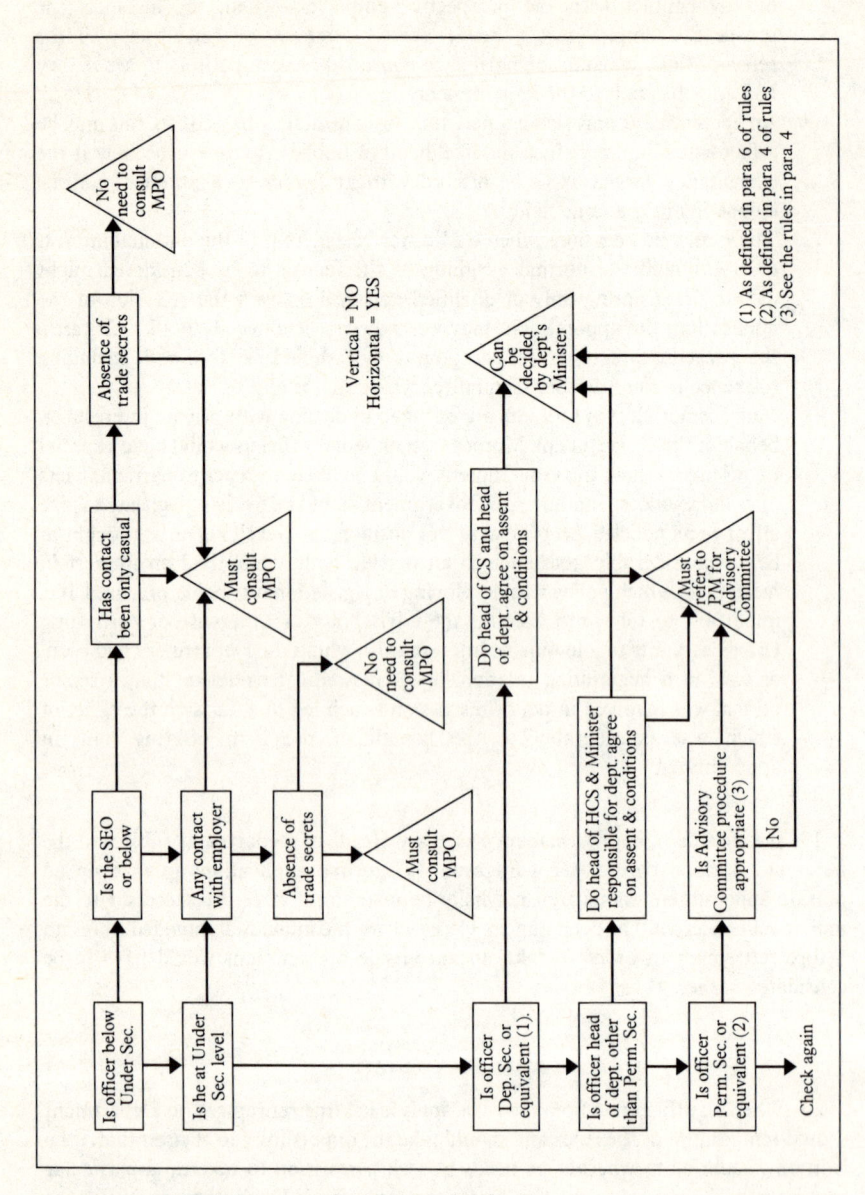

Box 52 The MPO's arrangements for vetting movement to the private sector

And the select committee's view

1.6 The second issue is related. We have had an overview of the movement of senior civil servants in general both in terms of their former Department, the private sector employment to which they went and the public comments made at the time of the move. We have the impression that there is now a steady and accepted movement of certain senior civil servants into certain areas of the private sector. The ease of the movement, the ready availability of employment and the often informal approaches made by the private sector suggest to us, at a time of increasing closeness and interdependence between government and the private sector, that the traditional independence and impartiality of the Civil Service is in danger of becoming eroded or compromised in the eyes of the public.

1.7 We return to the original purpose behind the introduction of the rules. The acceptance of business appointments by crown servants was seen as proper and desirable by the Government of the day. The rules were designed to ensure public confidence in the impartiality and integrity of the Civil Service. It was recognised that there may be public suspicion, however unjustified, or misunderstanding over certain business appointments. The rules were intended to allay this. We consider that that principle must remain paramount today, even at the expense of the freedom of movement of individual civil servants or the particular benefits accruing to them or to firms. It is essential that the traditionally high standards of the Civil Service should be maintained and seen to be maintained in the eyes of the public.

1.8 From our evidence we consider that Governments have failed to adapt the rules and procedures to changing circumstances. They seem to be unaware of the regular expressions of concern and criticism and they have not opened procedures and decisions—originally designed to allay public anxiety—to public scrutiny.

1.9 Consequently we believe that there is a danger that amid the generality of movements to the private sector to which we have no objection in principle, Governments may have allowed a pattern of transfer to develop which could be in conflict with the purpose of the rules. Indeed, the longer such types of appointments are allowed to continue and become seen as normal by both Governments and Departments, the more the rules and procedures could come to be seen as generally ineffectual and the greater the potential both for abuse of business apointments and for loss of public confidence in the integrity and impartiality of the public service in this country.

Appendix 4

Departments – responsibilities and ministerial duties 1989

NOTE: When ministerial reshuffles take place, responsibilities are often reallocated.

1. Ministry of Agriculture, Fisheries and Food
Whitehall Place, London SW1A 2HH   01–270 3000

1988 staff: 10,236 (plus 778 for Intervention Board for Agricultural Produce.)

Responsibility for administering agriculture, horticulture and fishing policy in England and for many food matters in the UK. Some responsibilities for animal health extend to Great Britain. In association with the Scottish, Welsh and Northern Ireland Offices and the Intervention Board for Agricultural Produce it administers EEC agricultural and fisheries policies and national support schemes. It administers the control and eradication of animal and plant diseases and assistance to capital investment in farm and horticultural businesses and land drainage. It is also responsible for applied research and development. The Agricultural Development and Advisory Service is part of the Ministry. MAFF sponsors the food and drink manufacturing industries and distributive trades. It is concerned with the supply and quality of food, food compositional standards, food hygiene and labelling and has certain responsibilities for ensuring public health standards in the manufacture, preparation and distribution of basic foods.

Ministerial duties

The Minister of Agriculture, Fisheries and Food has overall responsibility and deals with agricultural support policy; the EC, including price fixing and the Annual Review; and the Forestry Commission.

Three Parliamentary Under Secretaries:

1. (A Peer) deals with cereals, sugar, oils and fats; potatoes; processed fruit and vegetables and tropical fruits; horticulture; plant health; plant variety and seeds; pesticides and infestation control; regional administration; advisory policy; research and development; marketing, export promotion and trade policy; relations with all overseas countries and international organisations; and is the Minister's deputy.

2. Deals with meat, milk and poultry products; animal health and welfare; agricultural resources policy including labour, finance and taxation matters; fisheries; deregulation; central services; IBAP; emergency services; economics and statistics.
3. Deals with food policy; food standards and food science; alcoholic drinks; countryside matters including agricultural land use diversification; environmental and conservation policy; rural employment including the Farm and Countryside Initiative; EC socio-structural policies; land tenure; agricultural grants; flood defence.

2. Office of Arts and Libraries
Horse Guards Road, London SW1P 3AL   01–270 3000
1988 staff: 56

Concerned with matters affecting the arts generally and with museums and libraries, the National Heritage and the Government Art Collection. It funds a number of agencies including the national museums and galleries in England and those run by English local authorities, the British Library and public libraries in England, the Arts Council of Great Britain and other arts bodies. It has direct responsibility for expenditure on the British Library's St Pancras Project.

Ministerial duties

Minister for the Arts has overall responsibility.

3. HM Customs and Excise
New Kings Beam House, 22 Upper Ground, London SE1 9PJ   01–620 1313

1988 staff: 26,252

Responsible for collecting and administering customs and excise duties and Value Added Tax and advising the Chancellor of the Exchequer on any matters connected with them. Also responsible for preventing and detecting evasion of revenue laws and enforcing a range of prohibitions and restrictions on the importation of certain classes of goods. It also undertakes certain agency work on behalf of other Departments, including compilation of UK overseas trade statistics from import and export documents.

Ministerial duties

The Economic Secretary in the Treasury deals with Customs and Excise.

4. Ministry of Defence
Main Building, Whitehall, London SW1A 2HB   01-218 9000

1988 staff: 142,507

Concerned with the control, administration, equipment and support of the UK's armed forces. Research, development, production and purchase of weapons and equipment is the concern of the Ministry's Procurement Executive.

Ministerial duties

The Secretary of State has overall responsibility.

The Minister of State for the Armed Forces is responsible for the size and shape of the three services; arms control; military assistance to the civil authorities; and operations and exercises.

The Minister of State for Defence Procurement (a Peer) is responsible for defence industrial question; defence sales; equipment projects; collaboration; forward planning of the equipment programme; and civilian personnel.

The Parliamentary Under Secretary for the Armed Forces assists the Minister of State, with particular responsibility for the defence estate; low flying; and reserves and training.

The Parliamentary Under Secretary for Defence Procurement assists the Minister of State, with particular responsibility for R&D; contracts; 'Next Steps' policy and the New Management Strategy; and quality assurance.

5. Department of Education and Science
Elizabeth House, York Road, London SE1 7PH   01-934 9000

1988 staff: 2,555

The Department promotes education in England. It is responsible for the Government's relations with universities in England, Wales and Scotland and it fosters the progress of civil science both in Britain and in collaboration with other nations.

Ministerial duties

The Secretary of State has overall responsibility and specific responsibility for the Department's organisation and running costs, public expenditure, teacher's pay – schools, universities, PCFC sector and FE, and city technology colleges.

The Minister of State deals with the school curriculum including TVEI and religious education; tests, assessments and school examinations; LEA complaints; machinery; under fives; school governors; inner London education; teacher training; education research; grant maintained schools; section 12-16 of the Education Act 1980.

Two Parliamentary Under Secretaries:

1. Deals with open enrolment; local management of schools and charging; school and FE building programmes; Architects and Building Branch duties; special education in schools; European schools; inner cities policy; school/industry links and careers educations; information technology in schools; discipline in schools; health education (including AIDS, drugs and sex education); independent schools, the assisted places scheme and the music and ballet scheme; youth services; teachers' supply; teachers' misconduct; teachers' pensions. He assists the Minister of State with applications for grant maintained status and sections 12–16 of the Education Act 1980.

2. Deals with higher education, notably policy, individual institutions funding council matters, content and quality; science policy and the science budget; further education, notably financial delegation, governance and management, content and quality, special education needs and 16–19 year old issues; links with the Employment Department: the Training Agency (except TVEI); adult and continuing education; student support; student affairs; overseas students; international work.

6. Department of Employment
Caxton House, Tothill Street, London SW1H 9NF 01–273 3000

1988 staff: 41,358 (plus 12,012 – Training Agency; 3,412 Health and Safety Commission/Executive; 618 – Advisory, Conciliation and Arbitration Service)

The Department promotes a competitive and efficient labour market conducive to the growth of employment and the reduction of unemployment. The key aspects of its work are: to secure better arrangements for young people and adults to acquire and improve their skills and competences for work; to give positive help to unemployed people; particularly those out of work for 6 months or more, by providing a range of training programmes and job placing services and making payments of benefits to those unemployed and entitled to it; to promote the creation and growth of small firms and self employment; to promote a positive environment for work so that industrial relations continue to improve and a fair balance under the law is obtained; to ensure equal opportunity under the law and that the employment rights of individuals are safeguarded and to see that health and safety at work is maintained and improved. The Department is responsible for the Employment Service's nationwide network of Jobcentres and Unemployment Benefit Offices. It provides a wide range of training programmes including YTS and employment training. The Department is also responsible for the collection and publication of statistics on labour and industrial matters, liaises with the International Labour Organisation, and represents the UK on employment.

Ministerial duties

The Secretary of State has overall responsibility.

The Minister of State is responsible for Europe; other international matters; Small Firms and Enterprise; training, and Training and Enterprise Councils; the Employment Service; inner cities; Financial Management Initiative.

Two Parliamentary Under Secretaries:

1. Deals with employment training; YTS; ITBs; Open College; industrial relations legislation; health and safety; equal opportunities; Wages Councils; redundancy payments; ACAS; and also assists the Minister of State on Small Firms and Enterprise.
2. Deals with tourism; disabled persons; work permits; statistics; research; local/regional employment issues; employment agencies; energy conservation.

7. Department of Energy
Thames House South, Millbank, London SW1P 4QJ   01–211 3000

1988 staff: 991

Responsible for policy in relation to all forms of energy, including energy efficiency and the development of new sources of energy. It is also responsible for the international aspects of energy policy. The Department is responsible for the nationalised coal industry as well as the Atomic Energy Authority. It sponsors the nuclear power construction, oil, gas and electricity industries. It is responsible for the Government interest in the development of oil and gas resources in the British sector of the Continental Shelf and for the Offshore Supplies Office in its role of developing the ability of UK suppliers to meet the needs of the offshore operators on the UK continental shelf and worldwide.

Ministerial duties

The Secretary of State has overall responsibility and deals with major policy issues and matters of major public interest.

The Minister of State has responsibility for all oil and gas matters including the offshore supply industry. He also handles energy efficiency and renewable sources of energy.

The Parliamentary Under Secretary has special responsibility for coal, electricity and nuclear power.

International energy questions in any area of policy is a matter for the Minister with responsibility for that particular area.

8. Department of the Environment
2 Marsham Street, London SW1 3EB   01–276 3000

1988 staff: 6,594 (plus 21,468 – Property Service Agency; 1716 – Crown Supplies)

Responsible for planning, local government, new towns, housing; construction; inner city matters; environmental protection; water; countryside affairs; sport and recreation; royal parks and palaces; historic monuments. The Property Services

Agency is responsible for Government buildings, land and property holdings, and associated supplies and transport services.

Ministerial duties

The Secretary of State has overall responsibility for the direction of the Department and its policies, including the Property Services Agency.

The Minister for Housing and Planning is responsible for housing, planning, construction industries, and new towns and water.

The Minister for Local Government and Inner Cities is responsible for local government and inner cities.

The Minister for the Environment and Countryside is responsible for environmental protection, countryside, heritage, British Waterways Board and Ordnance Survey and water

Four Parliamentary Under Secretaries of State:

1. Supporting the Minister for Housing and Planning on housing, new towns, and construction; the Minister for local Government and Inner Cities on local government finance issues; and reporting direct to the Secretary of State on the Property Services Agency.
2. Supporting the Minister for Housing and Planning on planning; the Minister for Local Government and Inner Cities on inner cities; and reporting direct to the Secretary of State on sport.
3. Supporting the Minister for the Environment and Countryside on environmental protection, countryside and water (after flotation); and the Minister for Local Government and Inner Cities on local government issues other than finance.
4. Departmental spokesman in the House of Lords; and supporting the Minister for the Environment on Heritage, British Waterways Board and Ordnance Survey.

9. Foreign and Commonwealth Office
Downing Street, London SW1A 2AL   01-270 3000

1988 staff: 8,027 (plus 1,517 – Overseas Development Administration)

Provides, mainly through diplomatic missions, the means of communication between the British Government and other governments and international governmental organisations for the discussion and negotiation of all matters falling within the field of international relations. It is responsible for alerting the British Government to the implications of developments overseas; for protecting British interests and citizens overseas; for explaining British policies to, and cultivating friendly relations with, Governments abroad and for the discharge of British responsibilities in the associate states (mainly for defence and external affairs) and dependent territories. The Overseas Development Administration deals with British development assistance to overseas countries. This includes capital aid in concessional terms and technical cooperation (mainly in the form of specialist staff abroad and training facilities in

Britain), provided directly to developing countries or through multilateral aid organisations, including the United Nations and its agencies. (Eland House, Stag Place, SW1E 5DH 01–213 3000)

Ministerial duties

The Secretary of State has overall responsibility.

Four Ministers of State:

1. Deals with the European Communities and international trade and economic relations; Western and Southern Europe; China and Hong Kong.
2. Deals with overseas development and aid and certain overseas pensions.
3. Deals with the Middle East, Near East and North Africa, sub-Saharan Africa, the USSR and Eastern Europe, East/West relations; defence; arms control and disarmament; science, environment and nuclear energy; and security co-ordination.
4. Deals with the Far East (except Hong Kong and China); South and South-East Asia; South Pacific; and Maritime and Aviation issues. He also has responsibility for resource management, personnel policy and other administration issues, the Overseas Estate, security, training, communications matters and information technology. Also has responsibility for all FCO subjects in the House of Lords.

The Parliamentary Under-Secretary of State deals with the Falkland Islands; North, South and Central America; the West Indies; International aspects of narcotics control and AIDS. he also deals with claims; immigration and nationality; consular questions; information and cultural affairs; United Nations matters and Protocol. He is responsible for Parliamentary Relations. In addition he is spokesman in the House of Commons on the above Minister's responsibilities.

10. Department of Health
Richmond House, 79 Whitehall, London SW1A 2NS 01–210 3000

1988 staff: 8,794

The Department is responsible (in England) for the administration of the NHS; for the social services provided by local authorities for the elderly and handicapped people, socially deprived families and children in care; and for certain aspects of public health. It also makes reciprocal health arrangements with other countries; represents the UK in the World Health Organisation and in other international fora.

Ministerial duties

The Secretary of State has overall responsibility.
  The Minister of State has responsibility for NHS management, personnel and pay issues. Also personal social services (including child care services) primary and community care, AIDS and pharmaceutical issues.
  The Parliamentary Under Secretary has responsibility for preventative health care,

including drug and alcohol abuse, mental health, and hospital services including those for the elderly and children and womens' health matters.

11. Home Office
50 Queen Anne's Gate, London SW1H 9AT   01-273 3000

1988 staff: 40,122

Deals with those internal matters in England and Wales that have not been assigned to other Government Departments. It is particularly concerned with the administration of justice; criminal law; the treatment of offenders including probation and the prison service; the police; immigration and nationality; passport policy matters; community relations; certain public safety matters; fire and civil defence services; and also with broad questions of national broadcasting policy. It is the link between the Queen and the public and exercises certain powers on her behalf including that of the Royal Pardon. Other subjects dealt with include electoral arrangements; addresses and petitions to the Queen; ceremonial and formal business connected with honours; requests for extradition of criminals; scrutiny of local authority bye-laws; grants of licences for scientific experiments on animals; cremations, burials and exhumations; firearms; dangerous drugs and poisons; general policy on laws relating to the voluntary social services; and race relations and sex discrimination policy. It is the link between the UK Government and the Governments of the Channel Islands and the Isle of Man.

Ministerial duties

The Secretary of State has overall responsibility and deals personally with emergencies; Royal matters; security and chairs the Ministerial Group on the misuse of Drugs.

Three Ministers of State:

1. Deals with immigration and nationality; community relations; data protection; the Passport Office; broadcasting; refugee resettlement; shops; Home Office interest in deregulation; and obsenity issues.
2. Deals with criminal policy and justice, other than life sentence cases and mental health policy and casework; crime prevention; juvenile offenders; probation and after-care; criminal justice casework; magistrates' courts; gambling; voluntary services; sex discrimination; community relations and inner cities; extradition and House of Commons business on charities law and cults; fire; and civil defences.
3. (A Peer) Deals with police; fire service; Channel Islands and Isle of Man; civil defence; charities; law and cults.

The Parliamentary Under Secretary deals with prisons, liquor licensing; electoral matters; summer time; animal welfare; coroners; local legislation/bye-laws; mentally disordered offenders policy and casework; life sentence cases; and House of Commons business on police, Channel Islands and Isle of Man.

12. Law Officers' Department
Attorney General's Chambers, Law Officers' Department, Royal Courts of Justice, London WC2A 2LL   01-936 6602

1988 staff: 19

Serves the Attorney General and the Solicitor General.

Ministerial duties

The Attorney General is the Government's principal legal adviser; he deals with questions of law arising on Bills, and with issues of legal policy; and is concerned with all major international and domestic litigation involving the Government. He supervises the work of the Director of Public Prosecutions and the DPP in Northern Ireland, and he has specific responsibilities for the enforcement of the criminal law. His consent is required for prosecutions under certain statutes and his fiat is required in connection with relator actions.

The Solicitor General has responsibility for such matters as the Attorney General delegates to him from time to time, and shares with him the handling of matters referred to the Department by MPs.

Both Ministers answer in the Commons on matters for which the Lord Chancellor is responsible, and vice versa.

13. Lord Advocate's Departments
10 Great College Street, London SW1P 3SL   01-212 7676

1988 staff: 19

Serves the Lord Advocate and the Solicitor General for Scotland and acts as legal adviser on Scottish questions to certain Government Departments. As Scottish parliamentary draftsmen, it is responsible for the drafting of legislation relating exclusively to Scotland and for the adaptation to Scotland of other legislation.

Ministerial duties

The Lord Advocate (a Peer) is the principal law officer in Scotland and the Government's constitutional and legal adviser on Scottish affairs. A further officer in Edinburgh, known as the Crown Officer, assists him in his responsibilities for prosecution in the High Court, Sheriff Courts and district courts, and for fatal accident and sudden death inquiries. The Scottish Courts Administration, also in Edinburgh, assists him in his responsibilities in the civil law field in respect of civil jurisdiction and procedure, evidence, the enforcement and respect of foreign judgments, the law of diligence and limitation of actions, private international law, and related matters. The Scottish Courts Administration is, however, answerable to the Secretary of State for Scotland (see 16) for the organisation and administration of the Supreme and Sheriff courts. The Lord Advocate has oversight of the work of the Scottish Law Commission.

The Solicitor General for Scotland is responsible for such matters as the Lord Advocate delegates to him from time to time and shares with him the handling of matters referred to the Department by MPs. He is spokesman for the Lord Advocate in the Commons.

14. Lord Chancellor's Department
House of Lords, London SW1A 0PW   01-219 3000

1988 staff: 10,706 (plus 9,348 – Land Registry; 420 – Public Records Office)

Administers the Supreme Court and county courts in England and Wales and legal-aid schemes. The Land Registry registers title to land in England and Wales, and subsequent transactions. It is responsible for registering incumbrances and other matters where the title is not requested, and for agricultural charges on farming stock. The Public Record Office houses the records of central government and the courts.

Ministerial duties

The Lord Chancellor is responsible for promoting general reforms in the civil law, for the procedure of the civil courts and for the administration of the Supreme Court and county courts in England and Wales, and for legal-aid schemes. He advises the Crown on the appointment of Masters and Registrars of the High Court and District and County Court Registrars and magistrates. He is responsible for ensuring that letters of patent and other formal documents are passed in the proper form under the Great Seal of the Realm, of which he is the custodian.

15. Northern Ireland Office
Whitehall, London SW1A 2AZ   01-210 3000; Stormont Castle, Belfast BT4 3ST   (0232) 63011

1988 staff: 174

Serves the Secretary of State for Northern Ireland, with overall responsibility for Northern Ireland Departments.

Ministerial duties

The Secretary of State has overall responsibility for the Office and the Northern Ireland Departments. He deals personally with political and constitutional matters; security policy and operations; broad economic questions; and other major policy issues.

The Minister of State has responsibility for Law and Order and also for the Department of Finance and Personnel. In addition, he acts as deputy to the Secretary of State.

Four Parliamentary Under Secretaries:

1. Assumes responsibility for the Department of Economic Development and remains responsible for the urban renewal activities of the Department of Environment.
2. Remains responsible for the Department of Education, Political Affairs Division and the Information Services.
3. Assumes responsibility for the Department of Agriculture and for the activities of the Department of Environment other than urban renewal, with particular emphasis on transport.
4. Takes on responsibility for the Department of Health and Social Services and will be spokesman on all Northern Ireland issues in the House of Lords.

16. Scottish Office

Dover House, Whitehall, London SW1A 2AU   01–270 3000; New St Andrew's House, Edinburgh EH1 3SK   031–556 8400

1988 staff: 9,839 (plus 878 – Scottish Courts Administration; 259 – General Register Office, Scotland; 920 – Registers of Scotland; 120 – Scottish Record Office)

Serves the Secretary of State for Scotland, with overall responsibility for Scottish Departments.

Ministerial duties

The Secretary of State has overall responsibility for the work of the Scottish Office. He deals personally with life prisoners, State patients and the exercise of the Royal Prerogative of mercy. He has responsibility for a wide range of statutory functions administered by the Department of Agriculture and Fisheries for Scotland; the Scottish Development Department; the Scottish Education Department; the Scottish Home and Health Department; and the Industry Department for Scotland. In addition, he has responsibility in some degree for the Scottish Courts of Administration, the Department of the Registrar-General for Scotland, the Scottish Record Office and the Department of Registers for Scotland.

The Minister of State for Agriculture and Fisheries (a Peer) deals with agriculture; fisheries, forestry; the Highlands and Islands Development Board; Scottish Tourist Board; and the co-ordination of Government action in relation to the Highlands and Islands.

The Minister of State (Commons) is responsible for industrial and regional development; matters relating to oil development; new towns, urban renewal and local government finance.

The Parliamentary Under Secretary for Health and Education deals with Health

Boards and the Common Services Agency. He deals with the following services: hospital, GP, community health, ambulance, the elderly, children, disabled, mentally ill and handicapped; Also education (excluding universities); public libraries; sport and recreation; community and youth services; the arts; List D schools; children's hearing and the after-care of offenders and superannuation.

The Parliamentary Under Secretary for Home Affairs and the Environment deals with the police and fire services; civil law and criminal justice; prisons; the Scottish Courts Administration; town and country planning; housing; roads and transport; water sewerage and pollution; local government (excluding finance); building control and ancient monuments and historic buildings.

17. Department of Social Security
Richmond House, 79 Whitehall, London SW1A 2NS   01–210 3000

1988 staff: 85,627

The Department is responsible for the payment of benefits and the collection of contributions under the National Insurance and Industrial Injuries schemes; for the payment of child benefit and one parent benefit; and, on a means-tested basis, for paying Income Support and Family Credit. It also administers the Social Fund and pays a number of non-contributory benefits which are not means-tested. It administers resettlement units and is responsible for assessing the means of people applying for legal aid. It also makes reciprocal social security arrangements with other countries; and is responsible for pensions for UK war pensioners and war widows throughout the world.

Ministerial duties

The Secretary of State has overall responsibility.

The Minister of State has general responsibility for policy and all social security matters with specific responsibility for disability issues and co-ordinating Government policies for disabled people.

Two Parliamentary Under Secretaries:

1. Has day-to-day responsibility for income-related social security benefits, child benefit and benefits for the unemployed. He is also responsible for management issues including the operational strategy and for service to the public.
2. (A Peer) has day-to-day responsibility for all pension matters, including war pensions and occupational and personal pensions, other social security contributory benefits, national insurance contributions, resettlement units and the vaccine damage payment scheme.

18. Department of Trade and Industry
1 Victoria Street, London SW1H 0ET   01-215 7877

1988 staff: 12,477 (plus 1,631 – Export Credits Guarantee Department; 300 – Office of Fair Trading)

Responsible for: international trade policy, including the promotion of UK trade interests in the EC, GATT, OECD, UNCTAD and other international organisations; the promotion of UK exports and assistance to exporters; policy in relation to industry and commerce, regional policy and regional industrial assistance (some of this applying only to England); City Action Teams; specific interest in all manufacturing and service activities apart from those covered by other departments; policy in relation to British Shipbuilders, the British Steel Corporation, and the Post Office; competition policy and consumer protection, including relations with the Office of Fair Trading; the Monopolies and Mergers Commission; and the office of Telecommunications (OFTEL); co-ordination of policy on deregulation and the encouragement of enterprise; policy on science and technology research and development, Space, standards, quality and design; the National Physical Laboratory, National Engineering Laboratory, Warren Spring Laboratory, the laboratory of the Government Chemist and the National Weights and Measures Laboratory; company legislation and Companies House; the Insolvency Service; the regulation of the financial services and insurance industries; the regulation of radio frequencies; the Patent Office; and the Business Statistics Office.

Ministerial duties

The Secretary of State has overall responsibility.

The Minister for Industry and Enterprise deals with regional policy; inward investment; financial assistance under the Industrial Development Act; inner cities; general R&D policy; national collaborative R&D programmes; industrial research establishments; intellectual property; British Technology Group; advisory services; quality; design; standards; the market for iron, steel and other industrial materials; engineering markets; shipbuilding; consumer markets; vehicle markets; aerospace and space policy.

The Minister for Trade has responsibility for overseas trade policy; commercial relations and tariffs; relations with the European Community; Single European Market; export promotion (including invisible exports and exports to the European Community); British Overseas Trade Board; Export Credits Guarantee Department; Expo 92; he is also the departmental spokesman in the House of Lords.

The Parliamentary Under Secretary of State for Corporate Affairs has responsibility for competition policy; monopolies and mergers; restrictive practices policy; deregulation; financial services; company law; insurance; the insolvency service; EC aspects of the above; he is also the spokesman on overseas trade in the House of Commons.

The Parliamentary Under Secretary of State for Industry and Consumer Affairs has responsibility for the Post Office; management development; industry/education links; consumer protection and information; consumer credit; The Estate Agents Act; consumer safety; trading standards and trade descriptions; weights and measures; hallmarking; Nationalised Industries consumer Councils; Citizens Advice Bureaux; advertising and public relations; industry and the environment; material reclamation and recycling; information technology and electronics; telecommunications; radio-communications; films.

19. Department of Transport
2 Marsham Street, London SW1P 3EB   01-276 3000

Responsible for land, sea and air transport including sponsorship of the rail and bus services; airports; domestic and international civil aviation; shipping and the ports industry; navigational lights, pilotage, HM Coastguard and marine pollution; motorways and trunk roads; oversight of road transport including vehicle standards, registration and licensing, bus and road freight licensing, regulation of taxis and private hire cars, road safety; and oversight of local authorities' transport planning including payment of the Transport Supplementary Grant.

Ministerial duties

The Secretary of State has overall responsibility.

The Minister of State is the Secretary of State's second in command and continues as Minister for Public Transport, responsible for railways, buses, taxis, London Regional Transport, transport co-ordination in London's Docklands, the Channel Fixed Link and the export of transport expertise. He has special responsibilities for the Department's financial planning and for promoting private sector finance in all modes of transport.

The Parliamentary Under Secretary of State, is the Minister for Roads and Traffic, responsible for the motorway and trunk road programmes, local roads, London roads and traffic, road freight, road safety and traffic law, driver testing and training, road taxation, driver and vehicle licensing, vehicle testing and safety, transport for disabled people, tolled estuarial crossings and Departmental research.

The Parliamentary Under Secretary of State is the Minister for Aviation and Shipping, responsible for airlines and airports; all marine and shipping matters, including the Coastguard and pilotage, and for ports.

20. HM Treasury
Parliament Street, London SW1P 3AG   01-270 3000

1988 staff: 3,158 (plus 66,385 – Inland Revenue; 7,370 –Department for National Savings; 3,183 HMSO; 962 – Royal Mint; 784 – Central Office of Information; 132 – Registry of Friendly Societies; 54 – Government Actuary; 47 – National Investment and Loans Office)

238 Appendix 4

The Treasury serves the Government in allocating and controlling public expenditure and promoting the satisfactory functioning of the UK economy. It is responsible for fiscal, monetary and counter-inflation policies; balance of payments policies; the management of the reserves and international monetary cooperation; the aid programme and matters connected with the UK membership of the EEC. It prepares short- and medium-term economic forecasts and provides advice on financial management and accounting standards in the public sector. It is responsible for Civil Service pay, allowances and superannuation. The Central Computer and Telecommunications Agency, which falls within the Treasury's responsibility, advises and supports Departments in the field of information technology. The Chessington Computer Centre provides payroll and other computer services to other Departments.

Ministerial duties

The Prime Minister is First Lord of the Treasury.

The Chancellor of the Exchequer as Second Lord is its Ministerial Head and has overall responsibility.

The Chief Secretary deals with public expenditure control, including local authority and nationalised industry finance; nationalised industry pay; and value for money in the public services (including 'Next Steps').

The Financial Secretary deals with Inland Revenue taxes; the general oversight of the Inland Revenue (excluding Valuation Office); privatisation and wider share ownership policy; the Central Statistical Office; competition and deregulation policy; Economic and Monetary Union; and Parliamentary financial business (Public Accounts Committee, Comptroller and Auditor General, Exchequer and Audit Acts).

The Paymaster General deals with Customs and Excise duties and taxes; general oversight of Customs and Excise; the Paymaster General's Office; European Community business (other than EMU), including membership of the Budget Council; Civil Service pay, personnel management, recruitment and industrial relations; procurement policy; competitive tendering (including local authorities); and Central Unit on Purchasing.

The Economic Secretary deals with monetary policy; Treasury responsibilities for the financial system, including banks, building societies and other financial institutions; Department of National Savings, Registry of Friendly Societies and National Investment and Loans Office; the Royal Mint, Central Office of Information, Her Majesty's Stationery Office, the Government Actuary's Department, the Civil Service Catering Organisation, and the Central Computer and Telecommunications Agency; international financial issues and institutions (other than EC); industrial and export credit casework; Treasury interest in general accounting issues; legislative programme; Inland Revenue Valuation Office and Rating of Government Property Department; and the Paymaster General's business in the Commons.

21. Welsh Office
Gwydyr House, Whitehall, London SW1A 2ER   01-270 3000

1988 staff: 2,171

Responsible in Wales for ministerial functions relating to health and personal social services; education, except for terms and conditions of service; student awards and universities; the Welsh language and culture; local government; housing; water and sewerage; environmental protection; sport; agriculture and fisheries; forestry; land use, including town and country planning; countryside and nature conservation; new towns; ancient monuments and historic buildings; roads; tourism; a range of matters affecting the careers service and the activities of the Manpower Services Commission in Wales; selective financial assistance to industry; the urban programme in Wales; the operation of the European Regional Development Fund in Wales and other EEC matters; non-departmental public bodies; civil emergencies, and all financial aspects of these matters, including Welsh rates support grant. It has oversight responsibilities for economic affairs and regional planning in Wales.

Ministerial duties

The Secretary of State has overall responsibility. He deals personally with economic matters; industry; European Community issues; agriculture; forestry; constitutional issues; and financial rate support grant issues.

The Minister of State deals with education and training; the Employment Department; the Training Agency; small businesses; tourism; Development Board for Rural Wales; transport and highways; Welsh language; arts; National Library and National Museum of Wales; historic buildings and ancient monuments; Countryside Commission; National Parks; conservation; general issues relating to public appointments.

The Parliamentary Under Secretary deals with health and social work; housing, water, local government; land use planning; urban affairs, including urban programme and urban development grants; enterprise zones; sport.

Small Departments

1. Cabinet Office
70 Whitehall, London SW1A 2AS   01-270 3000

1988 staff: 1,591

Comprises the Secretariat, which supports Ministers collectively in the conduct of Cabinet business; the Management and Personnel Office (MPO) which is responsible for the management and organisation of the Civil Service and recruitment into it, training, efficiency, personnel management and senior appointments; the Central

Statistical Office; and the Historical Section. The functions of the Cabinet Office are in support of the Prime Minister in her capacity as Minister for the Civil Service, with responsibility for day-to-day supervision delegated to the Chancellor of the Duchy of Lancaster.

2. Paymaster General Office
Sutherland House, Russell Way, Crawley, West Sussex, RH10 1UH 0293 27833

1988 staff: 816

Acts as paying agent for Government Departments other than the Revenue Departments (Inland Revenue; Customs and Excise).
Also responsible for the payment of many types of public service pensions.

3. Privy Council Office
Whitehall, London SW1A 2AT   01–270 3000

1988 staff: 31

Responsible for the arrangements leading to the making of all Royal Proclamations and Orders of Council; for certain formalities connected with ministerial changes, for considering applications for the grant (or amendment) of Royal Charters; the scrutiny and approval of bye-laws and statutes of chartered bodies; for the appointment of High Sheriffs and many Crown and Privy Council Appointments to government bodies. It approves certain regulations and rules made by the governing bodies of the medical and some allied professions. The Lord President of the Council has responsibility for the work of the Office. The Minister for the Arts is his deputy. As leader of the House of Lords, the Lord President is responsible to the Prime Minister for the arrangement of Government business in the Lords. The Judicial Committee of the Privy Council is the ultimate court of appeal for the British Commonwealth except for the UK and those independent countries which have abolished appeals to it. It also has limited jurisdiction in the UK, including certain ecclesiastical cases and the hearing of appeals by members of the medical and certain allied professions against decisions of the statutory disciplinary bodies.

4. Treasury Solicitor's Department
Queen Anne's Chambers, 28 Broadway, London SW1H 9JS   01–210 3000

1988 staff: 443

Provides legal services for many Departments. Those that do not have their own legal staff are provided with litigation and conveyancing services and general advice. The Treasury Solicitor is a Permanent Secretary.

Sources: *Civil Service Yearbook 1989*; *List of Ministerial Responsibilities* (Cabinet Office 1989); *Civil Service Statistics 1988* (HM Treasury).

Appendix 5

All-Party subject and country groups

Adult education
AIDS
Alcohol policy
Animal welfare
Animals in medical experiments (replacement of)
Anti-slavery
Arts & Heritage
Action on Smoking & Health
Association football
Aviation
Barristers
Book publishing
Boys Brigade
British Limbless Ex-Servicemen's Association
Cable TV
Campaign for the Homeless & Rootless
CB radio
Channel Tunnel
Chemical Industry
Child and family protection
Children
Complementary and alternative medicine
Conservation
Cotton and allied textiles
Cycling
Defence study
Disablement
Drug misuse
Energy studies (alternative energy)
Energy studies
Engineering Development
Esperanto
European-Atlantic
Film industry
Firearms
Fisheries
Fluoridation
Food and health forum
Footwear and leather industries
Forestry
Franchise development
Human rights
Industrial common ownership
Industrial safety
Industrial study
Information technology
Inland waterways
Knitwear industry
Leisure & recreation industries
Licensed trade
Lighting
Management
Maritime
Media
Mental health
Minerals
Motor industry
Non-profit making clubs
Overseas development
Paper industry
Parliamentary Scientific Committee
Penal affairs
Pensioners
Personal social services
Pharmaceutical industry

Photography
Plumbing
Population and development
Pre 1973 war widows
Pro-life
Race relations
Racing & bloodstock
Railways
Reform (House of Commons)
Refugees
Retail trade
Retirement
Road passenger transport
Roads
RAF
Rugby League
Scotch Whisky
Scottish penal affairs
Scottish sports

Scout Association
Shelter
Social science and policy
Solicitors'
Solvent abuse
Soviet jewry (release of)
Space
Sugar cane
Televising Parliament
Tourism
Trans-Pennine
Transport safety
United Nations
War crimes
Westminster Hospital
Widows and one parent families
Wool textile
World government
Youth affairs

Afghan
Africa (Horn of)
Albanian
Algerian
American
ANZAC
ASEAN
Austrian
Bahamian
Bahrain
Bangladesh
Belgian
Belize
Benelux
Bophuthatswana
Botswana
Brazilian
Bulgarian
Burmese
Cameroon
Canadian
Caribbean
Chinese
Colombian
Cuban

Cyprus (Friends of)
Cyprus
Czechoslovak
Danish
East African
Ecuadorian
Egyptian
Ethiopian
Europe
Euro-Arab cooperation
European Atlantic Group
Falkland Islands
Finnish
Franco-British
Gabonese
German Democratic Republic
German
Ghana
Gibraltar
Greek
Hong Kong
Hungarian
Icelandic
Indo-British
Indonesian

Iranian
Iraqui
Irish
Israeli
Italian
Ivory Coast
Japanese
Jordanian
Korean
Kuwait
Latin America
Lebanese
Liberian
Malawi
Malaysia
Malta
Manx
Mauritius
Mexican
Mongolian
Moroccan
Namibian
Nepalese
Netherlands
Nicaragua
Nigerian
North Korean
Norwegian
Oman
Pakistan
Palestine
Papua New Guinea

Peruvian
Polish
Portuguese
Romanian
Saudi-Arabian
Senegalese
Sierra Leone
Singapore
Somali
South African
South Pacific
Southern Africa
Soviet
Spanish
Sri Lanka
Sudanese
Swedish
Swiss
Syrian
Taiwan
Thai
Tunisian
Turkish
Turkish Cypriot
Uganda
UAE
Venezuelan
Vietnam
Yugoslavia
Zambian
Zimbabwean

Index

accountants, 210
Adjournment Debates, 44, 116, 142
   typical week, 117
Administrative Executive and Clerical (AEC) System, 26
administrative legislation, 202
administrative officials, 26–7
administrative v. political issues, 129, 195–7
advance contact, importance of, 161
Adviser on Foreign Affairs, 5
advisers
   on dealing with Government, 206–12
   to Prime Minister, 3–5
advisory bodies, 34
advocacy
   techniques of, 127–9, 156–8
   understanding Government point of view in, 191–2
air courier industry, 183, 184, 192
All-Party Groups, 23, 40, 42, 145, 201
   contacting, 167
   details of membership of, 154–5
   influence of, 55
   listing, 255–7
Appointments Secretary, 4
Assistant Private Secretaries, invitations to, 171

backbench committees, 23, 40, 41, 104, 201
   contacting, 152, 167
   influence of, 55
   proceedings of, 155
banks, 210
Barnett, Joel, view on Ministers, officials and Cabinet Committees, 80
Bills
   amendments to, 197–8, 204–5
   see also legislation; Private Bills; Private Members' Bills; Public Bills
books, campaign against VAT on, 24–5, 130, 138, 191–2, 199
briefing of Government, 178–91
British Airways, 3
British Medical Association, 198–9

Budget formulation, lobbying and, 86–8, 205–6

Cabinet, 12–14
   meetings, 13–14, 99
   members in 1989, 13
Cabinet Committees, 4, 14, 25
   in 1985, 15–18
   proceedings of, 153
Cabinet Office, 3, 19–20, 229–30
   Management and Personnel Office, 20
   meeting of Deputy Secretaries in, 81
   publications, 141
   Secretariats, 19
Cabinet Secretary, 4, 13, 19
campaigning organizations, 150
Carrington, Lord, 9
Central Office of Information, publications, 141
CFRs (Confidential Final Revise of Select Committee reports), 134
Chairman of Ways and Means, 72
Circulars, 194
Civil Service, 19, 20
   and secondment to private sector, 20, 217–23
   Unified Grading Structure, 138–40
   see also departments; officials
Civil Service Yearbook, 138, 141
Closure, 120–1
Collective Responsibility, 9
Committee (1922), 40, 42, 172, 205
Committee on Overseas Trade (House of Lords), 111
Committee on Privileges, 38
Committee of the Whole House, 72
committees of enquiry, 201
Comptroller and Auditor General, 8, 113
Conservative Central Office, 20
Conservative Party
   backbench committees, 40, 41
   conference, 46
   guide for parliamentary candidates, 150
   manifesto, 47, 51

Conservative Party (*cont.*)
  organization, 48
  research department, 47, 51
  see also Committee (1922)
constituencies, areas covered by, 37, 147
constituency associations, 46
consultants, government affairs, 208–10
consultation periods, 127
contact with Government, 161–9
  impersonal, 161, 163–4, 168–9
  personal, 161, 164–6
contracts, 133
  tendering for, 83–5
courts, action against executive and administrative decisions through, 213–14
Crossman, Richard, 91
  quoted, 79
Cunningham, George, 103, 104
Customs and Excise, 225

dealing with Government
  common mistakes in, 122
  ethical considerations, 131–6
  honesty in, 132
  levels of approach in, 130–1
  prime considerations in, 123–4
  requirements in, xiv
  technique of, 126–7
  timing and, 127
debates, parliamentary, advance notice of, 137
Department of Education and Science, 226–7
Department of Employment, 227–8
Department of Energy, 228
  sponsorship by, 29
  structure, 28
Department of the Environment, 228–9
Department of Health, 230–1
Department of Social Security, 235
Department of Trade and Industry, 52, 236–7
  advisory units, 31
Department of Transport, 237
Departmental Special Advisers, *see* Special Advisers
departments
  advisory role of, 27, 31
  areas of responsibility, 24–6
  conflict of interests within, 25
  dealings with outsiders, 92–7
  developing information links with, 147–50
  enquiry points, 141
  Information Offices, 141
  internal memoranda, 153–4
  obtaining information on, 138, 141–2
  Parliamentary Branch of, 141–2
  and policy formulation, 31
  responsibilities and ministerial duties 1989, 224–40
  role, 27, 31, 33
  sponsorship by, 27, 93–4
  structure and staffing, 26–7
  see also quasi-departments
Deputy Secretary, 81
  working day of a, 88–9
divisions, Government defeats in (1970–88), 63
documents, official, access to, 134
Dod's Parliamentary Companion, 142
Dubbs, Alf, 99

Early Day Motions, 7, 44, 72, 117–18, 142, 144
EEC *see* European Community
Enabling Legislation, 58
entertainment, of MPs and officials, 131
ethics, in dealing with Government, 131–6
European Communities Committee (House of Lords), 111
European Community, legislation, 25, 58–9, 158–9, 196
European Legislation Committee (House of Commons), 111
executive agencies, 34
executive officials, 26
executive powers of Government, 2–24
executives, business, and exchange postings, 20
external organizations, 160

Films Bill, 65
  see also tape levy
Finance Bill, 88
  see also Budget formulation
Foreign and Commonwealth Office, xi, 5, 51, 229–30
Fringe Bodies (Cabinet Office publication), 141
Fringe Bodies (quangos), 33–4
Fulton Committee, 27

government affairs consultants, 208–10
Gow, Ian, 7
Green Papers, 60–1, 127, 137
  submissions following, 203–4
Grylls, Michael, 103

Haines, Joe, 81
Hansard, 142, 143, 144
Heath, Edward, 8

Home Office, 231
House of Commons, 37–44
  Bagehot on power of, 43
  Chamber, 42, 44, 55
  Crossman on power of, 43–4
  daily timetable of, 98–9
  debates, 99
  Library, 42, 54
  Order Paper, 142
  recesses, 100
  televising of, 42
  times of sittings, 97
House of Lords, 8, 24, 45–6
  Chamber, 56
  debate on Public Bills in, 64
  EEC select committee, 56
  Order Paper, 142–3, 144, 172
  Parliamentary Questions in, 46
  Private Members' Bills in, 119
  Select Committees, 111–12
  times of sittings, 97–8
House Magazine, 145
Hybrid Bills, 58
  procedure, 73, 77

Independent Retailers Group, 162–3
information
  assessing, 137
  difficult to obtain, 151–6
  need of Government for, 160–1
  obtaining, 136–56, 141–50
  supplying Government with, 156–7
  supplying officials with, 132, 135
  value of advance, 137
Inland Revenue, memorandum to Select Committee on Wealth Tax, 185–7
interests, disclosure of, 132–3

journalists, 146
judicial review, 213–14

Labour Party
  backbench committees, 40, 41
  conference, 47
  organization, 51
  research department, 51
  sponsorship of parliamentary candidates in, 46
  see also Parliamentary Labour Party
Law Officers' Department, 232
Law Society, 135–6
leaflets, production of, 199
legislation, 57–77
  administrative, 202
  change to, *see below*
  deficiencies in, 194

  delegated, 58
  drafting of, 61
  interpretation of, 57
  need for, 58
  parliamentary time spent on, 57
  and Standing Committees, 38
  technical, 206
  time scale in promotion of, 200–6
  types of, 58–9
legislation, change to
  alternatives for, 194–5
  Departments involved in, 195
  European Community law and, 196
  factors affecting, 194–200
  involvement of Prime Minister in, 196
  methods, 193–4
  support for, 198–200
  and timing, 196
letters
  to Members of Parliament, 167–8, 178
  to Ministers, 164–5, 168
libraries, law, 146
lobby correspondents, 146
lobbying, 130, 158, 159
Lord Advocate's Departments, 232–3
Lord Chairman of Committees, 73
Lord Chancellor's Department, 233
Luce, Richard, 9

Machine Tools Federation, 148–9
Management and Personnel Office (MPO), 20
mass lobbying, 130
media coverage, in presenting a case, 198–9, 201
meetings with Government, form and timing of, 170–3
Members' Interests Committee, 38
Members of Parliament
  attitude to lobbying, 102
  biographies of, 142
  briefing of, 178–83, 188
  and career politics, 101–2
  committee membership of, 38–42
  common characteristics, 97–8
  constituency days, 171
  contacting, 167
  contacting Ministers through, 165–6, 169
  correspondence received by, 99–100
  correspondence sent by, 101
  developing relationship with, 147
  disclosure of interests by, 133
  during recesses, 100–1
  and elections, 103
  employment by organizations, 133
  influence of, 53, 54, 102

Members of Parliament (*cont.*)
  invitations to, 98, 171–2
  lack of research support for, 101
  meetings with, 167–8, 171–2, 175–7
  mobilization of support by, 103
  need for contacts, 161
  numbers of, 37
  and publicity, 103
  retained, 210–11
  role of, 37
  sending information to, 135, 169
  targeting, 159
  timing of meetings with, 172
  voting against own party by, 103–4
  working day of, 97–8, 100
  writing to, 167–8, 178
memoranda, internal departmental, 153–4
Ministerial Enquiries, 141, 164
Ministerial Responsibility, 9
Ministers
  accountability to Parliament, 10
  advice given by officials to, 27, 31, 91–2
  appointment of, 8–10
  ascertaining views of, 152
  assistants to, 159, 160; *see also* Parliamentary Private Secretaries
  briefing of, 188, 191
  contacting, 160, 164–6
  Diary Secretary, 141, 164
  hierarchy of, 10
  income, 9
  information needs of, 160
  invitations to, 171
  limit on numbers in Commons, 9
  meetings with, 170–4
  numbers in 1989, 8
  outside interests of, 9
  and policy formulation, 31, 33
  power of, 53, 91–2
  Private Office, 77–9, 141
  representations to, through MPs, 190
  role of, 10
  Special Adviser *see* Special Advisers
  staff support for, 77–83
  timing of meetings with, 172
  visits by, 174
  working day of, 77, 78
  workload of, 91
  writing to, 164–5, 168
Ministry of Agriculture, Fisheries and Food, 224–5
Ministry of Defence, 52, 226
Mitchell, Austin, 197
monitoring of Government, 124–5, 136–7
motivation of Government, understanding of, 151–2

MPO (Management and Personnel Office), 20

National Audit Office, 113
nationalized industries in 1988, xiii
negotiating with Government, 157–8
Northern Ireland Office, 233–4

Office of Arts and Libraries, 225
officials
  briefing of, 190
  contacting, 166–7, 168–9
  developing information links with, 147–9
  grading of, 26
  information needs of, 160–1
  invitations to, 131
  meetings with, 174–5
  power of, 53
  presenting a case to, 202–3
  targeting, 159
  visits by, 175
  see also Civil Service; departments
OFTEL, 153–4
Ombudsman (Parliamentary Commissioner for Administration), 102, 214–15
Order Papers, 142–3, 172

Parliament
  before Second World War, xi
  information issued by, 142–6
  and policy-making, 36–7
  power of, 36–7, 129–30
  scrutiny of policy by, 104–21
  see also House of Commons
Parliamentary candidates, 159
  meetings with, 177
Parliamentary Commissioner for Administration (Ombudsman), 102, 214–15
Parliamentary Counsel, 61
Parliamentary Labour Party (PLP), 40–2, 51, 127, 147, 172, 205
  see also Labour Party
Parliamentary Private Secretaries (PPSs), 6–8, 23, 159
  contacting, 152, 166
  influence of, 54
Parliamentary Profiles, 142
Parliamentary Questions, 44, 46, 96, 113, 115, 142, 143–4
  approaching MPs to table, 134, 135, 156
  briefing MPs on, 182–3
  Oral, 96, 113, 115, 134, 144, 182
  rules governing drafting of, 155–6
  Supplementary, 113, 115, 144
  Written, 115–16, 155–6

Parliamentary Under-Secretaries, 9, 10
Parties, 46–56
  conferences, 47, 105, 150
  and constituency associations, 46
  research departments, 150
  see also Conservative Party; Labour Party; Social and Liberal Democratic Party
Patronage Secretary, 4
Paymaster General Office, 240
Peel, Sir Robert, xi
Peers, 45–6, 159–60
  briefing of, 188
  contacting, 167
  influence of, 56
  invitations to, 171, 172
  meetings with, 176–7
  number of, 45
  retained, 210–11
  writing to, 167
Permanent Secretaries, 19, 20, 79–81
personalities, securing support of, 199–200
petitions, 199
policy
  formulation, 2–24, 31
  implementation, 24–36
  management and administration, 77–90
  Parliamentary scrutiny of, 104–21
  scrutiny and endorsement, 36–46, 104–21
Policy Unit, 5–6, 12, 20
  influence of, 54
  members and backgrounds 1989, 6
Political Office, 5–6
political v. administrative issues, 195–7
power centres, identifying, 125–6
power structure, 1, 2, 51–6
  myths concerning, 129–31
Press, 146
press conferences, 198
Press Office, 5
Press Secretary, 5
pressure groups, 93–4, 128, 212
Prime Minister
  personal staff, 3, 4–8
  power of, 54
  role of, 3
Prime Minister's Question Time, 99, 115, 172
Principal Private Secretaries, 4, 77–9
  invitations to, 171
  typical working day, 89–90
Priority Questions, 142
Private Bills, 58, 206
  Commons proceedings as at 7 July 1988, 74–6
  procedure, 72–3
Private Members' Bills, 44, 64, 118–21, 197
  amendments to, 198
  in House of Lords, 119
Private Office
  Ministers', 77–9
  Prime Minister's, 4–5
Private Secretaries, 4, 77, 78–9
  see also Principal Private Secretaries
private sector, secondment to and from, 20, 217–23
privatization, 200
Privy Council Office, 240
Provisional Order Confirmation Bills, 58
Public Accounts Committee, 38, 113
Public Bills, 58
  Committee Stage, 62–3
  First Reading, 61
  procedure, 59–64
  Report Stage, 63
  Second Reading, 61–2
  Third Reading, 64
public corporations in 1988, xiii–xiv
Public Information Office, 147
public relations, 131, 198
public relations firms, 211–12

quangos, 33–4
quasi-departments, 33–6, 141
  listing, 241–59
  number and listing 1989, 35
quasi-judicial agencies, 34
Questions of Procedure for Ministers, 14

Register of Members' Interests, 142
Regulations, 58
  consultation document preceding, 206
  procedure, 69, 71–2
  source and form, 70
regulatory bodies, 34, 94–5
representative bodies, 207–8
research bodies, 150
research departments, of Party headquarters, 150
Roth, Andrew, 142

Science and Technology Committee (House of Lords), 111, 113
Scottish Office, 234–5
Scrutiny Committee, 71–2
secondment of officials, 20, 217–23
Secretariats (Cabinet Office), 19
Secretary of the Cabinet, 4, 13
Secretary of State, 10
  invitations to, 171
Select Committees, 38, 39, 98, 142, 201
  advance notice of investigations by, 137

Select Committees (*cont.*)
　Confidential Revise Form reports (CFRs), 134
　contacting, 167
　departmental, 39–40
　House of Lords, 111–12
　influence of, 55
　offices of, 147
　press releases, 145–6
　procedural structure, 104–5, 111
　publication of evidence given to, 154
　reports, 105, 111
　rules for officials giving evidence to, 106–10
　selection of agenda for, 113
　submissions to, 183–4
　typical days, 112
Services Committee, 38
Shadow Cabinet, 10, 99
Shadow Ministers, 10
Social and Liberal Democratic Party organization, 49
solicitors, 210
Special Advisers, 10–12, 20, 159, 190–1
　contacting, 152, 166
　influence of, 54
　meetings with, 172
Standing Committees, 10, 14, 23, 38, 62–3, 98, 137, 142, 143
　amendments lists, 144
　Clerks to, 147
　Hansard for, 143, 144
　and Statutory Instruments, 72
Standing Order 39 procedure, 119, 120
Statutory Instruments, 58, 69, 142, 143
　annulment of, 72
　Parliamentary control over, 71
　procedures for challenging, 71
supervisory bodies *see* regulatory bodies
Supply debates, 99

Table Office, 116
tape levy
　campaign against, 182–3, 194, 197, 200, 204
　Green Paper on, 94
targeting of decision-makers, 159–60
Ten-Minute Rule Bills, 58, 116–17
tendering, by Government, 83–5
Thatcher, Margaret, 3, 4, 5, 12, 14, 20
Thorpe, Jeremy, 8
timing, in dealing with Government, 127
tobacco companies, 135
Treasury, 8, 25, 52, 113, 195, 237–8
　and Budget formulation, 86–8
Treasury Solicitor's Department, 240
triangle of power, 51–2

Unstarred Questions, 46, 143, 144

Wealth Tax, inland revenue memorandum to Select Committee on, 185–7
Weekly Information Bulletin, 145, 154
Welsh Office, 239
Whips, 21–4
　meetings, 24
　opposition, 23
　power of, 54
　responsibilities of, 21–2
Whip, The, 23
White Papers, 61
Whitehall *see* departments